# MY
## BIG Lily

Manchester United's Biggest Supporter

---

# Keith Norris

BIG LILY Productions

First published by Big Lily Productions in
Great Britain in 2002

PO BOX 60

Carrickfergus
BT 38 9YA

A CIP catalogue is available from the British Library.


ISBN 095437620X




Printed in Great Britain by
The Universities Press (Belfast) Ltd

For my wife Yukari, my son Alex, my mother and father and our families and friends in Japan and Northern Ireland.

For the Shirts, Sir Alex, Paddy Crerand and all Reds across the globe.

## Acknowledgement

To my good friends and neighbours, Jim and Jo
Shields, my other United family, especially Alan and
Linda Jackson, wee Gary Callaghan, The Faceman,
Brian from Bray, all the Carrickfergus Reds,
the Cockney Reds, Kevin, Jamie, Brian and Big
Paul Barrett to whom I am eternally grateful.

I am forever indebted to Karen Banks,
Martin Noble, Jacqui Bennett, Paddy Crerand, Sir
Alex Ferguson, Walter Smith, Mo Mowlam, Richard
Kurt, Andy Mitten, Barney Chilton, Pedro Chueca
Remon, Fernando Hierro, Raul Gonzales Blanco,
Stephen Ryan, Paddy Harverson, Karen Shotbolt,
Jack Kennedy, David Wilson, Julian McGrath, Chris
Moore, John Mahoney, Patrick Griffin, Fernando
Garrido, Guillem Balague, Kerry Hannin, Steven
Moore, Phil McCord and The Universities Press and
all those that helped along the way from Andy Hill,
the computer wizard, my sales manager Stephen
Mitchell and my American friends Patrice Browne,
Karen Collier and Betty Burns Hastings who, not
only were believers but kept me encouraged from
the very start.

Contents

# Foreword

I was fortunate enough to play 392 times for Manchester United; privileged to play under the leadership of the great Sir Matt Busby and alongside such great players as Denis Law and George Best. Working for Manchester United, I have met, and continue to meet, thousands of United fans from all walks of life. One such fanatic I have met, both in Manchester and at various locations around the world, is Keith Norris from the Carrickfergus Branch of the Manchester United Supporters' Club. If United are playing anywhere in the world you can be sure Keith will appear with that huge flag of his, Big Lily - Brazil, Japan, Spain Thailand, to name but a few. How he transports it I will never know! The players, the Directors, Sir Alex Ferguson and every Manchester United fan know of Big Lily. What Keith and his friends, including the legendary 'Faceman', have done for community relations in Northern Ireland and public relations for Manchester United can only be commended. Supporters are the lifeblood of Manchester United. Keith Norris is an ardent supporter and I wish him every success with this truly outstanding book.

Paddy Crerand

# INTRODUCTION

To describe me as a Manchester United supporter is an understatement. I'm a follower, a member of a world-wide family of followers, the people who put the fan in fanatic. I don't remember how it began, it seems like it was always there, and a childhood relationship with a distant football club became a full-blown affair on my first visit to Old Trafford on 8 December 1979.

I am neither a historian nor a student of literature. Contained in the pages of this book are personal memories drawn from a life of dedication to a club, a team, a cause, a way of life that includes the European Champions League success of 1998/99 and 2000/2001 season in which United won their seventh Premiership in nine years.

My birthplace is Northern Ireland and I work in my family auto parts business. I live in Whitehead, a mostly graceful and genteel Victorian seaside town, the only town or village in Ireland that doesn't have a 'street'. The outbreak of the 'Troubles' in the '60s and the damaging effect on tourism coincided with the arrival of the cheap package holiday to the sun. Whitehead was deserted by its summer visitors, lost its three hotels and fell into a kind of shabby hibernation. The troubles deepened and recession stifled the economy, jobs galloped over the horizon to the Far East where the yarns and fabrics, oil tankers, passenger liners and the engineering flotsam and jetsam which were the lifeblood of our country, could be produced for a fraction of the cost.

I share my home and life with my Japanese wife Yukari. We met as a consequence of my trip to Tokyo to watch United play in the Toyota Cup. We fell in love and, most fortunate soul that I am, she consented to be my wife. Yukari and my two Samoyed dogs, Keano and Treble regularly take me for long walks along the idyllic Blackhead coastal path, whether I want to go or not!

And then there is the other love of my life -'Big Lily'. A larger than life celebrity who has travelled the world, made countless television appearances, lives in my garage and Yukari knows all about her! It has been said there may not be another as big as my Lily anywhere in the world. She covers 300 square yards and is an enormous red, white and black flag, the club colours of my beloved Manchester United. I created Lily and she accompanies me around the world in support of my team.

Life as a Manchester United fan hasn't always been easy, I have experienced less successful yet still exhilarating times following the Red Devils. During my boyhood years of the late seventies and early eighties the Scousers of Liverpool F.C. dominated the football league. Their typical continental, defensive based, boring style was, in my eyes, more suited to the Italian Serie A or the Germany's Bundesliga. You cannot deny them their achievements but the way they played football never appealed to me. Give me a team with 'hearts like lions' any day. To me football was, and still is, a game of flair, a game of attacking wingers and a swashbuckling 'never-say-die' attitude. It was easy being a fan of the Scousers and true Reds supporters were not as plentiful in those days. Times have changed and countless millions now follow 'my' team on every continent and probably in every country on earth.

During my early schooldays, it was the Scousers in my class who had the swagger of the glory hunters. Following the underdog was never as easy but it was always satisfying, as my big mate Paul Barrett from London so aptly puts it: 'It ain't all about glory and day tripping.'

The dominance of a well organised Liverpool F.C. and the physical Leeds United fuelled a fierce and protective loyalty among the fans of an off-song Manchester United. That club had recovered from worse setbacks than a temporary loss of form.

The Munich air disaster of 1958 had a profound effect on many people. The sadness and sorrow of this terrible accident are still felt today by many of those who watched the graphic scenes on the grainy black and white images of their television sets. One of the heroes that day was the fabulous Harry Gregg who, despite his injuries, went back into the stricken plane repeatedly to rescue his team mates. Harry was only one of a legion of Northern Ireland born players who helped make Manchester United Football Club the global success it has become. George Best, possibly the greatest footballing talent in history, was just one in a line of wonderful footballers who learned their skills on the streets of Belfast or the green fields of the Ulster countryside. Jackie Blanchflower, his blossoming career cut short by Munich, Jimmy Nicholl, Sammy McIlroy, David McCreery, Trevor Anderson, and Norman Whiteside, still the youngest player in history to play in the finals of the World Cup. Each of those names played their part in sowing the seeds of passion deep within me, it was so easy and natural to fall under the spell of these stars. When I looked at them I could see my own people and I was well and truly ensnared by the tradition and history they brought to the park each week.

To me the biggest thing about football is the match-going experience. It's not simply all about ninety minutes of football on the pitch. It is about the pre-match debate, the after-match analysis, the travel and most of all the people, be they your Red friends or match-day mates.

I often hear 'Oh, I can't afford to go' offered as an excuse, yet the same guy goes down the pub seven nights a week. When you have a passion you have to make sacrifices. Each time I walk down the Warwick Road I get the same buzz, the same tingling as I had on my first trip to Old Trafford all those years ago.

Recent seasons have seen dreams become reality both on and off the pitch for the team and members of the Carrickfergus Branch of the Manchester United Supporters Club. I hope you enjoy these words simply for what they are, the story of an unending love affair, unparalleled romance, a tale of passion, dreams, satisfaction and fulfilment.

# THE EARLY DAYS

*"So fare thee well, my own true love.*
*When I return United we will be.*
*It's not the leaving of Liverpool that grieves*
*me ..."*

The lads and I were already addicted at the age of nine. This was the old Clancy Brothers' tune that we sang every Friday morning at Drumahoe Primary School. This small country school sat high, surrounded by in-need-of-a-painting railings. It was in many respects the centre of the Universe for a young boy. I can recall the wonderful scent of freshly cut grass when the groundsman visited and the essential aroma of late autumn when the few remaining leaves were traceries of gossamer and the ground crackled underfoot from the hoar frosts that were common in that era. I can feel the adrenaline rush of the delicious expectation on football days and the equally strong desire to flee on the days when the homework wasn't done or had been scrawled down at the last trump in order to squeeze the very last ounce from the setting sun.

The school overlooked the Glenshane Road, a hectic artery often crammed with labouring, smoking diesels that thundered past laden with mystical produce from exotic Belfast.

We would sing along in our squeaky off-key soprano voices to the music emanating from the tinny speakers of a

15

primitive cassette recorder. We'd be looking forward to verbally ambushing the Scousers, of whom there were at least fifteen in my class. Fellow Reds Roost Henderson, Big Nick Gray, Scone McKeegan, Duke McClelland and I wouldn't sing the verses. Oh no. We preferred to save our voices for an explosion of noise during the line in the chorus, 'United we will be'. This would result, without fail, in the cane, or the 'licker', from our teacher Mr Dallas for our non-participation in the song as a whole and our over-exuberance at the mention of United.

This was always considered to be well worth it and was not insolence but more of an unadulterated defence of our Red Culture and of the team we adored. Our team, Manchester United, were not successful in this era but we loved the attacking way they played football, we loved their fascinating history, which was steeped in tradition. To us, Manchester United was an enigmatic legend, a way of life, more than a pastime or a hobby. Unquestionably we were living in the vast shadow of the prevailing Liverpool regime but we found there to be so much more to being a Manchester United supporter than all-conquering success. Besides, a stand had to be made, nothing like a bit of Scouse baiting, eh?

At our crescendo Mr Dallas, mid-forties going on one hundred, balding on top, well dressed in navy blue suit and matching tie, wearer of thick lensed, black rimmed glasses, would suddenly leap out from behind his desk, his face reddening with a mixture of frustration and anger, and switch off the tape recorder.

"Right, you lot, I'll not tell you again. Will you boys never learn? Get up here now, all of you. You're all getting the licker," he would proclaim.

Most of the other kids in the class would smile and laugh, the Scousers would scoff vigorously, glorifying in our anguish. The five comrades lined up, heads bowed, beside the large blackboard at the front of the classroom.

One by one, and in dictatorial sergeant major tones, he called our names: "McKeegan, McClelland, Henderson, Gray, Norris", and one by one he proceeded to cane us in turn with a firm whack on our outstretched right palms.

"You should know better, Norris, you're up here every week."

"Sir, it's not fair, we always get the licker, them Scousers started it, it wasn't us," I'd protest.

Then, hidden from Mr Dallas, I would make an obscene gesture with my left hand as I clenched my other fist and waved it defiantly in the direction of the rejoicing Scousers.

School years were always tribal. It's amazing that Red friends are still mates in later life and I guess this was the start of my Red Family- a junior branch of the Red Army.

Live television coverage was rare back then, we had to rely on the occasional Midweek Sports Special or the vintage Match of the Day, with the clock that seemed to move far too quickly. When United did not feature on the main game it was like being told Santa Claus didn't exist.

Even in those days club merchandise and in particular the replica team shirts were a much sought-after item-even if no one, and I mean no one that I knew had or could afford one. I longed for the white 'Admiral' away kit with the three black stripes, especially after Jimmy Greenhoff's headed semi-final replay winner against Liverpool at Goodison Park in 1979. The picture of Jimmy hovering in the air like a Harrier jump jet and heading that winning goal sticks in my mind to this day.

During this late-seventies period, many Manchester United players attended functions in Northern Ireland. Lou Macari, a diminutive yet charismatic Scotsman and one of our footballing heroes, visited a house in Tullyalley, about a mile down the road from where I lived. He was and remains good friends with a match-going supporter Jim Wallace with whom I travelled at the inception of my United vocation. Andy 'Scone' McKeegan used to live in the front row of the Tullyalley housing estate and told us about the craic the night that Lou was present.

Lou had been staying at the White Horse Hotel when Jim asked if he'd like to join him and his young family for a cup of tea. Kind-hearted Lou offered to pay for Jim to go Wembley with him the following morning. This was big news among our small working class community.

It is often said that schooldays are the best days of your life. For me they most certainly were, even though we were raised against a background of torment, division and conflict between the Catholic and Protestant communities. We had very little contact with the Catholic community. Only a few Catholics lived in the Drumahoe area, but there were some, and we played football together after school. We were friends even though we did not attend the same schools or go to the same churches.

Undeniably many atrocities did occur: bombings, shootings and killings, most of which made headlines across the world. I remember images of the carnage. The horrifying yet mesmeric pictures of the dead and pieces of bodies lying in the streets. I remember the all-too frequent bomb scares, the traffic jams and diversions, countless police and British army checkpoints, the regular noise of bombs exploding in the distance most of the time. The explosions were not always small and not always in the distance. You heard the sound of both low and high velocity shots followed by the braying of the ambulances and fire engines and the thunder of low flying military helicopters.

On a night of any such occurrence, the late night BBC Radio Ulster news was listened to with meticulous care and attention. However strange it may sound, you felt distanced from the whole situation. If it did not happen on your doorstep or didn't affect your immediate family, there was a kind of unreality or dislocation about the whole thing. As you got older, such things mostly passed you by unless they were particularly horrific. In a bizarre way you became hardened to it all because it was an everyday occurrence...until the moment when your doorstep wasn't far enough away. There was a terrible price to be paid for this proximity.

Terrorist killings, indiscriminate and often no-warning bombs, security force and government misdemeanours, all heinous crimes against humanity and mankind, all happened with all too much regularity and suffering came to all sections of the community. Far too many families in Northern Ireland, from both sides of the divide, were affected by the carnage.

Days of protest or election polling days were considered good entertainment and most importantly days off school when we could play football all day long. I recall one particular day of Loyalist protest when the country came to a complete standstill. Roads were blocked with everything from local farmers' tractors to commandeered and hijacked cars and lorries. The main Belfast road was blockaded by many people waving placards and demonstrating for who-knows-what. I had been standing down on the grass area in front of my house, which overlooked the main road, watching the proceedings. A bakery delivery lorry bearing the name Hyndman's of Maghera was driven through the protesting crowd parked across the road to great cheers from the mob.

"Keith, Keith come in to the house now. I'm warning you. You're not going to be standing about there if there's trouble," my mother shouted.

I pretended not to hear her but it was not long before she walked the short distance that separated us.

"It's all right, Ma, it's only a bun van. They're not going to burn it."

"Keith, I'll not tell you again, get up to the house now."

Not long after, as I watched from our large front window, a troop of men, women and kids in a tableau more reminiscent of a famine scene in far away Africa, walked in a straight line away from the protest and towards the Tullyalley housing estate, each carrying bountiful supplies of buns and cakes in wire baskets.

At school the following morning, all the talk centred around how many cream cakes and pastries each household had 'obtained'.

"What did you'se get?"

"My ma got a dozen jam buns and our Davy got six loaves of bread."

An overriding memory from childhood is sitting on a parked bus beside my mother, head resting against the window, looking up at a large advertising hoarding and seeing the words,

'7 YEARS IS ENOUGH DON'T MAKE IT 8'

I counted on my fingers and asked "What does it mean, mum? 7 years is enough? Enough of what? What does that mean?"

"What does what mean, Keith?"

"That, that poster, over there, '7 years is enough don't make it 8'"

"That means it has been 7 years of trouble, the fighting and bombing. They are asking people to stop fighting and then there will be no more years."

"Will they stop, mum?"

"Oh son, I don't know, I hope so, I really, really hope so."

This billboard poster referred to the seven years of 'The Troubles' that had poisoned our communities.

It was only at the age of eleven or twelve when we changed from primary to secondary school that we became more aware of our own cultural identity, and ties with our Catholic friends for the most part diminished.

Certain incidents were more evocative than others; The Dublin and Monaghan bombings of 1974 when the U.V.F. set off a series of explosions killing thirty-three people; the 1981 Hunger Strike, when ten Republican prisoners starved themselves to death and the bombing of the La Mon House hotel in which twelve members of a Collie Club were burned to death and thirty more injured by the I.R.A., caused emotional outpourings and raised tensions, thus creating a more divisive community.

My secondary school was situated in a predominantly Catholic area. Occasionally altercations would take place in the city centre between pupils from different schools. Friends we once played football with were now on 'the other side'. Obscene gestures and taunts with religious connotations would be traded, often with added choice expletives. Catholics were called Fenians or Taigs and Protestants were called Jaffas or Huns. Very little contact existed between the two sides. Each was left to its own devices, each entrenched in its own shielded web and each totally existing in its close-knit communities.

This book is by no means a political anthology and I hate talking about discordant issues when the very essence of this project is the exact opposite. I could never address the depth of Irish politics, nor would I try. Maybe they are like the Emperor's New Clothes. There may be no depth there at all.

Conflict between the two communities in Northern Ireland dates back hundreds of years and, in this last thirty years alone, has claimed in excess of three thousand lives. Most Catholics consider themselves Irish and would like to see the island of Ireland united, whereas most Protestants consider themselves British and wish Northern Ireland to remain part of the United Kingdom.

Terrible as events have been here, when I recall all my schooldays, Manchester United memories are always prominent. Often trivial things, like one touch or flick of the ball in the playground at lunchtime and we thought we really were our United heroes like Gordon Hill or Steve Coppell. Even our primary school headmaster, Mr Anderson, a real gentleman, in an effort to ensure we stayed in good behaviour mode would often get involved during the heated football banter. I'll never forget the morning after a 2-3 cup defeat in 1978, played at the Hawthorns, against his team, West Bromwich Albion. Mr Anderson, wearing a tweed suit and green tie, sat perched on his desk in front of me debating how and why United had just been dumped out of the FA Cup.

"What happened to your team last night, young Norris, eh?"

"You'se were just lucky, sir."

"Lucky? I don't think we were lucky. I doubt my wee team gave your boys a lesson. Do you not think so?"

He had a great passion for football and was one of those guys who could administer the cane one minute but in the next would ask about the most recent game. We respected him all the more for talking to us in the way he did and I think he actually liked us football nuts.

Another vivid memory from primary schooldays is the defeat at FC Porto. They 'chinned' us 4-0 away in the second round of the 1977 Cup Winners Cup. The build-up for the return tie at Old Trafford set the butterflies somersaulting in the stomach. I set the chairs out in the living room to resemble the Porto defence, emulating my first United hero, Steve Coppell. Oh how I hoped he would score. Bang, off the radiator, between the defenders (cushions that I laid on the floor), around the settee and into the goal with the TV and my coat (fur lined snorkel and all) as goalposts. Unfortunately a certain Mr Seninho destroyed all our dreams after a gallant effort.

Two Porto own goals, two from my hero Steve Coppell and one from Jimmy Nicholl - ecstasy in the making - then the reality set in, as Porto scored and we eventually won 5-2, but lost 5-6 on aggregate.

That was always the thing about United - you thought overcoming a four-goal deficit was possible. That was United during that era. Entertaining to the last - the nearly men. They would always take us so close to the edge. That hasn't changed.

# THE FIRST TIME

## The First Supporters

Manchester United were originally known as Newton Heath. In their early days, Mr Bird or 'Father Bird', a local chimney sweep, was known to encourage the team vocally from the sidelines. He was possibly the forerunner of modern day songster and folk hero Peter Boyle. He is known to have invited all the players to his home two or three times a week prior to important games for generous portions of Lancashire hotpot or potato pie. He was well known and well liked by the players and once posed with the players in a team photograph.

Mr Sedgwick, the stationmaster at Manchester Victoria Station, was also a regular attendee at North Road. Always immaculately dressed in the distinguished Victorian clothing of that era, Sedgwick was said to provide reserved carriages for the team's travel to away matches.

Another of United's first documented fanatics - and pioneer of the Red Army - dates back to the 1893/94 season. This was George Lawton. The team first played in green and gold, then later in blue and white. The famous red and white strip did not make its appearance until 1902. George was an accountant to a brewery named Walker and Humphries. He used to cycle to watch Newton Heath, even in the most adverse weather conditions. George was extremely friendly with the first club captain, a gentleman called Harry Stafford.

Once, while frantically cycling to a game, George collided with a horse and trap on Oldham Road. He picked himself off the ground and was just about to give the driver of the trap a piece of his mind when he realised it was none other than his own boss, brewery director Mr John Henry Davies. This led to a chain of events which culminated in Davies' involvement with the club. He was immensely impressed by the enthusiasm shown for the club by Lawton. Lawton and Stafford cycled to his home and appealed to his sportsmanship, deep pockets and no doubt good nature, when the club was in dire financial circumstances. Davies went to Bank Street, saw for himself the plight of the club and, recalling Lawton's passion, agreed to help.

This is not a history of Manchester United. What happened in between? The history, people and events are chronicled in great detail elsewhere and while fascinating and essential to the development of both the myth and the reality of the club, they play only a peripheral role in my story.

# Our Team

United won the League Championship the year I was born (1967) and the European Cup in 1968, and no doubt the newspapers of the time were full of the exploits of the underdogs, and of the team that had to be completely reconstructed after the horrific Munich air crash in 1958. I remember, as a boy, reading and being told the stories of all these great players. We felt that we knew them and there was a closeness and a great affinity towards the team and the club.

We already knew a lot about Manchester United, the players, the history, the results, the fixtures and statistics. We would know that Brian Greenhoff drove a Rover V8 and that his favourite meal was Steak Diane and we discovered that Stuart Pearson drove a Ford Cortina GLX and his favourite television programme was M.A.S.H. We knew that Gary Bailey's middle name was Richard and that Mickey Thomas was born in Mochdre, Colwyn Bay.

Just because we could not make the trip to Manchester, this did not stop us from being fervent in our support. We would try to outdo each other with questions.

"When was United formed?"

"1878."

"What was their first name?"

"Lancashire Railway Workers."

"No, it wasn't, it was Newton Heath."

"No it wasn't, we used to be Newton Heath LYR up to 1880, then it was just Newton Heath on its own."

"When did we become Man United?"

"1902 was it?"

"Aye, that's right, we changed it 1902."

"Who got the most goals in the League in one season?"

"Denis Law."

"No, you're close, you got the first bit right."

"Oh aye, I know now, Viollet, Dennis Viollet, wasn't it?"

"Yes, you're right this time."

Most of my memories from primary school days are related to United. I recall, as a nine year old, the atmosphere of the match against Southampton at Wembley in the 1976 FA Cup Final, the tragedy for us of the Bobby Stokes goal. Ecstasy for the Southampton fans, an ensuing feeling of emptiness for us. Despite this catastrophe I was still excited because of the newness of the experience.

Even at the age of eight or nine I knew I was never going to play football competitively but that did not stop me dreaming, nor from playing for hours on end. Our school team made it to the dizzy heights of our local Schools Cup Final, the schoolboy equivalent of The World Cup. It seemed as if the whole school turned out to lend their voices and psychic will to the team. 'Drum-a-hoe, Drum-a-hoe' was our chant from the touchline. I felt something stirring in me that when fully realised was simply this. I adored soccer. All of it. Not just playing but all of the other things that have to happen before a game is truly a game. I was going to be a much better supporter than player.

By 1977, at the age of ten, I had all the merchandising accessories and all the trimmings such as a clock, mirror, rug, lampshade, pillowcase and a very special tapestry of the club crest made for me by Auntie Joy in America. My uncle and good friend Larry Weddle, from Cincinnati, Ohio, still talks of how, when he was here on holiday, I used to draw the imaginary number eleven on his back with my fingers, representing the legend that was George Best.

## Home and Away

Every Saturday we would make the trip to my granny's country farmyard house at Curryfree. We would play football all day long. We would even permit our female cousins Wilma and Hilary, as well as my sister Cherith, to play to make up the numbers. I used to bring along the large Bush radio with the manual dial. This was as important as bringing the ball. We placed it on the windowsill so we could listen to the live match commentary and keep up to date with all the latest scores while we were playing.

My mum, Auntie Kathleen, Auntie Barbara and Granny and Grandad would go crazy every time the ball hit one of the windows near our 'pitch'- a concrete yard surrounded by house and porch on one side, coal shed on the left and various farm buildings, including a byre and pig shed that acted as our grandstand. The only break we took was for dinner. My granny loved having all her grandkids to lunch. She loved to bake and cook and would put on some wonderful feasts for us. A big favourite of ours was 'champ' (mashed potatoes with scallions and loads of butter) and lots of HP sauce.

Every kid has their own special place where they played football, their own home grounds and their own parks where they spent thousands of hours. The concrete yard at my granny Dougherty's in Curryfree was by far my favourite.

Auntie Janet was involved with Faughan Valley Youth Club. She organised trips to Old Trafford and had relatives in London. This later turned out to be a godsend as we could then stay with them during all our cup final appearances at Wembley Stadium. Thankfully her sons and my cousins, Adrian and Alvar, have also been lifelong match-going United fans.

Unlike our 'away ground' at Curryfree, Aidy and Alvar had a dream 'home-ground', a well-cut field behind our father's garage and adjacent to Auntie Dot's house on the corner of Gortree Road. The pitch was laid out properly with penalty areas, centre circle and touchlines all marked out with flour purloined from the pantry. This was the nearest thing to a real pitch we would get to play on. Because this belonged to the local farmer, it could only be used for a few months each year. When our ground was closed to allow for the 'crappy farming stuff' to take place, we would move a few hundred yards to 9 Gortree Road. This was a walled concrete yard at the back of Aidy's house.

Mrs Payne (Adrian and Alvar's granny) would often tell us off because we'd knock hundreds of stones off the pebble dashed walls or the ball would bang loudly against the large garage door that we used as a net to play 'shooty in'. Afterwards when we were exhausted and couldn't kick another ball, her stern face would relent and she would treat us to lemonade and biscuits. Those feasts were banquets. The cool, fizzy liquid was champagne and the sugary coatings on the biscuits manna.

I always loved that special feeling of scoring into the goal framed by the metal garage door and the loud, tinny bang would lead to delirious celebrations.

'Tackly shooty in', 'Passy shooty in' or 'Three gets you in' were all games or variations of games played into one net when one of us would be 'keeper and it depended who we were playing with as to whether we would pass to or tackle each other. Usually, if it was a particularly good friend or if only three people in all, it would be 'Passy'. You always tried to be on the side of your best friends who were inevitably United supporters.

These games were only temporary measures until enough of your friends arrived to play a proper match. Younger boys, overweight boys, even girls, would be humoured in a fashion to get them playing so as to make up the numbers for a game.

My own 'home ground' was 'the Square' in Faughan View Park housing estate where I spent the first twelve years of my life. We would have two large green plastic milk crates, parka jackets or duffle coats as goalposts. The big boys, like Sean Connor, Davy Dunn, Davy Laird (renowned for his big toe), Trevor McKinlay, Frankie and John McCool, Paddy Monaghan, Graeme Park (an avid Leeds fan) and the Rosboroughs played in a team every night while the younger ones, like Stephen Hetherington, Gary Quinlan, Alan Curley and I, would stand about until we were picked and told to join a team if there were unequal numbers of players. If there happened to be an odd number you had to stand about until someone else arrived. If nobody else turned up, some other urchin's door would be knocked. 'The big boys want you out for a game'.

'Aye, aye, I'm sure they do,' would be the disbelieving yet hopeful reply.

'No, Honestly. I swear the "big boys" told me to call for you,' we'd say in our most persuasive demeanour.

'All right, give us a minute to tell my ma.'

Some of these big boys were good players, especially Sean Connor and Davy Dunn. If you were in nets you would be terrified if they got anywhere near in case they unleashed a ferocious shot anywhere in your direction. Davy Laird always wore what I recall as work boots and was renowned for his big-toed pile drivers.

*

I used to have to go to bed after 'Crossroads' ended. I would try and make some plausible excuse to my erstwhile team mates and endeavour to slip into the house before my mother came out and commanded, "Ke-i-th. Bed-time," gleefully in a sing-song voice. This would be greeted with derisory jeers from those permitted to stay out later. If I was

31

late returning to the house, my mother would come out and an altercation would ensue.

"Come on, Ma. Please! We're nearly finished the game. Give us another few minutes," I would plead in supplication.

"Keith, don't be so cheeky, I'm warning you, if you don't come in right this minute, I'll take the wooden spoon to you."

I knew my mother was serious and I would trundle across the square towards our house while my mother stood waiting at the front door, accompanied by the mocking taunts of my friends.

'Huffing' (sulking) was a big part of street football culture and if you were lucky enough to own a ball in those days you were in a very dominant position - you could lift the ball and go home in a 'huff' at any time if a decision went against you. Owning the ball also meant that you were always assured of a game.

Christmas was always considered a bad time of the year because everyone had a ball and you lost a certain amount of control.

Football was more than a way of life; life was football. A net would be chalked out on every gable wall. On every street corner some form of football-orientated game would be taking place such as 'Kerby' (played across a street when you had to kick the ball, hit the opposite kerb and make the ball come back to you) or 'Keepy uppy', when you had to stop the ball hitting the ground using any part of your anatomy except your hands.

Football squash played against a wall was another favourite and like most games this also had variations. The most common was 'Lives' when we would try to make it as difficult as possible for whoever was following us. If you messed up in any way such as missing the wall (or sometimes the outlined net) you lost a life. The winner was the person left at the end with most lives remaining. It was most unusual for us younger boys to win these games but this did not stop us trying - if anything, we tried a little harder.

We played football anywhere, at any time, in any weather conditions and on any surface: tennis courts, living rooms (often with cushions, balloons or special house balls), bedrooms, kitchens, gardens, driveways, roads or fields. If no one else was about you played on your own, either practising to see how many times you could keep the ball up or kicking the ball off a wall, even setting up two nets at either side of the garden and playing an imaginary game. The fantasy games that drove me onward were those against Porto in the Cup Winners' Cup and against Liverpool in the 1977 FA Cup Final.

# The First Contribution

Uncle Bert took me to Windsor Park to watch Northern Ireland play Holland in 1977. This was to be the day that George Best would win his final Northern Ireland cap. United's midfield battler David McCreery was the hero that day - marking the legendary Dutchman Johan Cruyff out of the game - and it was the first match at which I made a proper 'contribution': I remember shouting from the Railway Stand, 'Break his legs, Jimmy!' at which point my Uncle Bert, Uncle Willy and about fifty of the crowd gave me a startled look. The sheepskin coat clad spectators turned in my direction. Many sported sideburns and wore their hair fairly long hair as was the fashion. Most wore the green and white favours of Northern Ireland.

Perhaps I was a little bit embarrassed but I remember a feeling of achievement - I had backed my team to the hilt and felt a glowing inner pride. I was now a proper football supporter.

## The First Trip

My first-ever trip to Old Trafford was on 8th December 1979. The result was a 1-1 draw against Leeds and I remember every detail vividly from leaving on the coach with all of us sporting scarves and hats, sat two by two, the noise similar to that of a boisterous gaggle of geese. We couldn't refrain from writing 'MUFC RULE OK' with our fingers in the condensation-covered windows. The big boys lounged at the back smoking and drinking cans of beer which was followed by the inevitable "Stop the bus I want a wee wee" song, and the eventual stop in a lay-by adjacent to the Glenshane Pass (the main road to Belfast where we caught the ferry to Liverpool) just south of Dungiven.

"Right, lads, that's it," we were instructed, "no more stops until we get to the boat. If you have to go, go now."

The ferry crossing on the old Liverpool boat from Belfast was a trip and a half. Eleven hours of either being sick or walking about avoiding the piles of vomit which appeared more and more as the boat rocked and the lads necked small cans of Carling Black Label by the dozen.

Having endured the all-night escapade and finally docked in Liverpool, we were shepherded on to the coach in preparation for our inaugural drive to Manchester.

There are certain days when something particularly memorable happens in the course of a lifetime. Your first day at school, your first kiss, or the first time you have to cope with death or tragedy. I'll never forget that Saturday morning walking down the Warwick Road. The crowds, the singing, the flags and banners waving. And I remember the first time I saw the 'Big Red Lady', which had only ever appeared in my dreams. The illuminated, red, MANCHESTER UNITED sign, the narrow turnstile, the eager anticipation as I climbed, trembling with expectation, up the steps from the concourse. At last - the bright green pitch, the floodlights, the scoreboard. Then the chanting and finally the huge roar as the teams came out.

This was the cementing of the relationship. This was the day of realisation, the deliverance, the consummation and the baptism. As a twelve-year-old, I had my first taste of unstoppable passion. Beaming, one of the other boys and I were swollen with pride as we recited the names of the players in our own pre-match interlude;

"Here we go, there's big Joe Jordan and wee Lou Macari in the middle."

"Aye, I can't wait. There's Stevie Coppell on the right and Mickey Thomas on the left."

"Big Kevin Moran and Martin Buchan at the back."

"Sammy McIlroy, Ray Wilkins and Ashley Grimes in midfield."

"Gary Bailey in nets and Jimmy Nicholl in defence."

"There's Dave Sexton down the front of the dugout."

An hour before kick-off, the deafening chant arose - "U-NI-TED, U-NI-TED" - and for the next few days all I could hear was the noise of that crowd reverberating inside my skull.

Tiny Leeds youngster Terry Connor opened the scoring in the twenty-second minute. We were distraught. And stunned. We didn't expect a bad result when we were watching for the first time.

"Oh no."

Old Trafford fell silent apart from the noisy Leeds fans in the ground. We looked at each other in disbelief.

About fifteen minutes later Trevor Cherry fouled my hero Steve Coppell in the area and we were awarded a penalty.

"YESSSSSSSS."

After all the years of support, all the years of reading about the team and results, watching goals on television, this was now the real thing and we were about to witness a United goal in the flesh - or so we thought.

Irishman Ashley Grimes struck what looked like a good penalty, only for Leeds 'keeper John Lukic, a tall stringbean of a man and a good 'keeper to make a great save. We were stunned and distressed. This wasn't part of the script we had written a hundred times in our dreams.

"Oh no."

"How'd he miss it?"

"It's going to be one of them days."

Going to the loo just before half time, I received funny looks as I walked towards the back of the South Stand bedecked in four scarves (including one on each wrist), hat, flag on my back and huge rosette pinned onto my chest. I look back now and smile. What amusement I must have given the 'Red Army' as I walked by - a fully-fledged 'Day-Tripper'.

Northern Ireland international Jimmy Nicholl crossed a long ball in, which was headed on by big Joe Jordan and then knocked in at the far post from a very acute angle by the flying Welshman, the long-haired Mickey Thomas.

The instinctive celebrations surrounding the goal are vivid. All of us getting bigger simultaneously in anticipation of an attempt at goal, then arms punching the air, hugging and kissing those beside us after the ball hit the net. Now we knew what it was really like to see our team score in 'real life', the smiles, the laughs, the relief, the glee, the unity, the mass togetherness ... truly incredible.

My other memories of the match itself were overshadowed by the ear-splitting noise. The old scoreboard was used to indicate the attendance figure. As it flashed up '57,471' (as I remember, although The Official Manchester United Illustrated Encyclopaedia states that there were 58,348) the stadium announcer called out over the Tannoy system.

'The biggest crowd of the season, thank you for your wonderful support.'

The announcement gave you a feeling that you were part of something extra special. I remember the raised eyebrows and the looks and smiles being exchanged between us. Everyone was thinking the same thing.

"Magic hi, this is class, isn't it?"

"Waaohh, I've never seen that many people in my whole life!"

It was also my first-ever encounter with crowd trouble. Several Leeds fans were dragged around the perimeter of the pitch to tremendous cheers from the United fans.

The draw may have been somewhat disappointing but the experience was one I knew would leave me counting the days until I was back again. You could say, though, that having our pictures taken with Lou Macari, Martin Buchan and Paddy Crerand in the executive lounge after the game more than made up for the result.

You can imagine a group of eleven to sixteen-year-olds, wearing baseball boots, bomber jackets and parkas on their first trip to their Mecca.

"There's Wee Lou at the bar."

"There's big Martin Buchan," said someone excitedly as they peered through the opening into the lounge where the players and families and friends were gathering.

"Aye, so it is, he's bigger looking in real life, isn't he?"

Well-to-do men and women, dressed in what to us was considered nighttime function attire - large collared shirts, big knotted ties and buttoned blazers. Meanwhile I was wearing a long-sleeved blue-checked shirt, with a Manchester United 1878-1978 Centenary scarf wrapped around my neck and stuffed inside my black tanktop with a huge rosette pinned to the outside.

Like eager kids on Christmas Eve, high-pitched shrieks of excitement and a noisy scrum, with anyone who entered having to excuse themselves two or three times as they pushed through us to make their entrance.

A bunch of animated, boisterous kids, all jockeying for position at the top of the stairs.

"Right, boys, c'mon now, don't be letting us down," one of the leaders exclaimed.

"Form an orderly queue or you won't be getting in at all."

After about twenty minutes one of the aforementioned blazered gentlemen swung the door open and stood at the threshold, with one foot inside and one out shielding entry to the lounge.

"Who's in charge here?" he asked.

Big Jim made his way to the door and was acknowledged. He evidently knew the man and instructed us not to rush up to the players but once again to form an orderly queue and we would all have the opportunity to get autographs and pictures taken.

"Everyone understand?"

"Aye."

"Yes, sir."

"No problem, sir."

"Right, in you all go."

I was about tenth through the door and, before contemplating my approach, I stood and watched as Lou Macari, who was sitting with Pat Crerand and two others whom I didn't recognise, was swamped from all directions.

"Any chance of a picture, Lou?"

"Mr Buchan, would you mind if we had a picture?"

"Give us a wee smile, Paddy."

I was not as forward as some of the other boys and sheepishly reached my match programme over Lou's shoulder, holding the pen in an encouraging manner, in total awe and unable to speak.

Lou, smiling and continuing a conversation with someone beside him, signed his autograph without even noticing me. He was used to this. As his head was turned in my direction a camera flashed.

"I got one of you and Lou, sir," someone exclaimed

There was such a crowd around the table I hadn't even managed to get either Paddy Crerand's signature or his picture. I moved back and sat on one of the red chairs staring at Lou Macari's name on my programme.

"Did you get them all?" someone asked.

"Not yet, there's too many people there."

"Away over and get big Buchan's, he's standing at the bar there around the corner."

Embarrassed and humbled, I shuffled timidly across the front of the bar and around two or three neatly set and as yet empty tables to where Martin was standing drinking from a glass and engrossed in conversation with two other people.

'Excuse me, sir,' was once again all I could manage. I reached out with my programme and pen beggingly.

"There you go, son," Martin said, signing the magazine.

I couldn't manage to speak to him but he had spoken to me!

"Keith, turn around," shouted whoever had my camera. As I did so, Martin put his arm around me and smiled.

Back in my seat, beaming and filled with pride, I now had only one more to get. With Martin Buchan acknowledging me I felt a new sense of confidence - at least for the moment.

But by this time Paddy had sat right beside Lou at the table, not quite directly opposite but with his side facing me. As I walked up again to the table, which was still the hub of activity, full of vocal intention, I stood motionless and without uttering a word, again thrusting my programme and pen out in front of me. Paddy was in conversation with his back to me. Standing for what seemed like an eternity, Lou gave Paddy a nod to signify someone was behind him.

"Och, sorry, son, I didn't see you there," said Paddy, in his strong Glaswegian accent, and proceeded to sign the front of the match programme.

The trend seemed to be for the players to sign the back of the programme where the team sheet was listed, so why did Paddy Crerand sign the front? Was it because he was not playing any more? Or was it because he was really important?

Once again whoever was taking the pictures told me to move to the side a little. As I did so, Paddy pulled the vacant seat on his right hand side around and signalled for me to sit beside him, placing his arm over my shoulder and smiling - as he did for everyone.

This was mission accomplished. Three superstars autographs and I had my picture taken with them. I knew every current detail about two of them and the other one

I had heard so much of from the 'big boys' and from many of the United books and magazines.

There is a certain 'friends for life' feeling for a kid when you get the opportunity to meet your heroes in the flesh - you think of them as best mates and I felt this in abundance.

I spent the final minutes in the lounge walking around the room gazing at the framed pictures which adorned the walls at regular intervals before we were ordered out. We heard rumours that the rest of the players were on their way - no doubt they were but our time was up. As we were led out of the door, our eyes moved swiftly, looking for any sign or glimpse of any more of our heroes.

As we gleefully walked out through the large iron gates into the tunnel beneath the South Stand, almost skipping to our coach, which was now parked in the forecourt, there was much showing of each other's autographs.

"Mine's clearer than yours."

"You can make mine out - who it is."

"Did you get them all?"

"Naw. I never got Buchan's. He was only there for a short time."

"Aye, class wasn't it, wee Lou Macari was brilliant."

# FROM DESPAIR TO SILVERWARE

## The Firm

At our non-football-playing grammar school, where rugby was the main sport, we would play soccer in the playground before school started (if you caught the early bus), a quick game at break time and then a 'big' game at lunchtime. Foyle and Londonderry College was a predominantly Protestant school in a predominantly Catholic area. There were only a handful of Catholics in my year and there was never any animosity.

One guy, Sean Corr, who could not pronounce his 'r's, was very loud: 'Ova, ova, ova,' he would shout for a pass any and every time you had the ball - even in defence. In these games it was a serious business rather than being a knock about between friends. And you would have first year pupils playing along with the older boys, although various groups had their own wee 'cliques' within the game.

You could always see who were the really talented footballers. I remember Jeremy Foster (thin and frizzy-haired, always with a pair of the most modern training shoes) being a tremendous player, Andrew 'Roost' Henderson (one of those who was naturally gifted at many sports including badminton and rugby) and big Nick Gary (the tallest boy in our year, who outgrew his trousers every few weeks, making his Derryman's socks very noticeable) was an outstanding goalkeeper. All these guys went to play at junior level like the BB old boys in Tullyalley or Institute in Drumahoe. One of the younger boys, Leslie Bryson who was particularly good, almost made it at Bradford although eventually returning home mainly because he was homesick.

Schoolyard football was weird: I was always intrigued how non-football supporters (well, they weren't as mad as some of us) would still participate in these games. Also it did not seem to fit that those who were 'boffins' (this broad category included anyone who took their work seriously or indeed was interested in weird subjects such as computer studies), such as Jeremy Black or Jonathan Boggs, would even play. It was almost an unwritten rule that if you were in any way intelligent you would not waste your break-time by playing something as ludicrous as football.

United supporters travelling around the country supporting the team had a bad reputation in this era. During the 1974/75 season, the Football League imposed 'away' match restrictions. They were made 'all ticket' matches and could only be sold in advance of the match, and at the same times by both clubs. No tickets were allowed to be sold on a match day. The self-styled 'Doc's Red Army', with customary white butchers' coats, was a common sight around the seventies and was copied by us during our girls' hockey 1st eleven team's exploits in the Schools Cup or the Rugby First XV in their cup competitions.

Big Davy Baldrick took over the organisation of the supporters from his brother Alistair and this was my era. The Baldricks were 'the firm' at Foyle College and this organisation was passed down like a family heirloom. Davy would make sure we all had coats and scarves while he would look after the drums and any other musical accompaniment we used in our support.

The white butcher coats, or lab technician coats, we often 'borrowed' from one of the science labs during lunchtime. We had patches and our school crest sewn on to the coats and to our scarves. We liked to think we were living up to United's bad boy reputation and we would chant in military style:

"Everywhere we go, People want to know

Who we are and where we come from …"

During this era we had plenty of support and no cups, although we were successful a few years later. Pupils throughout the school would travel, sometimes taking several coach loads of supporters, to watch our team in whatever competition they were in. We had a reputation.

We were even known to stone other school buses belonging to visiting schools' supporters. This was not uncommon, especially against the dominant Liverpool type schools of Campbell College or Methodist College from Belfast who won something every year.

## The Non Glory Days

Unlike nowadays, we had no distractions when growing up. As the world rapidly experiences technological revolution, five hundred million mobile phone users, the Internet, and the Sony Dancing dog, the street culture of football is not as apparent. Kids of today's generation have more and more distractions - Playstation, Sega Dreamcast, Gameboy, Pokeman or Harry Potter. To be honest, we were lucky we had no distractions: maybe this is why so few exceptional players have come through from Northern Ireland since Norman Whiteside, and it could be a factor in explaining why Britain has produced so few genuine world-class players in recent years.

It was heartening to see kids of all ages playing soccer everywhere in Brazil which I visited a few years ago. These poorer countries seem to keep producing exciting talented kids and World Cup winners, as if on a conveyer belt, and it's no coincidence that some of the world's greatest players hail from the poorest backgrounds - most famously Argentina's Maradona, Brazil's Ronaldo, Rivaldo and Pele, and Raul from Spain. Even quality players in the Premiership such as Kanu, Radebe, and our very own Quinton Fortune, all come from non-affluent backgrounds.

Nowadays if the temperature is below 15 degrees or there's the slightest hint of rain the kids will not even bother going out. This argument also may explain why teams like Croatia and the Czech Republic - and most recently Senegal and South Korea - do so well in world football.

I used to enjoy listing the United squad and then putting the country they played for or their nationality beside their name and then I'd read aloud:

'Stepney, England.'

'Nicholl, Northern Ireland.'

'Albiston, Scotland.'

'McIlroy, Northern Ireland.'

And so forth, right through the whole squad.

The time when Northern Ireland was drawn against the Republic of Ireland in the 1978 European Championship still sticks in my mind. This was the period when Northern Ireland was still producing exciting and talented players who had been signed up by the English clubs. An amazing six players from United were called into the squad. Tom Sloan and Tom Connell had just signed and were joined by Chris McGrath, David McCreery, Jimmy Nicholl and Sammy McIlroy. This was the largest ever number of Northern Ireland players who played for United at one time - six men from our wee country playing for our team.

Even in these early days I used to get the weekly *Shoot* and *Roy of the Rovers* magazines and, if fortunate, a couple of Christmas football annuals, which were also much sought after. If we weren't playing football we would be reading about it: collecting sticker albums of your own and other teams was a big part of our lives.

It is easy to overlook the 'non-glory' days but these are some of my fondest memories of following Manchester United. Being a Manchester United supporter was not about clinging to or latching on to something that was successful. Being a Manchester United supporter meant you were a part of something special. We did not know what real success was. At that time we had been relegated to the Second Division and made three trips to Wembley, twice losers - Southampton in '76 and Arsenal in '79 - but most importantly victors over Liverpool in 1977 and in so doing denying them an all-conquering Treble of European Cup, FA CUP and League Championship. We were not used to success but the hunger for it and the way United supporters were reviled made us even more zealous.

My next trip to Old Trafford was in February 1981, the opposition again Leeds United.

We had been in the middle of a bad patch, having been beaten away at Leicester City, a goalless draw with Spurs at Old Trafford in the last home game and yet another defeat at the hands of our biggest and bitterest rivals Manchester City the previous week at Maine Road.

47

We were seated fairly centrally in the South Stand and I was almost thrown out for having an air horn. My dad sold hand-held air horns in his shop at Gorticaw and I had a few spare canisters with me. As the players took the field I honked as long and as hard as I could. About five minutes later a tall, burly, bearded policeman came to my seat and told me that I was not allowed to use the air horn and proceeded to confiscate it.

We lost to Leeds that day. Seeing your heroes beaten by a rival is always hard to take, but this had a numbing effect, especially as we had counted the days from our last trip almost two years previously. This was a bad day. The United fans around us were depressed with the team's dismal recent performances.

"Three points out of ten. United, if we keep this up we'll be back in the second division." Gary Birtles, who had arrived from Nottingham Forest with a prolific goal scoring reputation, having won two European Cups and one League Cup, came in for particular abuse: "Fifteen league games and not one goal, you're a goat, Birtles," shouted a broad Mancunian voice behind us.

If it weren't for people like my Auntie Janet or Uncle Bert, I would probably not have been as passionate nor had the opportunities to see United 'in the flesh'. Uncle Bert was a match-going Scouser and I suppose because of this it was all the more appealing for me to support United. Family often influences your allegiance. If your father supports a particular team it is often the case that you are brainwashed from a young age.

On the other hand in choosing a team other than your father or brother's almost serves as an act of rebellion. My dad was not interested in football and it was Uncle Bert who was my footballing mentor.

Uncle Alwyn is tall, with a healthy crop of white hair reminiscent of Greg Norman and often dressed in trousers and sweatshirt, seldom with a tie; he has a very genial nature in contrast to his imposing build. He and my dad would buy thousands of gallons of Ford Oil and store them in a lock-up garage at the entrance to Faughan View Park - the estate where we lived. The kids in the neighbourhood would look forward to the lorry pulling up every couple of months, as this would mean a few pence for carrying the cases of oil. The money was not as important, though, as actually being involved with the unusual giant truck in our working-class neighbourhood.

Just as present day United started from very humble roots, so too, through hard work and sacrificial dedication, my father and Alwyn saved up (by fixing punctures and cutting grass) and bought a drum of Duckhams oil between them. This was the 'signing' that helped establish the pair as two of the shrewdest, most hard-working businessmen I have ever met. Through much graft and determination and several accomplished 'moves' including speculative acquisitions, as with Fergie, they have instilled the fire in the belly into their team - us, the staff.

My father Morley, neat, always immaculately dressed - always wearing a tie, glasses and neat side part in his hair, has few interests outside work and his grandkids whom he adores. Cricket (which he played to a good standard for many years) is his favourite sport (mind you, viewing anything more than four or five overs nowadays is considered overkill). Football is a no no - however I am assured by my mother that he does watch the European games and apparently did cheer when we beat Barcelona that night.

While Alwyn has watched United play in the flesh once (1983 Milk Cup Final) the only other game they've been to was Tenerife against Españyol a few years ago - then again this was on vacation and only because their Spanish friend Socas is a season-ticket holder.

The pair of them are two of the most genuine, honest and kind human beings I have ever met. I could never repay them for what they have done for me. I have utmost respect and I hold them both in the highest possible esteem.

## All we care about is United

If you were born in Manchester, for the most part, you either supported City or United. But, living in Northern Ireland, we were starved of being able to watch top-flight football and depended on the high-profile coverage of the big teams. Certainly we could go to matches but it involved either an expensive flight or a twelve-hour haul on the Liverpool or Stranraer ferries.

It is often said that we should all support our local teams. I most certainly did. I watched 'Institute' in the lower leagues and had flirtations with Irish League football but I treasured only one team and had only one place I longed to be: Old Trafford. For many in Northern Ireland there was always an element of 'peer pressure' to show allegiance to an English first-division team. With top-flight players such as Jackie Blanchflower, Harry Gregg, George Best, Sammy McIlroy, Jimmy Nicholl, David McCreery and Norman Whiteside hailing from Northern Ireland, many local fans followed suit.

Northern Ireland may be slightly different and, because of the political situation and the sectarian divide, most feel they have to show allegiances to Scottish football.

It is pretty simple (I jest!): if you are Protestant, it is assumed you support Rangers, and if Catholic, Celtic. For the most part this would appear to be an extension of religious and cultural background or identity.

You cannot take away from the Old Firm of both Glasgow Celtic and Glasgow Rangers the passion invoked and the loyalty of their support. Attending a Rangers game you sing the party tunes associated with the Orange tradition or Protestant culture whereas Celtic's tradition is built on a staunch Irish Catholic background

Because of the political connotations, many claim allegiance to both in Northern Ireland. I liken the rivalry between Rangers and Celtic supporters to the same armchair debates that follow many teams.

I know many avid supporters of The Old Firm, such as Chris Millar and Billy Brown, who are regulars at Ibrox and Celtic supporters such as Paul 'Arnie' O'Donnell or Ernan O'Donnell. I have more time for these guys because they make the effort to watch their team.

Up to a certain stage in Northern Ireland, many Protestants show allegiances to both Rangers and United but when it comes to it they have to decide - though obviously odd exceptions occur. You almost inherit an affiliation to either depending on 'which side of the fence' you were born on.

Religion also played a part, because of the division between Catholic and Protestant communities. We knew that United stalwarts, Sir Matt Busby and Paddy Crerand were staunchly Catholic and that among the friends and guests there would be many nuns and priests (in fact Denis Law used to wind Paddy up about how many priests he knew). But do you honestly think it mattered to Sir Matt or Paddy that George Best was a Protestant?

Exactly.

Or do you think the many Protestant Northern Irish players gave a toss how Manchester United may have been perceived? By the same token, do you think those who did happen to be Catholic standing on the Stretford End really wondered what school George Best went to or what church he attended as a kid?

Exactly.

I would suggest that most genuine match-going United fans from Northern Ireland, of whatever persuasion, while they certainly may have, or at some stage in their upbringing, had a soft spot for Rangers or Celtic, think about them in the same way they view Liverpool, Spurs or Newcastle.

"I've no time for either of them," I was told by a prominent Red recently.

During the heyday of Northern Irish players involvement at Old Trafford, little mention was made of historical or political differences - I didn't hear too many Catholics saying anything untoward about the likes of Sammy McIlroy or big Norman Whiteside who hails from the Shankill Road - a bastion of Protestantism. On the other hand, do you think many of us do not worship Roy Keane or Denis Irwin because they come from the Catholic faith?

Thankfully, with the on-going peace process, the two main paramilitary groups' cease-fires and the recent IRA decommissioning, sectarianism is not as rife and to some extent is slowly being eradicated. With ever-increasing globalisation and marketing of the game as a product, attitudes are becoming less insular.

If there were a Nobel Peace Prize for soccer, Manchester United would win it yearly. Quite simply, Manchester United unites and is unique in that it transcends all cultural and religious barriers which has particular, but not exclusive, relevance to Northern Ireland. United songster Pete Boyle sums it up:

*"We don't care if you're black, white or female,*
*We don't care if you're from London.*
*All we do care about is United"*

Northern Ireland's well-documented political situation possibly indirectly intensified our passion for our team. Anyone from Northern Ireland who achieved success or fame was idolised. Olympian Mary Peters, Formula One's John Watson, snooker's Alex 'Hurricane' Higgins and Denis Taylor, motorcycling's late and great Joey Dunlop, not forgetting our very own George Best. This was, I suppose, escapism and quite possibly our fervent support for United was symptomatic of our grasping at something from outside the realms of everyday life.

Having successful local personalities gives you a proud feeling of identity. With so many United players coming from our wee country again only increased our passionate support.

## What about you, Robbo?

During another visit to Old Trafford in 1983 (a league game against Southampton), we once again made it into the Executive lounge after the match. I was along with a bunch of lads from Drumahoe. The team under the control of the charismatic Ron Atkinson included Frank Stapleton, Dutchman Arnold Murhen, Irishman Paul McGrath and Remi Moses. We had just scraped a 1-1 draw with 'The Saints' with a goal from Bryan Robson who was fast gaining legendary status. That day we met nearly all of our heroes: 'Big Norm' (Norman Whiteside) Arthur Albiston, Mike Duxbury and 'Captain Marvel' himself, Bryan Robson.

"What about you, Robbo?"

"How's she cutting, Norman?"

I will never forget my cousin Johnny Norris's comment to Robbo as he signed our programmes, "Ye fair put that one in the onion bag, Bryan."

"Aye, it has to be done," smiled Robbo as he continued to sign autographs. I remember feeling very proud of Johnny, still wearing a United hat and dressed in burgundy bomber jacket, tight jeans and Doctor Marten boots: it was unbelievable meeting these guys in the flesh but he had the nerve to actually speak to them.

Throughout the late seventies and early eighties, memories of Old Trafford are still vivid: the crowd trouble, the taunting, the 'almost fear', the arrests from the cages where the away fans were hoarded, the forecourt battles, the police horses. United were then going through a transitional era - all the flair of Steve Coppell, the skilful goal-scoring and attacking of Gordon Hill and Mickey Thomas, the grit of Sammy McIlroy.

After that, with the exception of Cup Finals against Brighton in 1983 and Everton in 1985, my match going was put on hold. I had to rely on *There's Only One United, The Supporters Club Yearbook, Shoot, Roy of the Rovers* and *Match of the Day* in my attempts to follow the team. I was too old for the youth club and yet too young to go on my own.

I have been very fortunate to have been to Wembley on many occasions for most of United's FA Cup Final appearances (with the exception of replays). We all made huge sacrifices in many different ways - United supporters made and still make more sacrifices than those of any other team.

The first Cup Final I remember every detail about was the 1985 'Norman Whiteside Final'.

Flag tied up high on the corrugated iron backdrop, we sat on the ground eating our dinner watching the colourful spectacle as Reds arrived in their masses.

Wearing a ridiculously thin grey leather tie, grey canvas jeans, knitted jumper and red slip-on shoes, my cousin Aidy and I were behind the goal in direct line with Norman's shot. Our emotions veered from feelings of frustration and timid realisation of the potential for mass crowd trouble after Kevin Moran was sent off, to sharing in the absolute pandemonium when our very own Belfast boy curled one past Neville Southall in the Everton goal. When taken in its context, this may have been one of United's greatest-ever goals scored.

When the ball hit the net, I remember being carried about ten feet in the air and ended up almost on a woman's shoulder with her handbag around my neck. One memory of this incident was the fact that she had a tattoo of a red devil on her forearm. This was such a big thing to me at this time - what an act of dedication and passion, especially from a woman! But what I remember most was how we hugged each other and danced uncontrollably amidst the rejuvenated Red hordes.

I have had the pleasure of talking about this match to both Kevin and Norman. 'Big Norm' was a hero of mine. What he achieved in his short career was amazing. To me he epitomised what wearing the Red shirt was all about.

The legendary Faceman (my first Catholic friend, of whom I'll tell you more later) and I were in the company of Wilf McGuiness, Norman Whiteside and Paddy Crerand one afternoon after a game.

We knew that Norman and Paddy, like the Faceman and I, were of differing religions.

"Wilf, this is The Faceman, a good Catholic," Paddy introduced us, "and Keith another bloody Proddy from Ireland ... great lads."

"Norman and me arrived in Belfast this morning for an afternoon function," Wilf, forever the storyteller, began. "We had a few hours to kill and Norman suggested we go up the Shankill to visit his family."

"I'll tell you what, Norman - here's ten pence. I suggest you call them instead."

"Me, with a name like McGuiness, going up Shankill Road, you must be bloody joking."

There is something special about ex-United players. When you play for United you are (for the most part - with the odd exceptions for whatever reason) still a United supporter no matter where you play afterwards. United fans love to meet their old heroes and this was brought home to me when Kevin Moran sang with us in an Irish pub and we met Ashley Grimes in the street at the Toyota Cup in Tokyo.

## From Despair to Silverware

My next game was in 1988 when we played the Scousers. This was a day I would rather forget. Not having seen United play 'in the flesh' for almost three years, you can imagine how it felt when we were beaten by Liverpool. This period was again another transitional one. I remember thinking that the team did not have as many heroes in it. With the possible exception of Robbo, the team, in my opinion, consisted of fairly ordinary players. Of course if I had known then what I know now - that the new manager, a certain Mr Ferguson, would once more make us the greatest in the land - I would probably have been less pessimistic.

One of my biggest regrets is not making it to Rotterdam in 1991 - I could not afford it. Period. However this was the first season I was able to make the 'pilgrimage' to Old Trafford on a much more regular basis.

With the capture of the Cup Winners Cup, the European Super Cup and the Rumblelows Cup in 1992, you felt this was the start of something special. However, after the end of the 1992 season most United fans were still wondering if we were ever again to win the much-coveted League Championship.

Throughout my lifetime very differing managers have tried to emulate Sir Matt Busby's achievements. The flamboyant Tommy Docherty (1972-77) who bravely introduced an exhilarating 4-2-4 formation which certainly had attacking flair; and Dave Sexton (1977-81), who had an impressive reputation as a coach, did not have the personality required to follow such an act. And as for Big Ron Atkinson (1981-86), complete with King Edward and Champagne reputation, although he delivered a few trophies and the team played with flair, he was unable to deliver what we craved, namely the League Championship.

The early 1990s were an indication that 'the fire in the belly', which Sir Alex talks about, was well and truly lit. The emergence of a side with a blend of youth, experience and passion installed by 'the gaffer' was most pleasing to the loyal Red hordes. As another Peter Boyle song begins:

*"Many Reds doubted those barren first years,*
*When heroes like Norman were out on their ears,*
*For they did not realise Sir Fergie's own plan,*
*To once more make United the best in the land."*

However, you are judged on your success and already the signs of Alex Ferguson's unique talent in management were coming to fruition, in the same way that, all those years ago, Sir Matt Busby had invested so much in a strong youth policy.

1992 was the most disappointing end to a football season I can recall in my life of supporting Manchester United. We were so close to clinching that elusive League Championship. What made matters worse was that we lost at Anfield, home of our despised Scouse rivals in the title run in.

With about a month to go, we were the firm favourites to end the twenty-five-year League Championship famine but suddenly switched to major self-destruction mode. We (the fans) were nervous during the run in so I can only imagine how the players must have felt. This was my lowest season as a match-going fan. All the hype about winning the League being easier the second time most certainly seems to have more than an element of truth in it nowadays.

I made it to quite a few League and Cup games that season and what sticks in my mind were the number of 1-1 draws. Beaten by the Scousers and the title going to our other most despised adversary, Leeds. A trip to Wembley and winning the League Cup was scant compensation.

May 26, 1993 was the fulfilment of the dream for every Red (how our expectations have changed!) Twenty-six hungry years of being the nearly men, living in the shadow of the all-conquering Scousers.

My cousin Adrian and I caught the late-afternoon flight from Aldergrove to Manchester. We jumped straight into a taxi and headed for Old Trafford. Even accounting for the rush hour, everyone seemed to be heading for the 'Holy Ground' that night. You could feel the butterflies inside. We had already won the League Championship but the anticipation of the emotion was a special feeling. We had no match tickets (my normal sources had all sold out for extortionate amounts) but this was one of those nights that the house could have been up for sale or jobs could have been lost - you just had to be there.

As we neared the end of the Warwick Road, we could see endless ticket touts brandishing their wares. We asked the driver to stop and invited a tout (whom I recognised but didn't know) into the back of the cab.

"How much for tonight, mate?"

"How many you need?"

"Just the two."

"Three hundred for a brace.'

"How much?"

"C'mon sir, give us a wee bit of discount."

"Listen, lads, do you want them or not? They're getting dearer as we speak."

We had to fork out £150 each. Aidy, being the eternal businessman was a bit reluctant but all I wanted was to get the tickets in my hand so we could relax and savour the weird and wonderful atmosphere. We headed to the wee Greek café on the Warwick Road, had our usual pre-match meal of beans, eggs and chips along with the customary slices of white bread and butter which they dish out in abundance. You could almost smell the emotion among the Reds. Okay, we had won the League but how would we celebrate? And how would the Reds perform after what was surely 'An Almighty Session' at Brucey's the previous night?

We were simply not used to this - with of course the exception of a few Wembley finals and our triumphant night in Rotterdam in 1991. But this was different, this was 'The Real One' - the one we longed for and dreamed of

59

during the lean years. This was the night the Big Red Lady would rise like a phoenix - inspired by the maestro himself - King Eric.

We were seated in the South Stand Upper between the Director's Box and the corner. The game itself was not really important. Flags, scarves and banners made Old Trafford a colourful spectacle that night. Smiling joviality, final realization, uncontrollable emotions as a twenty-six-year craving was satisfied. Blackburn took the lead but we always knew that the lads would overcome them. Then the Giggs free kick, Incey's second after a majestically weighted pass from Eric and big Pally's superb right-footed shot buried safely in Flowers' goal. Let the party begin. To this day I vividly recall looking toward the Directors' Box and seeing Sir Matt slowly clapping and smiling as the tears ran down my own cheeks. Only twice in my life have I seen so many grown men and women cry as I did that night.

Emotionally drained after the game and the celebrations, we walked back to Piccadilly and the Britannia Hotel where we were staying. Big Drew Hamill, the local butcher from Carrickfergus and lifelong Red, was there, standing in the lounge, a glow of satisfaction over his bearded face that needed no words. It was full of Reds, as was the whole of the City Centre. A few 'Bitter Blues' caused a bit of a fracas in the downstairs bar (for a change) and the last thing I remember was coming back from the toilet and the place was swarming with the 'Old Bill' in riot gear. I pleaded insanity and sheepishly disappeared off to my room.

# MY RED FRIENDS

## The Jacksons

Alan and his wife Linda are two special people in my life. They are truly remarkable. As I mentioned earlier, it is easy being a good friend of other match-going Reds, there is a brotherhood amongst the besotted that is difficult to explain to those unfortunates who have not been infected by the Red virus. My dear friends live just around the corner from my workplace and are regular - almost daily - visitors. They'll come in, have a cup of coffee and we'll talk about our passion, United, the Supporters Club (of which Alan is Chairman) and the arrangements for the next trip.

Linda, shoulder-length hair, glasses (contacts when posing), attractive, with all the right bits in all the right places, hails from the Shore Road in Belfast. She has a distinctive 'townie' accent and uses many colloquialisms in her everyday conversation, such as 'Are you in the middle of your dinner?' (Are you eating?) or 'I've me dinner all over me' (I've eaten).

Alan, permanently tanned from his Teletext cheapies, is forty-something plus VAT, swarthy, hides the silver streaks deliberately by enthusiastically participating in many sponsored head shaves. Not only did he play football for many years in the Belfast District League (in fact had to retire because of a back injury) but he also possesses a sound overall football knowledge. Unlike some of us who are solely obsessed with United, he could give you answers to many questions regarding British, European and World football. Perhaps he should get out more often.

Attending the 1990 F.A. Cup Final at Wembley against an enthusiastic and talented Crystal Palace team was my first United game in the company of Alan Jackson. I remember stopping Alan in his red Mercedes as he drove up the North Road in the ancient Norman town of Carrickfergus.

"You going to Wembley, sir?" I asked.

"Have you got any tickets?" asked my erstwhile friend.

"Not yet but there's an advert in tonight's 'Tele' (Belfast Telegraph) advertising a package ... Skelton Tours, do you know those guys that do the trips?"

"All right then,' he said, 'if you can book me a place I'll definitely go."

Next morning I rang and was overjoyed when I was able to book two places. I couldn't believe my good fortune. It seemed that paradise was just over the horizon.

When we arrived at the airport we were informed that only one match ticket was available and when we arrived at the hotel we found only one bed in the room. Our complaints to the hotel fell on deaf ears and I slept fitfully on a floor which was as soft as titanium. I lay, covered in a coat with all the insulating properties of a broken window, to wake up shivering and the possessor of a neck so stiff that an angry dog couldn't have marked it with its teeth. Our adventure seemed doomed. How on Earth could we get a second ticket? By sheer chance we were able to buy a second ticket off someone we met and this set the tone for a wonderful weekend of soccer and doing the things boys do on such occasions. The game itself was the stuff of which cup final legends are made, a climactic six goal thriller that sent the blood pressure soaring. It ended in a draw and led to a replay which at that time was beyond our means.

I had just moved house to the Carrickfergus area and Alan was not only one of the biggest Reds I have encountered but also one of the most genuine people you could ever wish to meet. He's had the pleasure of seeing George Best in action at Old Trafford and when he downs a few 'cokes', the old times are revisited, such as how he was in the Stretford End the day George Best annihilated Sheffield United.

Since 1990 Alan and I have shared many occasions watching United play their way across various countries. Alan and Linda hold a place of affection in my life, as does their son - 'our Gary', as his mother calls him. They have an African Grey parrot 'Eric' and an Irish Red Setter 'Fergie', whom my dog Treble would like to get to know a lot better.

## Wee Gary Callaghan

1994 was quite a year. Some things just stick in your mind. The war in the Balkans wound its bitter way forward, Ayrton Senna was tragically killed, the Channel Tunnel opened, Nelson Mandela was sworn in as President of South Africa and the Provisional IRA called a ceasefire. It was then that I first met Gary Callaghan, another match-going Red whom I had often seen and acknowledged at airports but had never actually spoken to. I always thought he looked like Barry McGuigan, although by now his muscles were in major league relaxed mode.

Gary is about five foot six, wears nothing but Italian designer clothes (even if they were often intended for the much slimmer Italian male market) and for many years had a well-cultured rat (moustache) hanging beneath his nose. "If it's got a name, buy it," he can often be heard to say.

Gary is actually a hard-working, self-made man who is never off-duty. Even when on trips to Old Trafford and beyond, his mobile phone is almost permanently attached to his ear, often only switched off during the duration of the game. 'The wee man', as Alan and I call him (and he calls each of us), or 'Wee Barry' is one of the most fanatically loyal Reds I have ever met. Gary could quite comfortably pass as a 'suit' or executive supporter and could probably afford to buy each of us an executive box at Old Trafford. However, he's often an instigator of unique and witty terrace tunes, for example at the Spurs game in May of 2000 he could be heard chanting 'We won the Football League again …' and 'Bestie's off the sauce …'.

Gary's a great wee man to go anywhere with and between us we could write a book about our match-going experiences alone: the Leeds cup game, the QPR cup encounter, the 'bar diving' night in Sachas Hotel … the list is endless. The wee man is not quite as good as Peter Boyle at making up songs but they are always sung with feeling. When on a high, all any Red wants to do is sing.

I recall the taxi ride to the airport when the driver told us he was from Lahore. Picture the scene. We have just beaten Leeds and are heading back to the airport. The cab driver starts telling us all about Lahore in Pakistan and in no time at all the song began: 'Lahore in Pakistan, Lahore in Pakistan' (to the 'Go West' tune of 'Ohh, Ahh, Cantona'). We're both gifted enough that we can comfortably stand in the back of a black cab, which helps us in our roof beating in time with our singing.

On another occasion when we were coming in to land at Manchester airport, on another of our fortnightly flights,

I was bursting to go to the Gents but the 'Fasten your seatbelts' sign was well and truly lit - a bit like us in truth. We were flying so low you could see the buildings. I told Gary I really had to go urgently. He assured me that access to the toilet on board was permitted in cases of emergency as long as I was quick. I got up and ran towards the front of the plane - looking out, we were almost level with the rooftops.

By this stage nothing mattered. I had to go. On the way up the aisle I could hear a stewardess growling at me.

"Excuse me, excuse me!"

"Please sit down, sir."

No sooner had I made it into the toilet than the banging started on the door. I froze and panicked. Even before I could get my zip down and 'drain the spuds', I was thinking all sorts of things like being banned from flying or arrested for 'toilet rage'. I sheepishly opened the door, received a severe scolding from the stewardess and was shown to my seat like a humble wee mouse. Luckily enough it was only a matter of seconds before we landed and I was allowed special permission to 'dive to the bog' as we pulled up to our gate. Thanks, Gary, your advice was well appreciated.

It wasn't long before I had my revenge on wee 'Barry' Callaghan. On another after-match flight home, the morning after the Chelsea Cup Final, Gary was 'busting his gut' to go to the toilet even before we took off. About two minutes into the flight he said he had to go.

"Wee man, I'm not kidding, I'm busting my gut."

I assured him that it was OK and if he was stopped he should say he had a medical problem and all would be fine. Sure enough, the wee man got up as we were still at 45 degrees. He made it to the toilet and 'done the business'. Once again the stewardess banged furiously on the door.

He didn't respond but when he came out he was given a five-minute lecture at the front of the plane on air safety and civil aviation laws. Not one to be messed with, Gary told the stewardess exactly what he thought of her and how she was nothing but a glorified waitress.

About ten minutes later the flight supervisor arrived at our seats and started giving off again. I suggested to Gary that he take it easy as he ran the risk of being stopped at the other side.

Thankfully the stewardess did not take these comments too seriously (even though he really meant them) and we escaped yet again with a barrage of 'Oh what bad boys you are!' It was almost like being back in Drumahoe Primary School.

Gary and I have had hundreds of 'United nights' together. One of the highlights included a trip to Maine Road when we were brave, shirt-wearing Reds, deliberately worn with a purpose, I should add.

We arrived at Maine Road straight from the airport and tried to find a hostelry which might be 'Red friendly'. OK, I know we were a trifle naive. Gary was wearing the Red shirt with pride and me the black version - with collars turned up, of course. We moseyed around Maine Road looking for any Reds, but to no avail. A sign above the Social Club stated £1 or £2 admittance on match day. We asked if we could enter. "Sure thing, wee men," was the reply, "just watch yourselves."

To this day I will never forget the silence. About five hundred 'Bitters' must have been in the place, all pinting. As we walked towards the bar and turned left you could not only hear a pin drop but also see the pure shock on their faces. Either they were amazed at our brazen cheek or gave us the Irish 'by ball', but how we ever walked out of that place alive I will never know. At first I think they were respectful (just joking - more like dumfounded). Some clown walked by dressed in a judo outfit with a Barcelona scarf around his middle. I don't think he was too amused when I pointed out that it should have been a karate suit (in reference to Eric's two-footed attack on a loud-mouthed Palace fan and our team being dumped out of the European Cup by the Spaniards).

Luckily enough, two Reds were serving behind the bar and an old Irish Red bar steward who not only 'kept us right' but also gave us the nod to clear out before Armageddon began. This was the game in which the Reds were herded underneath the Kippax building site. It had been absolutely pouring down most of the day. After the game we walked to the bus stop and boarded what we thought was a 'Red' bus. As an almighty fight broke out just beneath the stairs it became fairly obvious that these were mostly 'Bitters' looking for any excuse to vent their frustration (we had 'stuffed' them 3-0) and we swiftly hid our 'colours'.

"Wee man, button up, quick, I'm not joking, we're going to get our heads kicked in here."

I remember another night in Sachas Hotel when Keith Gillespie joined our company with big Simon Blair - a Red whom we have not met since. This was a wild night of partying. I remember making up about twelve verses of 'Old Alex Ferguson had a farm' and running up and down the length of the lounge in an effort to get the Reds present 'wound up' enough to join in the chorus…It worked. All twelve times.

Then the 5-0 demolition of Manchester City when the 'wee man' had a fifty pound bet on United to win 4-1. Big Niall Quinn missed a sitter for City when we were 4-0 up. As the ball skied over the crossbar the pair of us 'got up' as if we had scored (you know that motion when you go through all the actions and then stop as the ball goes wide and you end up with a loud oooaaaaahhh noise). Then we realised we were actually United supporters in the East Stand - thoughts of the nearly-won bet were diminished when a few of the Red Army gave us looks as if we were 'Bitters'.

"Stuff the money - let's chin them properly," I remember Gary saying.

"You better believe it, sir - your big man was giving us some looks"

King Eric Cantona's return from his six month exile was on 17 September. I had my 'future ex-girlfriend' (now work that one out) Sue with me. I must admit if it had not been for her that day I would have been arrested or at least thrown out of the ground. Earlier we had bought a couple of 'gold-lined' tickets from a tout. A snip at £120 each. This meant we had about £50 to do us the rest of the weekend - though as usual we considered it good value.

"At least we got decent seats," I distinctly remember saying. You can imagine the horror when we went to sit down and there was someone in our seats. A steward came on the scene and asked us to make our way to the back of the stand where a burly police officer gleefully led us to a downstairs office.

Sue suggested she took care of the talking and explained that she had come over from America especially for this game. I stood outside where I could just about see, from the disabled entrance, the goal we were attacking.

After the 'inquest' the pair of us were led underneath the stands to a seat in the North Stand Lower Tier, which was then under construction. There had been many forgeries that day and most of the people had been ejected from the ground.

Sue was an American taking a vacation with some friends in Belfast when I met her. I had been skiing in Park City, Utah, the previous year. I received a telephone call at work one day from Des ('Macski, Ski Rentals') stating that he had a girl from Utah just stop in to say 'Hi'. He knew I had been to Utah a few times so he put her on the telephone to speak to me.

By coincidence, I had actually met her the previous year when she had been a ski guide. I noted her contact telephone number and although we planned to meet soon after, I had some already arranged Red commitments. About two weeks passed and I called her to ask if she fancied going to Manchester to watch a soccer game - United were playing West Ham. I met her at Belfast City Airport the morning of the game and instantly recognised her. I took her to The Dog and Partridge before the game and she hit it off with Boylie and the City shirt-wearing barmaid, Big Irish Anne.

It was all pretty weird for me because I had never taken any of my girlfriends to a game before. I felt then - and still do now - that it's primarily a lads' thing (although I do know some amazing female Reds). However I enjoyed taking her and recall that night sitting outside the Mitre Hotel trying to explain my 'fixation' with soccer and Manchester United. Sue's father had just died and she was very homesick, but I honestly believe she enjoyed the experience and I certainly had no problem taking her again.

She moved in with me shortly after that and it was not long before we went for a 'Double' at Easter. We played City on the Saturday at Maine Road and Coventry on the Monday at Old Trafford. That was the game in which the Sky Blue's player, David Busst, was horrifically injured in a clash with Denis Irwin. He lay in agony, his blood staining the grass after the collision. The 50,332 crowd - the biggest domestic attendance in nine years - was shocked into awful silence as Busst had his legs strapped together before being carried off. You could sense the players' heads were not really on the game after that.

I had obtained the tickets for City from John Kenyon who came to The Mitre Hotel to meet us on the morning of the game. John and 'Big Karl' had just starred in a documentary about ticket touting at Old Trafford. Kevin and Deirdre Woodside - two good friends of mine from Whitehead - were with us. Kevin had seen the documentary and proceeded to 'wind Wee John up - Major League style.'

While John and I were sorting out the tickets, a knock came at the door and Kevin shouted, 'Open up John, this is The Cook Report!'

John dived into the wardrobe and would not come out. He genuinely believed it was a film crew from The Cook Report and obviously did not fancy another starring role in a television documentary.

After the 1994 Chelsea Final, although we were soaked to the skin, we partied until dawn. After our stress on the way into the ground (officials drew us aside and informed us that our tickets were forgeries - which they were not), the rain was not going to prevent our celebrations when 'The King' destroyed the Blues with two penalties.

Another momentous night occurred when Gary, Paddy Crerand and I went to the Eubank and Naseem fights in Manchester. We had arranged to meet Paddy in the Chester Court Hotel after we had changed into our gear and he had finished his regular match day stint on the radio. Paddy took us to a nice Italian restaurant in Deansgate.

70

I recall Bryan Robson, sitting in the stand to our right, waving over to us (well to Paddy actually). Gary and I joked at the time, 'I bet you your man is saying, "Who is that old guy with Callaghan and Norris? No offence, Paddy.

Meeting Eric and Fergie for the first time were both memorable events.

We spent the 1996 Cup Final day with Walter and Ethel Smith in the Hilton Hotel at Wembley. Gary had obtained 'a good deal' from the Hilton and when we arrived on Friday night the place was full of Liverpool ex-players including David Johnson, and those Scousers who had sold enough stolen hub-caps to afford to stay there (just kidding, honest). There they all were, spouting with each other as to how great they were and how they were going to chin the Mancs the following afternoon. Gary and I were having a few cokes and chatting. It was a weird atmosphere being surrounded by them and having to listen to so much mad dog. As they drank they became louder and Big Time Johnson's cronies ordered a couple of bottles of champagne. We had such a laugh - it took them about twenty minutes studying the wine list to find the cheapest bottle of plonk. You know when someone orders champagne in an ice bucket how every head in the bar will turn to see who the Flash Harry is. Along came another one; obviously they must have taken a whip-round between them.

Gary was having none of it, so we moved to the other end of the lounge. Not long after, they began to sing their anthem 'Wa-lk on, Walk on'. There must have been about one hundred and fifty of them in full voice. Where they issuing us a challenge? One brave big-mouthed, big-moustached, big-haired shell-suit-wearing guy came over and asked if we knew any songs about Liverpool.

We didn't need to be asked twice and so broke into 'Sign on, sign on, cause you'll never get a job' and followed up with 'In your bitter Scouse slums, you don't go to Wembley you don't win no cups'. I continued with:

"United, United, ra ra ra
City, City, ha ha ha
Leeds, Leeds, ba ba ba
Scousers, Scousers, rob your houses!"

Now what would happen? If we had thought about it properly we should have sung something less hurtful, such as 'He's only a poor little Scouser' - that might have made them happier. Sure enough, Gary and I were surrounded by about twelve of them threatening all sorts of nastiness. Within about thirty seconds a few vanloads of police arrived and as the Scousers ran away (isn't there a song about that?), on Gary's advice, we sneaked off upstairs. The Wee Man is fairly sensible when he knows the 'Fat Lady has sung'.

Oh boy! Did we make the correct decision! We appeared down for breakfast the next morning to be told by staff that there had been a mini riot. Chairs and curtains had been slashed with knives in a fracas among themselves. We often laugh about it now when we realise that we had annoyed them so much they started fighting with each other.

The next day provided some of my fondest memories as a football fan. The Hilton Hotel was full of Reds - and the Scousers were in hiding. About 10.30 a.m. Gary and I were having breakfast when a well-dressed couple with two boys walked into the lounge. You know when you see someone you recognise but can't place them in that particular situation?

Gary said, 'There's your man! What do you call him? Walter Smith, the Rangers' manager.'

No one else was in the room so Gary sent a waitress over with a drink. In a little while a waitress appeared and asked if we would like anything from the bar. We looked across and Walter smiled, so we decided to join him. He introduced us to his beautiful wife Ethel and their two sons Stephen and Neil. We must have spent about two or three hours talking football, Rangers/Celtic, United/Liverpool. To hear Walter talk openly and so passionately about football and his wife, a real lady, join in the conversation was an unforgettable experience. I remember asking about Gazza and how he was getting on. Walter's boys told me of how he often took them on fishing trips and was generally a great bloke to be around.

They were such genuine people and I persuaded Walter to have a photograph taken dressed in a United scarf to show to my Rangers friends back home. As kick-off approached, Walter said he would meet us after the game before they got the evening flight to Glasgow. After Eric's momentous Scouse-busting winner, we headed back to the Hilton where we met up with big Martin and a few other Reds. We were telling them about the fantastic morning we had experienced and that Walter and the family were coming back. They all thought we were full of bull, but were silenced when about twenty minutes later I felt a tap on my shoulder and was asked, 'What are you having, wee man?'

I have met many of the footballing fraternity but can honestly say that Walter Smith is one the most down-to-earth and genuine of them all. He spoke openly to all the lads with us. Even the Celtic fans in our company shook his hand and passed comment on his very likeable character and his beautiful family. When we returned home, I sent Walter a letter thanking him for adding so much to our great day. It said it all when I received a letter back from him, passing on his regards and stating that he would be pleased to meet us again.

## Martin 'Faceman' Cleary

Another guy with whom I have shared many United experiences, and who is more than partially responsible for me embarking on this project, is the legendary 'Faceman' - Martin Cleary, another lifelong Red. The Face is one of those guys who has a heart for United as big and as strong as the Special Brew he drinks.

A tall character with a receding hairline , sometimes loud - 'Ahhhhhhhh I'm the Faceman' he would growl - but for the most part mild mannered and sentimental. The Face is often mistaken for Bruce Grobbelar to whom he bears an uncanny resemblance and he's never without his black United baseball cap. This hat could win a prize for some of the angles and positions it ends up on The Face's head (especially after he has been visited by the sauce doctor).

When I first moved to Whitehead, I had heard so many stories of this baseball-wearing Manchester United fanatic in the town but a couple of months passed before I actually met him.

'What about you, sir? I hear you're the biggest red in Whitehead'

'Oh aye, I heard there was a wee United man from Derry moved into my town. I heard the boys talking about you. I'm the Faceman, you're Keith I take it?'

'Aye, I'm Keith, sir. Keith Norris, nice to know there's another Red in the town anyway. 'I'm from Londonderry by the way, not Derry,' I joked.

'Aye, I suppose you say "wan" and call everybody "sir" like the rest of them from Derry stroke Londonderry or Stroke City as Gerry Anderson (local radio presenter) calls it ?'

In Northern Ireland it does not take long in a conversation, or tribal exchange, to establish someones religion. Faceman had said Derry, I had said Londonderry. He must be a Catholic. He knows I'm a Protestant. I thought to myself but never put much pass on it but I felt happy like coming out of the religious closet, if you like. This was Whitehead, County Antrim, after all, a friendly and mixed community I had heard so much about, all that political stuff shouldn't matter here, I thought.

'Oh sir, there's plenty of Reds in Whitehead. I'll introduce you to them.'

'I just moved here. Do you fancy going over to a game sometime? The Faceman? By the way, if you don't mind me asking, why are you called the Faceman? What's your real name?'

'Ahhhhhhhh I'm the Faceman', he growled and laughed. 'Few know the legend of the Faceman', he continued and produced a picture of a long haired, hippy like character. 'You are privileged, wee man, it takes years for people to see that picture.'

'Privileged? Scared more like, Faceman', I joked.

'Martin Faceman Clearly. That's me twenty years ago,' he announced and reached his hand forward. We shook as if we were a pair of highfalutin businessmen about to sign some colossal deal.

It was obvious Faceman and I would be good friends from the start. When two Reds meet and Manchester

United is the common denominator, NO barriers whatsoever exist.

Following the defeat by Everton in the 1995 FA Cup Final, The Faceman, Cousin Aidy and I decided to walk to London from Wembley. We headed out along the road and were soon passed by joyous Evertonians heading back to Scouse Land. The first ten or fifteen coachloads were giving us the two-fingered salutes, but as they continued to pass they became friendlier.

'Those tail-end Scousers aren't so bad,' exclaimed The Face. Little did we know that we were actually walking along a one-way system (the same coaches were passing us again and again). By the tenth drive past, the Scousers were waving and inviting us on to their coach. We eventually made it to Tesco's where we hi-jacked a taxi from some old dear carrying several bags of groceries. The Rasta taxi driver had never seen Northern Irish money. He became really upset when we advised him (in a nice way of course) that for his own safety he had better drive rather quickly.

'Yeah, man, no worries, brother, quick as I can.'

As we reached town, the driver was getting stressed. He dumped us out right in the middle of a bunch of Evertonians - was he really that clever and was this payback? We assumed that we were about to be harassed (Face was wearing his United cap again that Billy Moore had presented him on his fortieth birthday), but thankfully we saw a wine store right on the street corner. Acting the diplomat, I insisted we buy them a bottle of champagne. I knew it was a cheap thing to do - well, cheap sparkling wine works a treat on any Scouser. We were invited to join them in their after-match celebrations.

Eventually it ended up with Face and I wearing Blue Noses chanting 'Barry Horne, Barry Horne!' and the

Scousers were singing 'Ohh Ahh Cantona!' It was like being part of a UN Peacekeeping Force; always on edge but never any real threat of trouble. That is one thing about the Evertonians as compared to the real rival from across Stanley Park - a different type of Scouser, if you know what I mean.

The Face is one of those guys who is totally unpredictable. He gives any player he meets his autograph. We met Ole Gunnar Solskjaer in Manchester one day after a game. 'Ole, I'm The Faceman. Here's a wee souvenir for you, son.' Ole Gunnar, obviously startled, politely smiled and accepted his gift. He also gave Paddy Crerand his autograph one day in the Mitre Hotel.

The habit has intensified. Face and Paddy were enjoying festivities in the Amblehurst as usual following the last game of the Century at Old Trafford (Bradford on Boxing Day). The pair of them were signing autographs for American tourists. Okay, Mr Crerand is a legend but who will the Yanks tell their kids The Faceman is?

The Face was, is, and always will be Eric's worshipper. A few years ago, I bought a shirt in a frame which had been signed by Eric. I had pulled a muscle in my back and could barely walk. I even had to lie on the floor in the Trafford Bar while the boys were playing pool. Face guarded 'Eric' (the framed shirt) in the hotel and carried him like a child on the way home. Even on the flight home the next morning he had the passengers in stitches by insisting that 'Eric' was given a special seat of his own at the front.

Face's most legendary night was after the Barcelona game in '94. The Mitre Hotel bar had closed, so we sat chatting for an hour or two, trying our best to persuade Stan to serve some pints of refreshment.

'Ahh, Stan, any chance of serving the Faceman a few pints?' Face asked growling in his friendly way.

'No pints, Faceman, I can only serve you half-pints.'

'Okay then, can I have eighteen half-pints please, Stan?' asked Faceman.

'Okay, give me a few minutes.'

Stan actually did serve the eighteen half-pints. He could have been a part-time tax inspector - in fact, he was.

Then we heard the sound of a vacuum cleaner and assumed that as the sun had come up the hotel cleaners had started their daily chores. Lo and behold, time stood still, at the sight of The Faceman dressed only in thigh-length boots, and a 'Nick Cotton Is Innocent' T-shirt with - you've guessed it - the Hoover. This was Face's way of getting the boys an extra pint.

Meeting Keano and Pally a few hours earlier in Chinatown obviously wasn't enough for him. We had just finished a Chinese feast after the Barcelona game and were about to jump into a cab when we heard a mumbling that Keano and Gary Pallister were in a nightclub, I think it was named Brambles. Sure enough, in we trooped and there were Keano and Pally who had obviously consumed the price of a ton of coal. We had no paper on which to get autographs for the kids back home so I lent Davy 'Root' Nelson a £20 note. I eventually got the money back on my thirtieth birthday. It was given as a present this time and was the actual one I had lent him a few years earlier.

## Andy Cole RIP

I have one other story to relate concerning the murder of my beloved cat, 'Andy Cole Norris'. The Faceman has a lot to answer for.

During the last European Championship, The Face, Dave 'Root' Nelson and I watched every evening game at my abode. At the time I had two cats, 'Andy Cole' and 'Andy's Brother' (their registered names). It was the norm that Andy and his brother would lie sleeping on the mat in front of the fire as we watched the game. One night Face got up go to the bathroom. Before he left I shouted, 'Face, quick, watch this!' as a free kick was just about to be taken. Face rushed in, put his hand on my as yet unattached mantelpiece. Bang, off it came, on to the new gas stove, against the new brickwork and right on top of Andy Cole Norris, killing him immediately.

'I've killed Andy, sir. I've killed wee Andy Cole!'

'He's alright Faceman. He's only dazed sir, don't panic. Andy will be okay'

'Oh poor Andy Cole,' he sobbed. 'I'm so sorry sir, it was an accident, I would never hurt your cat, not wee Andy.'

'He's alright Faceman,' I tried to reassure him.

'He's NOT alright, NOW GET OUT OF MY WAY.'

Faceman lifted Andy and ran outside to the garage adjoining my house where Andy's brother was sitting frightened behind the lawnmower.

'Get Andy's brother out of here now, sir. I don't want him to see his brother in this state.'

'Right, no worries, sir. Calm down, Faceman, look Andy's dead sir, there's nothing we can do. It was an accident, you didn't kill him. If it's anybody's fault it's mine, that mantelpiece should have been fixed to the wall.'

'I DID KILL HIM, I killed your cat, I killed wee Andy Cole Norris'

My neighbour Jim appeared on the scene, startled by the commotion in my driveway, directly opposite Jim's house and clearly visible from his living room window.

'What's wrong lads? Are you boys okay?'

'Jim, Andy's dead, we had a wee accident.'

'We didn't have an accident, I killed Keith's cat, Jim…I killed Andy Cole…I'm sorry…. I'm away home.'

'What happened?' he enquired.

'You know that new fireplace Jim? The slab of hardwood for the mantel wasn't attached. Face was going to the toilet and one of the teams had a free kick. I shouted to Face to hurry back and watch. He ran in and leant against the wood and it fell on to the fire and then wee Andy who was sleeping on the floor.'

'Come on, we'll bury him round the back, sir and I'll make a wee headstone in the morning.'

Jim dug a grave at the side of my garage, placed Andy Cole in a plastic bag and then into the grave. We both filled the grave in silence, both heads bowed in respect.

'Jim, I'm worried about the Faceman, he's in a bad way'.

'Face will be okay as long as them boys in the pub don't give him a hard time, Keith.'

Accidents do happen, and I was equally to blame for not ensuring that the mantelpiece was properly secured. Faceman took it very badly. I tried to console him but he was having none of it. I tried calling him over the next few days but to no avail. It was the talk of the town. He was getting some serious abuse. 'Murderer', 'Catman', 'Cat Killer', were the jibes, but what nearly put the big man's head away was the fact that when he walked into the Whitecliff Inn at the weekend all his mates were wearing black armbands and making loud meowing sounds.

'Meeeeooooowwwww … meeeeeeooooowwww.'

'Here, kitty, kitty, kitty.'

'Hey, Faceman, when are you up in court?'

'You'll get three years with no parole.'

Face is a warm-hearted, sentimental guy. He appeared at my house again the following Monday night and asked to see where Andy was buried. I showed him around the back and he asked for a few moments on his own. I walked around the side of garage leaving him to it. He had paid his respects and said his farewell to Andy.

The next morning I was going out to feed Andy's Brother and peeked over at the grave to see Face's personal and treasured United badge sitting reverently on the headstone. That's the kind of guy he is. His devotion to United has been blamed by some for costing him his marriage. I must admit he didn't help matters when a recent press interview stated that when challenged by his wife that he loved United more than he loved her, he replied that he loved Manchester City more than he loved her!

While I loved Andy to bits, I actually felt worse for The Faceman. I now have another two cats, Scholesy and a new Andy along with two Samoyed dogs, Keano and my latest addition, Treble. Needless to say when The Face comes around for a game I keep a careful eye on him and he is allowed nowhere near the pets. Face and I are best mates forever. Differing religions maybe, different jobs maybe. This is one guy I would trust with my life - I did say life, not wife!

In case you think the Face is 'always with the sauce doctor' he is one of the most genuine guys and staunchest Reds around.

## The Cockney Reds

When you share a similar passion new acquaintances are easily made. When that passion is Manchester United this is amplified tenfold. The mutual respect and esteem which Alan, Gary and I hold for four, differing fellow Reds who happen to live in London is very hard to put into words. It's not talked about - it's simply there in abundance.

Emotional greetings, goodbyes or daily contact are all non-existent. In fact we have very little in common - except, that is, a match-going obsession with the Mighty Red Devils.

Residing in the infamous K-stand, home of many of United's hardcore support, these guys watch United home and away in the Premiership (a feat we can only dream of), are veterans of numerous 'Euro aways' and have given many years service to the Red cause.

We first met Jamie and Paul when we happened to be sitting next to them on the flight from Gatwick to Copenhagen and have shared many experiences including eventful trips to Milan, Tokyo and Brussels. 'Kev' and his father Brian - or 'Da Brian' as we call him -were introduced to us at a subsequent game at Old Trafford. Jamie, a school caretaker, and Kevin, a supervisor making ejector seats for aeroplanes, are both more than six foot tall, and could easily pass as male models, especially as they usually sport clothing worthy of such.

Paul, some sort of electrical wizard involved with repairing credit card machines, bears the old club crest tattoo on his chest and is slightly smaller, has slightly less hair and often wears a designer baseball cap, but like the others, he is always kitted out in up-to-date name-branded clobber.

'Da Brian', sixty-something, well spoken and always well turned out, is extremely passionate about the Reds and has several United-related tattoos on his body.

Following your team, you have many match day mates, but these guys have become genuine friends. This was epitomised in August 2000 when Alan and Linda, Gary and Marie and Yukari and I were invited to Kevin and

Jackie's wedding in London. When Linda started to address the envelopes in response to the invitations we encountered an absurd problem

'What's big Cavan's (Kevin's) second name?' Linda asked.

'Haven't a clue,' said Alan.

'What's Jamie's and Paul's?'

'Dunno,' I replied.

That shows the satisfying naivety of genuine friendships. We may have travelled with the lads, had them as guests at functions in Belfast and Carrickfergus and socialised with them often, but we didn't have a clue as to their surnames.

On the day of the 'United' wedding we were asked to dispel our already purchased flowers and replace them with red and white ones. The three-tiered wedding cake had a United player sporting the red 'Vodafone' shirt, and the speeches were very much United orientated. It was an unbelievable day, which included our being entertained by 'Marky', one of Tottenham's firm, who thrilled us with tales of his escapades and adventures over the years. This was capped when 'Da Brian' dropped his trousers to reveal the biggest tattoo of the European Cup we have ever seen on his right thigh.

These four characters play a big part in our United lives.

## Brian From Bray

'How's it going, Keith, I'm Brian.'
'What about you, sir, where's that accent from?'
'I live in Bray, just outside Dublin.'
'Are you going into the town?'

'Aye, c'mon, are you coming with us?' I asked.

'Brian from Bray', as we immediately christened him, joined us as we prepared to sample the sights and more importantly the sounds of Milan in the afternoon prior to the Champions League Quarter Final in 1999.

Brian almost always wears colourful, bear-like fleeces, black jeans and caterpillar boots. Short (well he is bigger than me - then again that wouldn't be hard), mousy-coloured short gelled hair (in the morning anyway).

'I've heard that you're the one with a big mother of a flag, Keith,' he continued

'Yes, I have a flag all right, Brian. She's only a wee child but she'll be a big girl some day, I'll have to let you meet her.'

'What do you call her, Keith, is it Lilian or something?'

'She's called Lily.'

'Ah, Keith, that's a lovely name for a big girl, I'd love to meet her.'

You never get tired of talking to Brian - his accent is musical, his attitude enlivening. Throughout the Treble season of 1999, especially in Milan and Barcelona, I was very much indebted to this mild-mannered man from Co. Wicklow … as you will find out.

## Late again

Another memory for me following the heartbreaking 0-1 home defeat (0-2 on aggregate) to Borussia Dortmund in 1997 was their amazing fans. I was working until 6.00 p.m. that day and had to catch the 7.00 p.m. flight from Belfast, meaning I would only miss the first half-hour of the game. Some folks said I was crazy but it was worth it just to be there. It was, after all, the semi final of the European Cup; I simply had to be there.

Having lost 1-0 at Westfalenstadion two weeks previously, we knew what we had to do. It was pretty simple - beat Dortmund in order to progress to the final of the European Cup.

I arrived at my seat in the South Stand at 7.30 p.m.

'Any score, sir?' I enquired of Alan.

'Wee man, we should be about four up.'

Numerous opportunities, chances squandered, an uncharacteristic lack-lustre performance from King Eric, this was not to be our night. It had a nervousness about it which ended in a 1-0 defeat at the hands of the Germans.

We all knew we were a better team than Dortmund, the eventual winners of the competition, and should have beaten them. 'Maybe we were not ready yet', was a fairly lame excuse bandied about repeatedly.

The only consolation were the Dortmund fans and their contribution to another memorable night. I thought at first there was going to be a riot after the game when hundreds of Reds made their way, running and jumping over rows of seats, towards the German fans in the right-hand corner of the South Stand. Unlike Feyenoord the year following, who sang Scouse songs and waved Liverpool scarves, the Dortmund fans broke into 'Oh Manchester is wonderful' and, if nothing else, eased the pain of defeat - at least a fraction.

One certainty whenever United are beaten (thankfully it is not too often) is that everyone makes a special effort on those sad nights and they often turn out to be especially memorable.

Against FC Kosice the following season (1997/1998) my brother-in-law Richard 'Duke' McClelland (one of the original Scousebusters in Primary 6), Sean, David, Gary and I had to charter a wee plane to get to the match on time. It seems crazy but it was cheaper for us to hire a light aircraft than to fly British Airways. Alan and the lads were already installed in the Mitre having driven down from Stranraer. We headed to the 'Dog' fairly early and the craic was good. As with all European nights, the atmosphere was electric. The floodlights seem to magnify the colourful spectacle, the crowd filled with fervent expectancy.

A comfortable 3-0 victory with goals from Cole and Sheringham and an opposition own goal set us up well in celebratory mode. After the game we went back to the Mitre for an hour or two and then hit Charlie Chans in the middle of Chinatown for our customary feed. I think about ten of us were at our table. At the table next to us was another group of local Reds. It wasn't long before the singing started by two separate suits sitting to our right. The waiter serving us bore an uncanny resemblance to United legend Bobby Charlton and seemed happy enough to let the boys chant away.

You know how a situation can change from one of good craic to almost mayhem? In short, one of the suits (well-dressed) began mouthing off how and why 'out-of-towners' came from Ireland to watch football and how he was a 'real Red' and lived in Manchester.

We accepted that much. However, when he said he had been three times that season so far, that summed him up. By that stage (November) most of us had at least a dozen trips under our belt. Anyone can be given a 'by ball' (be excused), to a certain extent, but when he remained persistent I could foresee a bit of argy bargy. Once again, being the diplomat, I sneaked down to the cashier and paid our bill in full. I happened to mention that a couple of guys were starting a bit of trouble, that we were good customers and had nothing to do with it. Besides he recognised me, as I had always given him a good tip as a sweetener.

The Chinese heavies began to appear from all corners of the room with all sorts of instruments - non-musical, I assure you. The action moved towards the big-mouthed suits who were refusing to pay their bill because of the singing - which they had actually started.

The next thing I saw was the fatter of the two big-mouthed suits getting slapped by Piper Al and sent sprawling over a table. Within seconds we heard police sirens approaching so we crept downstairs and outside. We had only walked about thirty feet when two vanloads of the Old Bill arrived. In case we had been spotted and falsely accused of anything we all changed coats. Big Sean, all six foot two of him, with my coat (what a sight), short arms and halfway up his back. I wore Sean's and looked like a banshee - it reached my ankles. Piper Al had Richard's trendy overcoat and, of course, we looked even more suspicious.

Every game attended brings a new story, a new memory. Old acquaintances and Red friends may change or drift away but one thing always remains the same. That is the buzz you get every time you walk down the Warwick Road. Some games are obviously not as memorable as others. Could you imagine forking out a full week's wages, for three trips in a row, to watch three 0-0 draws - Spurs, Leeds and Chelsea in 1995? I, and many others, did. The only solace amidst these three results was the 4-0 drubbing of Leicester City away. I had a ticket for the game at Leicester but had no way to get there, so I resorted to taxi - which I had paid to wait for me. All games play their part and we must accept they all cannot be glory nights.

Every supporter will have their own unique favourite or memorable experience. For some it was the intimidation in

Galatasary, the apprehension and fear in Porto. For others the last 'pay at the gate' game against Chelsea (before they built their new Stand) when about two thousand Reds casually strolled from the Shed end and never got touched by the home fans was especially memorable.

Certain games such as Aston Villa or Norwich away in 1993 are remembered for pure football. Others are memorable for exceptional atmosphere such as Barcelona in 1984 and 1994, Porto in 1996, Juventus in 1997. Particular goals from the likes of Whiteside, Hughes or Robson, specific results or something simple like one move or turn of brilliance: such as Gordon Hill's Brazilian flick or Eric Cantona's nutmeg of Shearer are what feeds our addiction. The same can be said about beating the Scousers in the last minute of the Cup or the Sheffield Wednesday game when big Steve Bruce set us on our way to that first title in so many years.

I spoke to a well-known Red recently driving his cab in Salford. He told me he had been to watch United in Europe fifty- seven times. This is some feat in itself but what made it even more interesting was that his particular favourite was the 4-0 defeat in Barcelona. One of his mates had prevented a kid from being knocked down by diving and grabbing her, movie-style. Spotted by some high-ranking Barcelona official, the lads were cordially invited to the Directors' box where they shocked a few well-known United personnel with their appearance there, including Mr Crerand sitting in the press box below.

When I asked this guy his favourite moment, he recounted the time he gave Eric Cantona a lift home over the Pennines from a game at Leicester and took him into his local pub for a drink.

# How do you classify a Red?

League match ticket-book holder, season-ticket holder, K or J Stander, Stretford Ender, Premier Suite holder, or someone able to attend five matches, fifteen or fifty? Certainly those that never miss a game are a unique breed. For most of us this is a dream and an impossibility. Every day we are talking about United in some form or checking the excellent Internet fanzine sites. United are omnipresent in our lives. Whether a scarfer, a casual or a shirt wearer, who are we to judge anyone else? The following appeared in the United fanzine United We Stand issue 83:

"I've written so much about the clothes we've worn, the swaggering attitude we've had. At this moment in time it's all bollocks. Scarfers, mums, dads, kids and casuals, we stood together as one in the Nou Camp, together in complete bliss as we watched history being made."

To me this says it all - when it really matters no-one cares who or what you are as long as you are a Red. Football is now a fashionable game. It is considered trendy to be a 'supporter'.

Just as there are more celebrity 'supporters' - I use that word loosely - so players now receive pop star acclaim. Fans are also changing but still a hard core of lifelong supporters remain.

The collectiveness and unambiguity of being involved in the community spirit of a football crowd at a match is an amazing and unique feeling. Football fans are often judged as intellectually deficient but if you ever heard the culture and speed of terrace wit and repartee, you would certainly form a different opinion.

United fans lead the way in their caustic chanting: 'Are you City in disguise?' sung to almost anyone we are beating easily is a firm favourite of mine.

Individuals over the years have suffered particularly hostile receptions: Alan Shearer for his attitude, Arsene Wenger because of his appearance (and for having a go at Sir Alex Ferguson), the Geordies for their crying, and individuals for personal misdemeanours such as Stan Collymore, Graham Rix and Lee Bowyer. Leeds, City and Liverpool suffer the brunt of our venom if judged by seventy-five percent of all our songs.

On special occasions like Euro away trips you will always hear songs from the seventies. Nothing silences a packed bar like someone singing an emotional version of 'The Flowers of Manchester' (dedicated to those who perished in Munich).

'You're pissed and you know you are' (to the tune of 'Go West') is directed at any player with a 'sauce' problem - notably Paul Merson and Tony Adams. These and many others suggest that United has more than its fair share of lyricists within the ranks of the Red Army, of whom Pete Boyle is the most famous.

I remember Paul Merson making a gesture as if he were 'snottered' to the United end a few years back after we sang 'There's only one Paul Merson ... he plays in Red he's out of his head. Walking in a Merson [unprintable] wonderland'. He also gave a swagger recently while playing for the Villa. Fair play to him was the general consensus. At least we respected him more for involving us. If I'm not mistaken, we actually gave him a clap that day.

At Manchester United you have to prove you're worth your salt. You have to prove yourself to the fans and be accepted. You cannot be bigheaded, obnoxious or bigger than the club ... as Paul 'Charly' Ince found out.

Famous tunes are used to sing about certain players. 'When the ball hits the net and if it's not Cole it's Poborski' (sung to the tune of 'That's Amore') or 'Gary Neville is a Red,' ('London Bridge is Falling Down') are two of my all-time favourites. 'If you follow Leeds United then ...' ('If you like a lot of chocolate on your biscuit') and other TV adverts such as Quality Street will have the words rearranged, such as 'Magic moments ... we'll never forget the bulge in the net when we beat the Scousers.'

## Brush with the Law Man

Most clubs have supporters from across the country because of resettlement, work, family allegiances or place of birth. To give you an example, in Northern Ireland alone we have several Liverpool, Manchester City, Spurs, Chelsea, Newcastle, Celtic and Rangers Supporters Clubs.

The old anti-United jibes of 'Do you come from Manchester?' or 'Cockneys, Cockneys what's the score?' are jealous cries from our bitter enemies. And if you look at any club's official website or listings you will see this is repeated throughout the British Isles.

Being a football fan costs you friendships, relationships and the financial strain can bring along other problems.

On one occasion I caught the Nightrider crossing from Larne to Stranraer. To be totally honest, we were in no fit state to go anywhere. I am not proud of what occurred although I must admit it was an experience I won't forget in a hurry.

Only eleven cars were on the boat and we had just docked in Scotland. Kenny English (the local painter) who was driving my car fell asleep on the upper decks and we were waiting for him to surface. I was standing joking and having some great craic with several of the dockers who worked on the ship when one of the security guys appeared on the scene and said to me, 'I hope there's not a bomb in your car, wee man.'

'Of course there's a bomb in it,' I replied in total jest. What did he think I was going to say?

On leaving the boat I was cordially led to Stranraer police station to be held until Monday before being charged with causing a breach of the peace. I remember the big burly police officer looking at my little gold United crest on my necklace and smiling, as if to say: 'You won't be seeing any football today, son!'

No-one knew where I was. I had only decided to go very late on Friday night.

Several Whitehead locals had gone to Scotland for a football weekend earlier in the day. We had intended to visit them during the night and then head down to the match early in the morning.

In the holding cell, which was about fifteen foot square, I went through all possible emotions of guilt, remorse, fear, apprehension, shame and humiliation, before realising that I was going nowhere for a few days...

To pass the time I reverted back to my childhood and started playing football with a plastic teacup. Firstly playing 'Keepy up', then actually running about the cell shooting into the goal, which consisted of a putrid grey blanket and the corner of my bed (a stinking floor mattress).

I never denied saying what I said, but the context in which it was taken was totally wrong. I was advised to plead not guilty but later changed this and was consequently dealt a three-month custodial sentence - thank you, your honour - which was reduced to a substantial fine on appeal although I had to serve a further seven days in Dumfries (some weird Jock law about a seven-day lie down).

When I first heard mention of 'a seven-day lay doon', I thought that was Jock slang for a week in the Algarve. However this notion soon left me when I discovered I would be spending seven days at Her Majesty's Pleasure in Dumfries prison. The journey from Stranraer up to Dumfries was, to say the least, eventful. I was handcuffed to a psychotic balloon head who had tried to kill himself in his cell the previous evening. The police had given him one of their shirts to wear because his own was covered in blood. Unfortunately 'Sergeant John' as he called himself had taken his new attire way too seriously. He believed he was now a policeman and proceeded to tell me how I should uphold law and order at all times. He was a fully fledged looper, had a strange, almost wanton look on his face, his head scarred and eyes staring in opposite directions (one looking to Glasgow, the other to Aberdeen).

After he fell asleep, the policemen informed me that Sergeant John was a regular punter and was arrested this time for robbing his own solicitor's office and in doing so dropped a piece of paper with his name and address on it.

The thought of going to jail was much worse than actually being there. I was amazed at the almost lacksadaisical atmosphere and availability of many illegal substances.

The news made it back to my hometown of Whitehead. Consequently at the next home match of Whitehead Eagles, The Faceman appeared brandishing a huge 'Free Keith Norris' banner. The Faceman still claims he was solely responsible for my early release.

# Unconditional Love

Throughout your life football is always relevant. Not a day passes when football doesn't matter. Even at the recent funeral of a very special friend, the uneasy silence was broken by the minister, a Leeds fan, and a jest made about 'that aul' team of yours' referring of course to me and my love of United.

Weddings and other special occasions also bring out good football banter. Recently I could not attend a wedding (how could my cousin Trevor have picked the day we were playing the Scousers to walk down the aisle?) and instead sent him and his beautiful bride Cathy a telegram wishing them all the best but asked had I taught him nothing over the years?

Everyone has his or her own recollections of United: my good friend and Carrickfergus Club Secretary Gary Callaghan actually went to Old Trafford for his honeymoon to watch the West Ham game in 1988; Club Treasurer Billy Manderson was shown around Old Trafford by Sir Matt Busby and Bilko Rainey peed in the same urinal as Stuart Pearson.

'Did you see the football last night?' is often asked, no matter who is playing. Although you adore your team, really you are in love with the game. Being a football fan means not reading about the deaths in the papers. We scour the sports pages for any snippet of news about our team. Football, while not controlling your life - how sad would that be? (choking) - plays a major role. Family, work, politics, environment and social issues all come well down the list when you have an addiction ... you will do anything to get that fix.

Even while travelling, CNN is often your only insight into the real world. When you are away watching United the whole match scenario dominates your thoughts. Wondering if Keano would sign a new contract was more important to Alan and me than any possible signing of the Belfast peace agreement during the Toyota Cup in Tokyo. Roy Keane was and is a major name in the history of our club. When he decided to stay, it was a boost not only for us, the fans, but also the players. It showed his commitment to the cause and his winning the Player of the Year award in 2000 was just reward for his endeavours.

Even stories like the Russian invasion of Chechnya or the bombardment of Grozny or other world catastrophes mean very little, terrible as they may be. We would rather have a United story in the headlines and the 'less important' news after. We switch between channels to catch any possible mention of United.

Football fans come from all sorts of backgrounds and have many varying opinions. Just as the teams and the ground evolve, so too does the supporter. In the seventies, the Doc's Red Army, complete with white butcher coats as previously mentioned, were to the fore. The early eighties was a time of scarves, rosettes and flags while later in the decade came the emergence of the casuals.

'Scarfers' seem to be almost looked upon as being uncool by certain sections of our Red family.

I had it all: rosette, two scarves and a United flag draped over my shoulders as a kid - and to be honest I would be way too embarrassed nowadays.

I know many good Reds who nowadays never wear a replica shirt because in their eyes it has become unfashionable and almost a daytripper thing to do. As big Paul rather eloquently puts it, they, the hardcore supporters, love the team but hate anything official. You won't catch these guys in the Megastore buying any merchandise.

From what I can ascertain, this non-shirt-wearing began in the eighties when 'firms' of most clubs cottoned on to the idea that they could create more hassle and escape the undue attention of the police if they were well dressed, hence casuals.

Success brings its own problems. So-called 'Celebrity' Reds jump on the bandwagon, as do millions of 'Glory Hunters' who all of a sudden show allegiance. Many more executives and daytrippers have unfortunately infiltrated our club. This worrying trend has had an affect on the atmosphere at home games and many Reds apportion blame to these quarters.

From my first visit to see the Reds in the flesh, my team has gone through what can only be described as a miraculous transformation. It is now a public limited company and worth an estimated one billion pounds. We have one of the most modern all-seated stadiums in Europe with facilities second to none. Merchandising and astute marketing have helped United become a globally recognised product. Even in war-torn Kosovo, it was amazing that some television news footage showed Manchester United shirts worn by both sides of the warring factions.

With two hundred and five official supporters clubs across the world; forty thousand season ticket-holders; one hundred and seventy thousand official members stretching from Australia, Hong Kong, Japan, Mauritius, Scandinavia and the US; megastores in Dubai, Kuala Lumpur and Singapore, United can certainly claim to be a global institution. It has been estimated that United now have over forty million supporters worldwide who claim allegiance. There are forty official supporters clubs in

Northern Ireland alone. They are by far the most supported club and have always represented something particularly unique in that they transcend the religious divide between the Catholic and Protestant communities.

Since their humble beginnings as Newton Heath L.Y.R. and the tragedy of Munich when a team with the world at its feet was so cruelly wiped out, the club we love has become truly gargantuan. But we must never lose sight of the fact that global branding cannot be allowed to rip the soul from the club. The most important thing is the team on the pitch. I have to agree with the fanzine view that the PLC, for many years, were only interested in money and had little or no regard for the match-going Red. Even so, Mr Kenyon's appointment as Chief Executive, recent consultations with IMUSA, the new Stretford End 'fanzone' (although I detest that term) and the Fans Forum are positive steps in the right direction. The new regime at the helm of the PLC has been making all the right noises but it is now time to start delivering if the real fans are not to be totally ostracised. Paddy Harverson in particular has been a breath of fresh air in club/supporter relations.

Every Red has memories, dreams; every Red thinks he is the biggest Red. That is not so. We share the same passion, feel the same joy and experience the same pain.

Uppermost, we share the same unconditional love for Manchester United.

# THE SUPPORTERS' CLUB

I moved to Whitehead, Co. Antrim in 1991 to be close to my work in Carrickfergus - a town of thirty five thousand people, which lies about nine miles north of Belfast and on the edge of Belfast Lough. It is famed for its medieval castle built by John de Courcy in the late twelfth century.

Whitehead, four miles to the north again from Carrickfergus, is a small coastal town whose most notable landmarks are the Blackhead Lighthouse and tranquil Blackhead path. It lies at the mouth of Belfast Lough. Scotland - which is only 11 miles away -and the Isle of Man can be plainly seen on a clear day. Of all the locations I have visited throughout the world, this is my favourite, and Yukari and I walk the coastal path daily with Keano and Treble.

I was not involved with the local branch of the Manchester United Supporters Club and did not know too many people who actually were members but did meet the 'Faces' at quite a few games. I used to get tickets from the Club when my own tout sources had run dry. I much preferred to make my own way and get my own tickets. Because of my work commitments, I could not travel with the lads as they usually left on Friday afternoon and were not home again until Sunday.

Having met the members of the Carrickfergus Club at the Black Swan, Altrincham and the Landsdowne in Fallowfield, I considered them to be a good bunch of lads who enjoyed the craic and knew how to let their hair down. To be honest, I felt a bit guilty about getting increasingly more tickets from the Club and was persuaded to join by the Chairman at the time, Salford-born Keith Cassells.

I joined the Club in 1994 and at my first meeting I remember being impressed with the raw passion of the members. The place was buzzing with tales from last week's game and looking forward to the next one in a couple of weeks. Meetings were fortnightly so we had no time for hanging about making arrangements. It was obvious these guys were not only match-going companions but also real friends.

Shortly after I became a member, the Club organised an 'Evening at the Races' function. I offered my help with raising funds through sponsorship of horses and obtaining actual race sponsors. The whole situation gave me a major buzz. Over the next few months I began telling my other match-going Red friends about the Supporters' Club.

Gary was wary at first, just like me, preferring to do his own thing and get his own tickets, but did join. The Faceman, my best friend and fellow Whitehead local, had heard stories about some incidents that had happened in the Club previously. He was yet to be convinced. He, like a few other Whitehead Reds, were members of the Carryduff Branch, which held its meetings in Belfast. He, being a Catholic, hinted to me that one of his and my other Catholic friends had suffered sectarian taunts from a former committee member of the Carrickfergus Club. This reputation had a left a bad taste among my new-found Catholic friends in Whitehead.

'Ah c'mon sir let's give it a go Faceman, the Carrick Club is not a loyalist or Protestant club. It's a United Supporters Club. Sure there's Catholics in the club now, sure you know them, don't you? To be honest I don't even know what religion half of them are Face, that's the way it should be. We're all reds-all United supporters-that's all that counts.'

'No, sir, I'd like to but I'm going to finish this year at Carryduff. I'll see how you boys get on.'

'Face, I'm annoyed. Do you honestly think I'd be staying about if that's the craic?'

'Wee man, I hear you and I know what you are saying but I'll join next year if everything goes okay. Fair enough sir?'

This pained me greatly and although it was going to take much time and effort on my part, I knew convincing Faceman and my other friends to join the Club would be easier if they heard positive vibes from other club members. My actions would have to be constructive and include enthusiastic participation. Looking back, I have to say that this was the catalyst for my war of a PR campaign and my relentless mission. It was like being told I couldn't have something I really wanted which, rather than cave in, or give up, only served to make me work with re-energised endeavour.

What possibly could be so bad that people, my best friend included, would not join a Manchester United Supporters Club, a supporters club with which I was involved?

## Meeting the King

Although an active member of the Club, I never went on any Club trips (still preferring to fly), until the game against Spurs in 1994 when we presented Eric Cantona with the player of the season award.

We had all stood around for about an hour waiting for Barry Moorhouse (Membership Secretary) to bring King Eric from the changing rooms. The kids queued at the programme kiosk underneath the South Stand with their programmes ready to get the King's autograph. We heard a door open and then close, strong footsteps and muffled voices. What a feeling when Eric walked around the corner. He was almost Madame Tussaud-like. I'll never forget that day.

I waited until fairly near the end of the queue, happily feeling his presence and watching him. When it came to my turn I walked up to Eric, open-armed as if to hug him. Eric gave me one of those 'I don't think so looks' and shrugged his shoulders in a humorous manner. Realising I was not going to kiss him, he gave me a huge hug and laughed. It sounds poignant but I was literally speechless.

I was so in awe of this colossus-like man and what he had done for the team I had worshipped since boyhood. I would not even dare try to describe Eric's contribution to the cause that is Manchester United. Sufficient to say in his one hundred and eighty one games he played for United he scored eighty goals and led us to not one but four Premiership trophies and two Doubles. In my opinion, his inspired signing from Leeds was not only instrumental in delivering that title we craved for so long but also the impact he had on the players and the standards he set paved the way for recent unprecedented successes. What Cantona created in his time with United and the way he acted as mentor to the 'young guns' will never be overlooked.

Thank you, Eric - Long Live the King!

# Going Places

The 'fix' I got that afternoon encouraged me to become even more involved in the Club. What was even more pleasing was that Faceman eventually joined and, when he realised what sort of a club we were and how efficiently we marshalled events, he ably assisted me in various fundraising ventures on his first evening in attendance.

'Well, sir, what did you think?'

'I have to admit, I'm impressed, it looks like you boys have got the club going well.'

'Faceman, this is what I was trying to tell you last year. We are a mixed club. We are Manchester United supporters, Reds together-that's all that counts. We have something special here and we need to bond the members together.'

'I got a buzz out of doing that fundraising last week. The club made ninety quid. You're right, wee man.'

'Good work at the fundraising, Faceman, You did well, the only snag is you are going to have to give me a hand at the rest of the club functions. We do have an opportunity here to achieve something for the good of the whole community. We are a unique club. Manchester United transcends all barriers, Faceman, I've told you that since I first met you. We can make a difference here. I don't know how we are going to do it, yet, but trust me, we will.'

To see the membership grow and the passion within the Club develop was most encouraging. The Club had, by now, received a substantial allocation of tickets for every home league game. We organised about seven or eight large 'weekender' trips a season where we would transport up to fifty members to Old Trafford. Most European games we would also receive a large allocation and these were always special nights. We met with and presented Nicky Butt and Ole Gunnar Solskjaer with Player of the Season awards. These were great days - for the junior members especially.

Like any organisation, we have had our problems. Accusations, arguments, fights, bitching, backstabbing seem to be an integral part of any club or society.

During a particularly rough period for the Club when funds were at an all-time low, there were rumours and allegations that certain influential members had been falsifying accounts. When this came to the fore, certain members of the committee either resigned or were voted out of position.

# Club Trips

## An emotional start: Leicester - home
## (15 August 1998)

The season kicked off with a home draw against Leicester City in August. Deep into injury time Beckham produced one of those free kicks we were becoming accustomed to and we earned our first League point of the campaign in a hard-fought 2-2 draw.

'Did you enjoy that, Jordy?'

'Aye, Keithy,' he said, watching in amazement as the thousands of 'big' people made their way to the exits.

This was an important day for me. I had taken my sister Cherith, brother-in-law Richard and their two kids, Jordan (aged six) and Jessica (aged two) to Old Trafford for their first time together. Richard had been a few times before.

It was nice to have my sister beside me and hear her say how much she enjoyed it. Did she now understand her brother's twenty five-year obsession?

'What do you think, folks?'

'I really enjoyed it, Keith, now I know why you're so mad,' quipped Cherith.

'Brilliant seats, wee man, you appreciate the speed of the game down here,' Richard added.

The first home match of the season is always something of an anti-climax. You long for it for three months and even though it is great to be back, the result is never crucial. It takes a few weeks to get a few games under the belt and you can feel this among the Red Army who are for the most part sunburnt and pie-laden. We had a large contingent of members from our Branch of the Supporters Club over for the Leicester game.

We had arranged for our Club President, Paddy Crerand, to come to the Mitre Hotel the next afternoon to meet the Club members for a bit of craic and be presented with a crystal decanter. Paddy, as usual, was on top form with a word for everyone and the craic lasted long into the afternoon. Although not many realised it that afternoon, this set the scene for a memorable season. Norman and Ian, lifelong and ardent Reds, could not believe they were sitting beside the legend that is Paddy. No matter whom he meets, he always has a word for them, and even if he does not remember their name he will remember where and when he met them. This certainly applies to the Faceman. Paddy was signing autographs for some of the members when the Face casually strolled over, reached him a piece of paper and said, 'Paddy, I am the Faceman, here's my autograph!' Paddy, the eternal diplomat, calmly thanked Martin and placed it in his wallet with pride.

The trip home was quite eventful. As we boarded the bus to take us to the aircraft the lads spontaneously broke into song - 'We'll Keep the Red Flag Flying High!' We were the only people on the bus with the exception of a couple of blue rinse, bingo-playing-type elderly ladies. Obviously not impressed with our light-hearted choral melody, they stormed off the bus hurling insults in our direction.

About five minutes later, the Captain (a Julian Clary lookalike) appeared and gave us a lecture on aircraft etiquette before we were permitted to board the plane for the short flight home.

It turned out that the two old dears were delayed and had been on the wrong bus anyway. They had had a few too many Irish coffees and were content to complain about our jovial singsong.

One day we will never forget, for all things enjoyable soon changed, from general joviality to a shocked, numbed, depression was as the full story of the Omagh bomb broke. The bomb in Omagh on Saturday 15 August 1998 resulted in twenty-nine deaths and hundreds of injuries. It was the single worst incident in Northern Ireland during the current conflict.

No more jokes, no more laughter, no singing United songs. This was the devastating reality of the horror felt by all at this carnage.

We had been enjoying relative peace for the first time in our lives in Northern Ireland. Our group was totally mixed, Catholic and Protestant, friends together. You could sense disillusionment, hopelessness and shame, but most importantly togetherness in our despair.

# An emotional beginning.

## Eric's Return: Farewell to a Legend
## (18 August 1998)

This was the night we all paid homage to the King, Eric Cantona - a night of sheer emotion. It was fitting that the King graced us with his presence for the Munich testimonial.

'Eric Cantona', 'The Munich Disaster' and 'Sir Matt Busby' will forever be synonymous with Manchester United. It was he, after all, who was instrumental in helping the Club move into a new era, the catalyst for things to come.

It was Eric who brought the team along, nurtured and guided them, setting the standards and leading by example. As Gary Neville said, 'Everyone thinks of Eric as full of fancy flicks. Eric was, as all great players, one of the most ardent trainers.'

He has to have been the buy of the century - a masterstroke from Fergie. Could even the great Sir Alex Ferguson have envisaged the influence Eric would bring to bear? I guarantee that if you had asked any member of that squad who was most instrumental in their success, they would name Eric. He was, by his sheer presence, a father figure, an icon and a natural-born leader.

After the Borussia Dortmund semi-final defeat in 1997, I think Eric believed that his chance of European success was over. This was signified by him removing his shirt before walking down the tunnel after the final whistle was blown. I remember his expressionless face when we won the Premiership against West Ham. While we were all saddened by his decision to retire, it was no real shock and it was time for the 'seagull to finally fly.'

The Munich Testimonial was his chance, and our club members, to exchange farewells. He had been responsible for destroying City on several occasions, played in many Scouse-busting and City killing matches and left us many memories. This was the farewell we craved.

# The King is gone. Long Live the King.
## Barcelona - home (16 September 1998)

Wee John from Rathcoole, Pete Boyle and I were still standing in the Dog and Partridge having a laugh with Anne the barmaid at ten minutes to eight. When we realised what time it was, we had to make a quick jaunt down the Warwick Road and into the stadium. We arrived late, only to find we were already one goal up.

'What happened, mate? Who got her?' I enquired of the middle-aged man beside me.

'Beckham crossed. Giggs headed it in. We should be two up. Yorke landed one on the roof of the net just before.'

To cap it off I had to 'drain the spuds' and missed the second goal a few minutes later. As I stood relieving myself in the toilet, the North Stand erupted in an earthquake of vibration and noise.

'No way, we've scored again, that's the second one I've missed the night,' I muttered to a guy beside me and ran towards the flight of stairs leading to Tier 3.

'What happened this time, mate?'

'Yorkie hit a bicycle kick, Hesp punched it away and Scholes scored.'

'Cheers, mate, I'm not moving from here again.'

108

What a second half! Barcelona were electric, we were shell-shocked and they tore us apart. In saying that, there were a few controversial decisions. Their front two players ran us ragged. Rivaldo was superb and if it had not been for Beck's free kick towards the end, our European ambitions would already have taken a severe blow. Nicky Butt handled the ball on the line and Luis Enrique stepped up to score Barcelona's second penalty and equalizing goal, 3-3.

'That ref cost us the points.'

'We were lucky to hold on for a draw.'

'Fair result in the end though.'

'How was that for entertainment, wee man?' someone asked.

'Amazing, what a game.'

## Toffee Trepidation: Everton - away
### (31 October 1998)

This was the first time we had been in opposition in the Premiership since Walter's move from Rangers. I rang him a few days before the game. His first words said with amusement were: 'All right, wee man, how many tickets do you need?'

I told him we didn't need tickets but we would like to meet him for a few minutes - although, as he had mentioned it, we were one ticket short. His immediate response was, 'Come and see me at two p.m. in the Main Entrance. Just ask for me.'

Now here was a man with the biggest game of his Everton career taking the time to meet Gary, Alan and me one hour before kick off - that really sums him up.

The front entrance at Goodison was jammed solid with autograph hunters and Fergie was hanging out the door signing away for all he was worth. Normally we would have tried to speak with him but this time we excused ourselves and pushed past him into the Reception.

'You must be Keith,' said the very attractive receptionist. 'Mr Smith will be right out.'

'Thanks very much, Lily,' I said, smiling.

Sure enough, Walter came out, shook hands and we had a yarn with him. While I thanked him for the complimentary tickets I also told him I hoped that his team would be stuffed. Walter laughed and told us to come back at five p.m.

There we were talking to Fergie, Bobby Charlton and a few of the Everton players. Okay, it was more a case of acknowledging each other but it was still overwhelming. Once again I managed to go off on a tangent when shaking Alex's hand. I have this uncanny knack of talking gibberish like 'the wee man from Strabane'(the fastest talker in Ireland).

I uttered something like 'How's it going, Alex? Keith Norris, fax you, Wednesday, office, machine, yes.'

You should have seen the look on Fergie's face. He cordially smiled and just as he was about to answer me another Scottish voice behind me called him away. Thank goodness. What I had tried to say was that, yes, it was me who had been in touch with his office via fax on Wednesday past (something to do with a television documentary).

This was the third time in the space of two years I had met Alex in person and the third time I appeared as someone requiring, at the very least, a speech therapy course.

The day after the Feyenoord game in October 1997, I went to the Motor Show in London by train. As we waited for a taxi, I spotted Alex, about ten people in front of me in the queue. Just as he was stepping into a cab I leaned over the barrier, extended my hand and shouted, 'Alex, have you got a wee second, sir?'

A perplexed Fergie walked back towards me, and once again extended his hand. I cannot recall exactly what I mumbled (something about Barnsley, I think). Sufficient to say when he returned to his cab and it pulled away the look on his face was one of relief and bewilderment.

Three players booked and a United opening goal within twenty minutes ensured we were in for a lively afternoon. As Yorke scored, the three of us punched the air and jumped up in celebration, as did about twenty throughout the Scouse-filled stand.

'Watch yourself, wee man.'

'Be wise, boys.'

'Forgot myself there. Thought I was in with the Reds.'

These comments were followed by a loud Liverpudlian accent proclaiming 'Manc twats' in our direction. It is easy to forget yourself at an away ground when you are seated in the home section - you become so engrossed you forget than you are only a few shouts short of a good punch. About three minutes later we were up again after an own goal by Craig Short, this time louder and backed up by more Reds dispersed in the stand. Obviously they had got braver knowing there was a fair scattering of Red brethren in the Toffees stand.

Duncan Ferguson rose to a cross from Ball to knock a powerful header past Schmeichel to narrow the deficit.

Everton had a few chances but United regained their two-goal advantage after Blomqvist ran down the left and supplied a ball to Cole, which he calmly slotted inside the post in the fifty-ninth minute.

'That's enough now, lads. How are we going to face Walter if we tank them seven?' I jested.

Six minutes later, we were once again on our feet cheering as Blomqvist scored United's fourth. As the travelling Red Army in the away fans' section became increasing more vocal, several Everton fans launched bottles and missiles at Schmeichel and then at the referee. Bitter Blues or Scouse appreciation of a class act?

After the game, having chinned the Toffees yet again (no offence, Walter), we had time to kill and decided to try the bar directly opposite for a wee Coke. The place was jammed full of despairing Scousers. Ten deep at the bar. I kid thee not when I tell you that Gary's tiptoes were no use to him. It was like a Chinese takeaway counter - only higher.

The wee man was leaning on a Scouser's shoulder, and had one foot perched on the foot rail at the front the bar in an effort to be served. It must have taken him a good half-hour. While he was at the bar, the Scousers were in mourning and debating among themselves how poorly their team had performed. Alan, shaking his head disconsolately, said to me, 'Terrible, terrible, wee man,' out loud and then added under his breath, 'That bloody Everton team is terrible.'

We had to look glum - you know what I mean.

We made our way back across the street to Goodison reception just before five and waited for Walter. His wife, Ethel, and their new neighbours were there and once again we renewed old acquaintances.

'Hello there,' she politely said and introduced us as United fans she had met in London. We had brought an engraved crystal vase with us as a token of our appreciation for Walter's hospitality.

'Walter, here's a wee token of appreciation for looking after us. Thank you very much, seriously, sir,' I gestured.

'No problem, Keith, a pleasure.'

Now there's a first - a Manchester United Supporters Club presenting an Everton manager with a gift.

As Walter was packing the crystal into his bag, he smiled and whispered quietly in my ear, 'Thanks for the present, wee man, good to see you again, but don't ever ask me for tickets.' (Or words to that effect.)

We arrived back at the Adelphi hotel to find a Red Dwarf Conference coming to a close.

Sure there may be nine million fanatics but, of the half dozen loopers we met, they had either been drinking all weekend or were seriously off their rockers and candidates for genuine Space Cadets.

When I was bombarded about the outstanding suitability of Northern Ireland for a rocket-launching site and if I would be seriously interested in getting involved I knew it was time for bed.

## Ramadan: Forest - home
### (26 December 1998)

On the way to Old Trafford, our cab driver explained it was Ramadan and that Moslems did not eat during daylight hours. I was intrigued by this and remember thinking that could be handy when the end-of-season diet came into operation.

Ronny Johnsen scored twice, United looked as if the Christmas turkey was still settling, Forest were poor, the crowd similar and the atmosphere for the most part distinctly lacking.

We were more than happy with the result and headed back to Sale. The hotel was fairly quiet and we were the only two people in the lounge where Stuart entertained us with his exceedingly dry wit.

About ten minutes later, the door opened and in walked Big Norman Whiteside. His first words were, 'Oh no, not the Carrickfergus boys again.' I had spoken to Norman on a few occasions and he was once more on top of his game in his new field of podiatry. As I found out later this was someone who provides a fully comprehensive foot health service for those conditions affecting the foot and lower limb. He explained how he had studied, qualified and was now busy working with over thirty League teams. Norman has not lost his ambition and wants to be the leader in his field once again.

We had been talking for about an hour when in walked Paddy, his son Danny, son-in-law Neil, Johnny Flacks and a few of Paddy's cousins from Donegal who had travelled over for the game. The banter and craic was festive and everyone was having a great time. To listen to two genuine Red Legends talk football and hear them reminisce about opponents, grounds, matches, football in general and United in particular was amazing. I think about seven or eight of us were sitting talking football the rest of the evening. Paddy and Face were having their usual banter, slagging each other off in a friendly manner. Norman would say he had to leave as his wife would kill him, but then would start telling another story or be asked more questions:

'Norman, who was the hardest player you ever played against?' someone asked.

'Jimmy Case, yes without a doubt, he was a hard man but fair,' replied Norman.

'Who was the dirtiest?' asked the Faceman.

'Souness.'

the documentary.' She shuffled as if to make a dancing movement.

Looking at Mo, who was wearing casual trousers, matching jacket and smart white jumper, it was hard not to notice her hair loss as she recovered from her own personal trauma of a tumour. I couldn't help thinking why on earth she even bothered trying to advance a very difficult political situation when she had her health problems. Respect.

After our discussion, the Secretary of State even offered to mention the project at the House of Commons during Northern Ireland Question Time. While we were sitting for photographs for the media, I was resting on the arm of Mo's chair. I started feeling very uncomfortable as I sensed she was staring behind my ears or neck.

Oh boy - everything went through my mind. Had I cleaned my ears properly? Was there a mark on my shirt? In an effort to break the tension I turned around and asked, 'For Pete's sake, what are you at, missus?'

'Oh it's OK, Keith,' she replied cannily, 'I was just checking to see how many facelifts you have had. I was on the Parkinson Show the other night and I counted five on him.'

After the photo call and just before Mo left, I presented her with a crystal candlestick holder and placemats on behalf of our Club. In jest, I said to her, 'That'll be handy when you're smoking the dope, Mo.'

I immediately wished I had not said it.

However, after a deafening silence that seemed to go on forever, she gave me a startled look and smiled, saying something like, 'I'm a child of the sixties ... that was a long time ago, Keith.'

After the meeting, we left on an inevitable 'high' and it was very nice to receive a letter the next day stating that it had been a pleasure for the Secretary of State to meet us and thanking us for our gifts on behalf of the Club.

Dear Keith

It was a pleasure meeting you today. Thank you very much for your gifts. I'll certainly remember them when I am having my next candlelit dinner.

Wishing you all the best for your plans for the documentary.

Mo

MARJORIE MOWLAM

The following morning we were proud to read in several local newspapers:

The Secretary of State, Dr Marjorie Mowlam MP, praised the cross community initiative of a Manchester United Supporters Club. She was meeting Keith Norris and Alan Jackson of Carrickfergus Manchester United Supporters Club who told her about their plans to produce a TV documentary series highlighting their efforts to promote community harmony in Northern Ireland.

From that point on, we were given tremendous support and pointed in the right direction by the appropriate civil servants for assistance with funding. We were also told to get in touch with Dr Mowlam's secretary if we required any further help. It was now up to Peter Browne and Michael McNally to obtain a commission. Unfortunately Mr Browne did not appear to have the appropriate drive and Michael was involved with many other projects.

The idea was to make a six-part fly-on-the-wall documentary, following the fortunes of Carrickfergus Manchester United Supporters' Club in the climax to the season. During the filming at Carrickfergus, Old Trafford and Wembley, Michael for some reason started to film other subjects (non-Carrickfergus members) at matches. I felt this was because we were insisting on having some

118

editorial input (as originally promised). He was less enthusiastic about 'Carrickfergus United' and was looking for the bigger picture. Possibly Michael was encouraged to do so to appeal to a wider audience so I cannot really blame him.

The home game against Sheffield Wednesday (17 April 1999) was a club trip and we agreed to be filmed throughout the day for the documentary.

About one p.m. we went to the Trafford Hall via the Amblehurst where again we had to endure embarrassing filming. We met the Cockneys as usual who wanted no part of the - in their own words - 'tacky, tasteless official Club venture'.

Our Supporters Club was to make a presentation to Andy Cole after the game. Unfortunately Andy was injured and could not make it. I felt especially sorry for the kids who were looking forward to meeting their hero.

Although deflated, the younger members of our Club unfurled our flag outside Old Trafford (just below the Munich clock) for the cameras almost in a defiant gesture. It was interesting to see the look of disgust on the faces of the suits coming out of the executive suites as they crawled underneath her.

We shall not be moved!

## How Bad is a Six?

On 5 May 1999, Gary, Alan, the Faceman and I left Carrickfergus harbour at six a.m. with the intention of sailing across the Irish Sea to Liverpool. Gary had just bought a boat and like fools we agreed to be filmed by the documentary crew again on this trip of sheer madness.

Sailing across Belfast Lough to Bangor to fill up on fuel, the waves were already starting to throw us around. It became so rough we could not walk about or indeed move without being thrown about like rag dolls. Gary radioed through, requesting a shipping forecast for our planned seven-hour journey. When I heard 'Force 6' mentioned I immediately thought, 'Oh, oh! What have I let myself in for?' As we fuelled in Bangor (about twenty-five minutes across the bay) marina, thankfully the conversation centred on whether it would be wise to continue.

'How bad is a six, wee man?' I asked.

'She'll be rough enough out in the channel lads but it's up to you guys,' Gary replied in a serious tone.

The documentary crew and Michael McNally in particular were already in bad shape. The Faceman had turned green and I knew the film crew were genuinely frightened. We had to get to Anfield that night so I suggested that we hire a plane - as we had done before.

Eventually it was decided that the production company would pay half the cost of the charter flight - we had no option.

We then had a high-speed car chase to Belfast International airport where we caught the afternoon flight to Liverpool, eventually arriving in the Adelphi Hotel at about four o'clock.

As the Reds started to gather, we were standing downstairs with the documentary crew who were once again following our every move. As they tried to film the United fans out on the street, they soon returned to us with their equipment 'recalibrated'. It was obvious that the Cockneys were not the only ones who thought this a 'tacky, tasteless, official Club venture'.

The Scousers celebrated the draw as if they had won the League, flags raised and waved defiantly in our direction. How sad they are. A once great team like Liverpool celebrating a home draw so feverishly (Two-Two in your Cup Final or what?).

They thought they had stopped us winning the League.

An air of despondency prevailed among some of the travelling Reds, but although disappointed we were still hopeful.

'We threw it away, wee man,' Gary said, as we watched the players disappear to the tunnel.

'That point will win it, sir, we'll have the last laugh,' I encouraged him.

Our grateful thanks to the Scousers for the championship winning point and special thanks to the many Arsenal (yes, I did see at least one Arsenal top) and Bayern Munich (several scarves) fans present that evening.

The filming continued at Club meetings and most members played an active part. The documentary, The World of Manchester United, was broadcast on Sky Sports One in the summer of 1999.

Although I was originally disappointed with the impression of United fans it gave to the world, I found it particularly pleasing that many of those who had initially laughed at my idea actively participated enthusiastically.

## An Evening with Legends

'The Eagle has Landed, wee man,' was the message on my mobile telephone, obviously referring to George Best's arrival.

I met up with Paddy Crerand and Denis Law at seven p.m. in the hotel reception. Club members started filtering in to the reception room we had set up adjacent to the main function suite. Denis and Paddy signed autographs for the jubilant members. The question on everyones lips was, 'Where is George?'

Someone came in and said they had seen George walking along the road towards Carrickfergus town centre. I must admit for a brief moment I panicked, but all our fears were banished when George and Alex walked in a few minutes later. George had gone for a walk to find somewhere he could play the National Lottery and had not 'done a George' as Alan suggested.

The three legends signed autographs for about half an hour. This autograph session was for Club members only. The Faceman kept a vigil and acted as bouncer as several other non-members and guests were trying their utmost to gain entry to the already packed room.

After the introductions and formalities, I was asked to present a welcome on behalf of the organisers.

I was shaking, not only with nerves but also in awe of the whole occasion.

My speech went according to plan and it was encouraging to be given an enthusiastic round of applause. After the meal, Paddy, Denis and George addressed the audience individually, followed by an off-the-cuff question and answer session, which Denis conducted. The three of them enthralled the audience with stories from their era including the 1968 European Cup Final. All three held Sir Matt Busby in great esteem.

This evening was achievement, fulfilment, ecstasy and satisfaction all rolled into one - a dream which literally came true.

# Ups and Downs

The week following the function, a local newspaper carried a story of how some local dignitaries were apparently shocked by some of the language heard on the evening.

This was most disappointing, as those in question had personally thanked various committee members for an outstanding evening. Their slur in the media was, in my view, an attempt to gain some cheap personal publicity. No mention was made of the considerable time spent with the disabled kids or the general feeling of exhilaration felt by many at having three living legends in our hometown.

Following the newspaper article, several committee members were approached by people who offered information about those dignitaries and their behaviour on the evening. We could quite easily have turned it back in their faces by relaying some of their own antics to national newspapers.

Instead, the committee issued a statement on behalf of the Club, merely registering our disappointment at those in question and called for all United supporters to reflect their disgust in any future elections. I was most displeased with former Club friend Mr Sean Neeson, then leader of the Alliance Party in Northern Ireland.

Sean personally shook my hand and thanked me for a great night and yet the next week was quoted in the local media criticising the evening and some of George's comments.

Several other local dignitaries, including the Mayor and Mayoress, claimed they had been insulted and hurt during the evening. Yet they had asked me for the guests' autographs.

After the articles appeared in the paper, another guest at the function who had been sitting at the next table to those in question approached me. He told me that he could not understand how a certain councillor was so insulted because she had drunk a substantial amount of red wine and had to be helped outside into a taxi. Furthermore when she got home from the function she had no money to pay the taxi driver.

I met Sean Neeson a few weeks later while he was canvassing in Whitehead for the upcoming elections.

'Don't be expecting too many votes from United supporters, Sean,' was all I said.

'Keith, they only printed a small bit of what I said.'

'You Judas'd us, Sean, you'll not be getting too many United votes, sir.'

I have to admit that two days later, when he appeared on television highly distressed after his abysmal performance, I and many others had more than a smile to ourselves.

One of my father's traits that I have inherited is to say what you mean and clear the air. If something is bothering me, I have to get out and not bottle it up. I cannot be nice to someone who has in my eyes wronged me, my friends or our Club.

I had spoken to a friend of mine in the business community one day regarding our Club and a future publication. He had approached among others a local estate agent and a certain local councillor.

A friend informed me that Mr House Seller had said in so many words that if I was involved he didn't want to know. When I met him in a hotel some three hours later he was nice as you like to me. 'How's it going, Keith?'

I was absolutely seething and leathered into him, telling him what a two-faced gentleman he was - or words to that effect.

He could not understand how I knew what he had said to a certain gentleman about me. He was gobsmacked and, typically, denied all knowledge.

When I eventually told him who the third person was, he left the hotel....

During the 'lecture' I was giving to Mr House Seller, Sean Neeson walked in and stood beside me. I bet you now he wished he hadn't. I had to tell him all over again how happy I was he had not been elected after what he had said in the press regarding our function and how many of us laughed when he was looking so dejected on television after his defeat.

A prominent local solicitor, with whom I had absolutely no argument, was sitting between the three of us. He didn't have a clue what was going on and why I was 'going off'. This is probably the reason he suggested to a taxi-driver friend of mine that I was paranoid a few days later.

Sean Neeson is friendly with the owner of a shop adjacent to my work. After a newspaper article he made a comment to the owner of the shop, smiling at our apparent 'bad press'.

Little did he know that Alan's daughter was working behind the counter. She immediately interrupted and mentioned the fact that her father was involved with 'those boys' about whom he was talking. I am reliably informed that Mr Neeson went a horrendous bright pink colour and promptly left.

Maybe this is a vindictive attitude on my behalf but I cannot help it. Being two- (or sometimes three-) faced is something I cannot stomach.

Certain local councillors and some local businessmen wannabies are the scourge of modern-day communities. Carrickfergus has its fair share of both.

For all the positive publicity we have brought to the Carrickfergus Borough and the community integration we have helped develop, the local Council and bureaucrats tied up in red tape have never recognised our Club in any fashion. I have approached several councillors directly and indirectly through other parties. My personal belief is that, because of a controversial business planning application in which I was involved, certain influential councillors choose to ignore our Club.

We had never planned to make a profit on the evening with the legends. We had based our figures on a total attendance of three hundred and fifty. Unfortunately not all Club members attended the function, leaving us with a potential loss-making situation. It was not a case of the Club losing money, it was more a case of our spending money we had raised through fundraising and sponsorship to put on one of the best ever nights Carrickfergus and Northern Ireland had witnessed. The fact that we had spent over twenty thousand pounds putting the evening together, was our prerogative. The fundraising committee had raised the money over the previous few years in order to put on such an event.

Once again, two members of the committee (one of whom did not even attend the function) mysteriously resigned their positions.

In what I can only surmise was an effort to put a slur not only on the evening but also on the Club, certain individuals approached a Sunday newspaper with a 'costings' statement from our function.

It always amazes me that those who make the least effort make the most noise. During my involvement with the Club it has always been those who participate the least, whether it be at meetings, supporting Club functions or fundraising activities, who grumble the most.

What annoyed me about this escapade was that those concerned were considered good friends. Two particular members caused a fracas at one particular meeting which led to the members having no option but to expel them from the Club for the detrimental effect they were having among members. Furthermore, a member of the committee was verbally abused and threatened by one of the men's sons who was also expelled.

Women and children regularly attend our meetings. Many expressed their disgust at what was happening and how they felt intimidated by those in question. Certain members stated that they would leave or not return while these men were members of the Club and were causing such a disturbance at Club meetings.

This was the time when I was at my lowest ebb since joining and was very close to resigning my position. Why were these guys trying to destroy what was a truly remarkable club? Could they not see the underlying trend of togetherness and achievement? Was this pure jealously or were personal vendettas being waged on those of us who gave considerable effort?

'I think I'm going to quit, Faceman, the time has come to pack it in, I can do no more.'

'Wee man, if you leave, the club will fall apart; that's exactly what these guys want,' Faceman added convincingly.

'Maybe you are right, sir. After what we tried to do, why should we let them win?'

Although disappointed by the actions of certain members, and with indebted thanks to the Faceman, Alan and Gary who persuaded me to remain, I continued my efforts with renewed vigour. As a club we are now much stronger without them and the feel-good factor has returned.

As supporting United has its many ups and downs, so too does the everyday running of the Club and, no matter what prevails, we never lose sight that our sole purpose is to support Manchester United.

# FA Cup Withdrawal

Following the announcement regarding United's non-participation in the FA Cup, we contacted our local MP, Mr Roy Beggs, and tried to orchestrate a campaign to lobby Tony Banks (then Minister for Sport) on the fans' behalf. It was our wish to see United compete in both the FIFA World Club Championship and the FA Cup. I received a letter back from Mr Beggs along with this:

Dear Roy,

Thank you for your letter of 19 July. Enclosing representations you have received from Carrickfergus Manchester United Supporters Club, expressing concern at the announcement by the Manchester United Board on June 30 to accept the Football Association's offer of 27 June to exempt the club from the 1999-2000 FA Cup competition. This enables the club to compete in the inaugural FIFA Club World Club Championship in Brazil next January.

I recognise that Manchester United's involvement in the Club World Championship will help the Football Association to develop further its ties with FIFA, its support for the game worldwide, and its bid to stage the 2006 World Cup here. However, Manchester United's exemption from next season's FA Cup was ultimately something which only the FA could offer and only the Manchester United Board could decide to accept.

As I have stated on a number of occasions, I would have liked to see Manchester United playing both the FA Cup and the Club World Championship. Unfortunately the FA and Manchester United have advised me that given the fixture congestion this has not so far proven possible.

Tony
TONY BANKS

When it was confirmed that United would not be playing in the FA Cup, we contacted our MEP, asking him to make further representation on our behalf.

I received this from Mr Paisley on 17 November 1999:

Dear Mr Norris
Please find enclosed a copy of correspondence from Kate Hoey MP regarding matters which you brought to my attention.

I hope this is of some interest and use to you.

Best wishes
Yours sincerely
I. Paisley
IAN RK PAISLEY MP MEP

Dear Ian
Thank you for your letter of 25 October, following representations you have received from Keith Norris of Carrickfergus Manchester United's Supporters Club about their team's participation in the FA Cup.

Manchester United's exemption from the competition was ultimately something which only the FA could offer and only the Manchester United Board could decide to accept.

I very much hoped a solution could be found to the difficulty Manchester United encountered in competing in this season's FA Cup, and did my best to help. Regrettably a solution could not be found that was acceptable to both the Football Association and Manchester United and the Manchester United Board confirmed on 29 October that the club would not be competing in 1999-2000 FA Cup

Best wishes

Kate

KATE HOEY

Minister for Sport

Although the decision remained unchanged, at least we endeavoured to take some action and not merely talk about it.

## Safe Standing

I contacted every Northern Ireland MP asking for their support regarding the Private Members's Bill (Roger Godsiff MP-Football Spectators Bill) supporting the relaxation of the 'all seater' policy imposed by the Government on all football clubs.

It was our wish to be given the choice to stand if we so chose. Personally I believe it is only a matter of time before common sense prevails. When you are standing you do sing more and therefore add to the atmosphere.

Thankfully nine Northern Ireland MP's agreed to sign the Early Day Motion 239. I must admit a wee smile to myself-in that we had achieved something fairly unique regarding Northern Ireland politics- cross party support.

# We'll Keep the Red Flag Flying High

The Club has grown in stature among the local community, gaining respect for its professionalism and fundraising. From highly successful businessmen to taxi drivers, unemployed, rich and poor, young and old, Catholic and Protestant, we are all 'United' through our passion for the 'World's Greatest Football Team'.

I do feel somewhat responsible for the strength of the Club. Not solely, mind you, I know the heart of the Club is now in the hands of the present committee. Mandy, Joe Black, Faceman and Tony Lunn have breathed fresh enthusiasm into it and Gary and Alan continue their dedication with vigour.

While we are extremely proud of our own Supporters' Club, forty such branches exist in Northern Ireland alone. Considering all the positive publicity that we bring for United, it pains me that certain members of the United hierarchy and indeed certain players seem to dismiss genuine supporters' events and co-operation.

We are now well into the new millennium and as our team continues an unprecedented run of success, Carrickfergus Manchester United Supporters' Club also continues to flourish. We were the subject of a four-page article in the March 2000 edition of the Official Manchester United Magazine, featured strongly in 'The Irish Connection' video by VCI in 2001 and have been the subject of several television documentaries including Terrace Talk on MUTV and The Red and the Green, broadcast nationally in 2002. To hear our local MP, Mr Roy Beggs, sing our praises on national television and United legend Paddy Crerand refer to us as 'ambassadors for Manchester United' encourages the members, and probably unnoticed by most, continues to promote wider community harmony- something in Northern Ireland that politicians could only dream of. Now we see each other as primarily genuine friends and United supporters, NOT as Catholic or Protestant.

As far as Carrickfergus Reds are concerned, 'We'll Keep the Red Flag flying high'.

# CREATING A LEGEND: BIG LILY

Before the 'Scouse-busting' FA Cup Final of 1996, I decided that I would make a large flag as a token of my appreciation of Eric Cantona - the greatest Manchester United player I have watched in my lifetime. The final result was a huge French flag with the words 'Eric the King' emblazoned upon it.

Unfortunately I was sitting on my own in the first row, second tier of the grandstand at Wembley. Gary, as usual, had jibbed his way to an Olympic Gallery seat, which was excessively high for maximum flag exposure. During the singing of the traditional Cup Final hymn, 'Abide with Me', I enlisted the help of a few fellow Reds beside me to unfurl my pride and joy. Eric (as I called the flag) danced playfully and swept around behind the goal and then passed all the way overhead to the end of the United section and disappeared down towards the concourse in the middle of the stadium.

Alan and I went to Copenhagen for the Brondby game, in the Champions League group stages in 1998, where we met Jamie and Paul from London for the first time. This game partially led to the concept of another flag -but we nearly didn't get there.

Millwest Tours was our last option for tickets for the game. 'Are the tickets definitely in the United section?' we asked.

'Oh yeah, no problem, mate,' (in Mancunian) was the reply.

That was good enough for Alan and me, as we had tried unsuccessfully and been chubbed - yet again - in our efforts to get tickets through the Club.

Alan and I are not exactly tall so everyone is a 'big lad' to us. As we took our seats on the aircraft, down the aisle walked a tall, mean-looking dude sporting a baseball hat with an even taller, well dressed 'minder' behind him. After the polite 'What about you' there was not much conversation, only the usual 'Where you from?' 'Going to the game?' 'Woz you there Saturday?' (a cockney Red?)

As soon as we arrived at our hotel and our hosts had taken our passports as security, we arranged to meet up with Paul and Jamie for a look around the town.

We were in one establishment for about ten minutes when this big bruiser of a guy came over and, in pidgin English, started talking about football. At first he seemed like a sound bloke. He was wearing a pair of dungarees and big knee-length boots. Now this could be taken as national dress in Denmark but when he introduced himself as Big Nillie, I have to admit I became more than a trifle suspicious.

Nillie and Paul headed off in search of The Dubliner while Alan, Jamie and I walked across the square towards the town centre in search of the Red Army. It was not long before we heard a vociferous rendition of 'The Banks of the River Irwell'. From the outside it looked like a quaint wee establishment but when we got in, there must have been about sixty Reds singing and partying. This was what we were looking for and exactly what Euro Aways are all about - especially the night before the game.

We were not in the door two minutes before this guy, bedecked with more chains than B.A. Baracus, asked if we wanted anything from the bar. After Friendly Nillie, we were starting to think in terms of best-ever city and how decent everyone was. We were amazed when we realised that B.A. Baracus was buying everyone in the bar a drink. We reckoned the round of drinks must have totalled around three hundred pounds. This went on for about two hours. No one was allowed to buy.

'No, you are Manchester United, I buy!' the guy would say.

No wonder the Reds were in such good voice and we joined in the singing before returning to our hotel about nine-thirty pm.

Up fresh in the morning, we eventually found the Dubliner where we sampled healthy portions of some good home cooking.

'I think I was in 'ere last night with Nillie,' said Paul.

He continued, telling how Big Nillie had been even friendlier than we had initially thought - he had tried to 'plant the lips' on him the previous evening.

The three of us were in stitches when he told us how he knocked Nillie through a shop window. The moral of the story has to be, 'never trust a guy in dungarees.'

Our Millwest tickets placed us right at the back of the home supporters' stand with the Red Army directly opposite. Definitely not in the United end. Few police were present nor were they required in the stand. And the hundred or so Reds alongside us tried their best to out-sing the home support. With only two minutes on the clock, Wes Brown crossed to an unmarked Giggs who scored from close range. Alan, Big Paul, Jamie and I hugged and danced at the back of the stand. Another superb cross from Blomqvist saw Giggs head United's second in the twenty-first minute, then seven minutes later Yorke and Cole combined well to kill the game off.

We had beaten Brondby 6-0 in a pre-season friendly. This score was looking as if we were going to surpass this and more.

Big Paul remarked, 'Yeah, I think we'll do 'em right and proper now.'

'I hope so, sir, ten would be nice,' I responded.

'You're getting greedy, matey,' said Jamie.

'What do you mean "getting greedy", Jamie? The wee man was born greedy,' Alan joked and the four of us laughed and I gave Jacko a pretend punch in the nether regions.

Daugaard pulled one back for the Danes when he curled a free kick inside Schmeichel's post.

Keano scored United's fourth, Dwight Yorke added the fifth and Solskjaer completed the rout with a fantastic shot a few minutes later.

'Fergie must have Danish family, he's feeling guilty,' someone uttered beside me.

'I think we'll get another one at least,' I gestured to Alan.

'Aye, you couldn't beat them Danes enough,' he replied, jesting.

A late consolation goal by Brondby could not spoil what had been a great European football match. We wanted goals and we got them in abundance.

It is not a nice experience being at any away game when you haven't been able to obtain tickets for the United section, whether it is in the Lego stand at Leicester, or in the main stand at Goodison Park. You feel as if the Red Army is singing at you and oh how you really want to show them that you are in fact a Red.

These were my exact thoughts during the Brondby game, even though the ground was mostly full of Reds albeit of Scandinavian origin. I remember thinking that next time I would have a flag that everyone (especially Reds) could not miss and more importantly, a flag that would help create a better atmosphere. Faceman and I had discussed creating a club flag to continue our campaign and as a follow-on to our Club CD and a forthcoming television documentary. All these factors synthesised in the idea of a flag.

I couldn't make it to Munich so I decided that the Inter Milan game at the awesome San Siro stadium would be the place for the flag's first outing.

I rang around to obtain an estimate for a red, white and black flag with 'Carrickfergus Reds' written in the middle. This would give the Supporters Club members a sense of identity and be the next stage in Faceman and I's personal crusade. I wanted the Manchester United Football Club crest inserted in the centre. Some didn't bother to reply and others laughed, assuming that I was 'extracting the Michael'. By chance, I obtained the name of Karen Banks from Carrickfergus who agreed to make the flag (minus the crest) in time for the St Patrick's Day assault on Milan.

So, a few days later, on the afternoon of March 14th, she was born. A birthday she shares with Albert Einstein, Michael Caine and Billy Crystal. There she was, in all her glory - all set for her trip of a lifetime.

Only one thing was missing - a name for her.

Naming a child can be an arduous task. Does it sound right? Will her friends shorten it? What will her nickname be? Will it suit her?

It is common in our community when we encounter a stranger at home or abroad to say, 'What about ye, Lily?' if female, or 'What about ye, Walter?' if male. Lilys and Walters come in all shapes and forms. She may be a foreign waitress who doesn't understand a word you have said or a hotel commissionaire - 'Good man, Walter', who will simply smile politely, hoping for a bigger tip. A prime example of a 'Lily' is the wee old lady in the Mercedes advertisement on television who is standing at the bus stop as the other two women sing, 'Oh Lord, won't you buy me a Mercedes-Benz.' The look on her face and the initial reaction to her makes her my fondest Lily. Even the name 'Lily' can create strife in Northern Ireland - Orange Lily as glorified by the Protestant culture or the Easter Lily as glorified by the Republican movement. My Lily was going to be Red;-neither Catholic nor Protestant, black nor white.

So the flag became known as 'Lily' and she was ready, packed neatly into a small grey and red MacGregor sports bag for her first ever 'Euro away'.

## Inaugural Trip

Her inaugural trip began on St Patrick's Day, 17 March, 1999 for the crucial Champions League Quarter Final against Inter Milan. We arrived at The Grand Hotel on the shores of Lake Maggiore late on Tuesday evening and even before we had checked in, Lily was unfurled in the large lounge - much to the appreciation of the one hundred or so Reds already gathered.

Amidst all the celebrations, an Italian waiter (an Inter fan) had seen enough of Lily and promptly marched her away to solitary confinement somewhere deep in the hotel cellar. I suppose I knew then that she was going to be a troublesome child.

It was at breakfast the next morning that the stark reality set in that she was actually missing. Several Reds organised a search party: the lobby, the reception, the workers' quarters, the kitchens, the bar. I asked four reception staff if they had seen Lily anywhere, only to be given the 'I no understand' response.

'Have you seen big Lily anywhere, sir?'

'Excuse me?' one of the receptionists replied.

'Biga Lily, le flago, el banderra, el losto!' I shouted (in the usual fluent Italian of Brits abroad) and gestured the enormity of her like a contestant on the seventies game show, Give Us a Clue.

It was strange that the previous evening they had had no language difficulties when I had been exchanging currency - Bitter blues?

Another flag, another disappointment. I had been there before, but this was different. Back in 1996 'Big Eric' had been a quiet, almost reverent character. In Lily's short life to date, she had shown fun-loving and almost roguish characteristics. Already she had won hundreds of friends and admirers and contemplating such a premature parting was a bitter pill to swallow.

United had a chance of making it to the Champions League Semi-Final, so I headed for the coach, downcast and Lily-less. Although feeling like we had just been knocked out of an FA Cup Semi-Final, the singing began on the coach regardless, so I put on a brave face although I was hurting underneath and missing the big girl like crazy.

How can you fall so much in love in such a short space of time?

We had been sitting for about fifteen or twenty minutes as the final stragglers made it to the coach and a few of the boys got their last fix of nicotine before the two-hour journey to the game when I heard that Lily had been found hiding near the grand piano in the lounge. Despite her incarceration in some deep cellar, she managed to make her stealthy way to freedom by hiding inside the grand piano until Brian from Bray liberated her.

139

When Alan and I spotted Brian struggling towards the bus with my prodigy, it was better than Christmas.

'Ah, wee man, you're a star. Where did you find her, sir?' I asked.

'Lying behind the piano, I think she slept there all night, Keith,' he replied in his broad Bray accent.

Brian is now a friend for life - obviously. Cheers, wee man.

The atmosphere in Milan was fairly calm throughout the day - pockets of Reds were doing their own thing and no real trouble ensued or at least we couldn't find any.

Lily did, however, make one appearance in the City Centre just in front of the amazing Duomo, which dominates the central square, where about two or three hundred members of the Red Army were taunting the locals with their unique Mancunian humour.

"Adorned with more than three thousand statues, Perego's Madonnina, who has kept her vigil from the cathedral's highest spire since 1744, is the most loved. From the roof terraces, visitors may examine the Duomo's spires and statues while enjoying a breath-taking view of Milan and, on a clear day, the snow-topped ring of the nearby Bergamo Alps."

As I read this extract from a tourist guide while sitting in the square I couldn't help smiling as I gazed up at this wee Italian Lily, wondering what she was thinking of my Lily's performance in her square.

Like anyone on their first foreign holiday, she was riffling in her bag, keen to experience the sights and sounds of continental Europe. We were then herded to the stadium at least two hours before kick-off. Alan, as usual, had the majority of the Lily bearing to do - it's good for his back.

140

As kick-off approached the carabinieri were becoming restless and I had visions of her not being allowed inside the ground.

One's first impression of the Giuseppe Meazza Stadium (San Siro) is mesmerising: huge concrete stair towers supporting a steel and transparent polycarbonate structure high above. Modified for the 1990 World Cup, it is a true shrine of world football.

The police on duty at the stadium were absolutely disgraceful that night. Only two turnstile gates were open in the United section. It had potential for serious injury, especially with the crush against the barrier just to the right of the turnstile. I remember being crushed against none other than Membership Secretary Barry Moorhouse who was livid at what we were witnessing.

One moment of humour amidst the crush was when Alan and I spotted two guys bunking the queue by climbing over a rail. As we were giving it to them, we realised they were two cockney K-Standers - our friends Jamie and Paul.

The police were mental. At least ten of our group missed a large portion of the match and a big guy from Dublin was split open with a baton for absolutely no reason. Lee Sharpe stood about ten rows in front of us in the United end.

'If we get one here it'll kill them off, sir,' I remember saying to Alan.

'I think we'll definitely score, wee man.'

The atmosphere in the steep-sided San Siro was more than I ever dreamed of: flags, banners, flares and the smoke, the Ultras in full voice in expectation. This was an experience in itself. The war of words between Fergie and Inter coach Mirclea Lucescu and the 'will he/won't he' play furore surrounding Ronaldo had given the tie that extra bite which was reflected in the hostile atmosphere.

Lily, although weighing a ladylike thirty-four kilos, is fairly bulky and the police were not only searching and shepherding us like sheep but many Reds were either getting turned away or beaten-up. Alan reckoned he should carry Lily through the turnstiles because he was taller and she would therefore not look so big - aye, right.

'Here, wee man, put her over my shoulders, I'm the tallest, she won't look as big.'

I didn't argue because if I carried her it would look like an ant with a keg of Bud Ice. Lily was more than a trifle embarrassed by such unbecoming treatment and having her person manhandled by men dressed like hotel commissionaires (Italian police) Eventually she gained her entrance and things began to look up.

The lower tier behind the goal where we stood was jammed full of expectant Reds in full voice, hoping for a victory over an Italian team on Italian soil.

Ronaldo was playing and Fergie announced a defensive line-up including Jaap Stam and Henning Berg at the back, with Ronny Johnsen in midfield instead of Paul Scholes.

Every time a United player touched the ball, the Ultras hissed, whistled, booed and jeered.

Inter threatened on several occasions but at halftime we were relatively happy with the scoreless situation.

Ze Elias, the Brazilian substitute, went down in a heap in the penalty area. The whistle went and the ref reached for his pocket.

'Oh no, sir, Keano's off,' I said to big Peter McMinn beside me.

The Italians were delirious but their mood soon changed to anger as Ze Elias was booked for diving. What a relief. What was it Fergie warned about diving Italians?

Inter were piling on the pressure in search of a goal which eventually came from Ventola who looked as sharp as he had done at Old Trafford.

But with full-time looming United broke away: Andy Cole headed a ball into the path of Paul Scholes who calmly sidefooted it into the net, 1-1 and bar a miracle we were through to the semi-final of the European Cup for the seventh time in our history. There was no way they were going to score three in two minutes.

Simone off, Ronaldo off, a strong ref, resilient defence, Schmeichel on top form, a never say die spirit shown by the Reds and a killer Scholes goal led to pandemonium at the final whistle among the buoyant Reds.

Bring on the Old Lady of Turin!

*

The best time to unfurl a flag is either at the start of a game or at the end, during the celebrations. I could not dare bring her out during the game. Even the Red Army would not tolerate that - unless we were about 5-0 up of course.

You can imagine the feeling after Scholesy's goal - let the party begin

We were locked in the stadium for about an hour after the game. This was Lily's cue and so out she came, wary at first, above the outstretched arms of the Reds. She was passed around the centre lower tier, really enjoying herself. Definitely Lily's finest hour so far and it gave me a great thrill after all the pre-match stresses. As I returned from the Quentin Hogg (as Big Paul would say) at the back of the grandstand there she was making her way back to me

- helped along by Big Jamie and Paul, who had followed her, knowing that eventually they would find Alan and me.

'Alright, matey, yeah we thought we'd find you 'ere, we just followed the flag,' big Jamie said.

'Yeah, you were pretty hard to find with all the height of you,' added big Paul jokingly.

'Where was you stood during the game?' he added.

'About twenty rows behind you, we were shouting at you in the first half,' I said.

'Me and the wee man were getting blinded with the floodlight bouncing off your napper,' added Alan smiling.

'Yeah, very funny, Jacko,' replied big Paul smiling as he uttered a few unprintable superlatives.

I sensed that Lily had enjoyed her wee run out and this was the moment that I realised she had certain exhibitionistic traits.

'She's going to be a nightmare to look after, sir,' Alan suggested.

'No, sir, she's going be a legend,' I replied. 'Trust me.'

That night, due to the result, we were obviously on a major high. Alan and I sat on the balcony of our 'ship' (our small room had two single beds in a line and overlooked the beautiful lake) and after eating the contents of the mini-bar we got a bit bored so had a throwing competition consisting of socks, toilet roll and towels. The mini-bar and television were too heavy although I had to restrain Alan from making a gallant effort. We rang Linda (Alan's wife) at about four a.m. She was very pleased we called - not!

## Leading the Invasion

Lily's next public outing was at Villa Park and the FA Cup Semi-Final replay against Arsenal's pretenders. We were

*Lily resting in Barcelona*

*Celebrating in Milan after the momentous result in 1999.*

*Big Lily in Nou Camp, 1999*

*Lily paraded at Old Trafford* (Pic. John Peters).

.Lily used as a human tent as fans sing and dance underneath her.

Brian from Bray, Steve McManaman, Me, Joel and Pedro Chueca Remon

Brian from Bray, Raul, Me, Joel Taggart, Luis Figo and Peter McMinn.

A young Norris.

United folk legend and my good friend, Peter Boyle.

From left - Neil 'Raff' Rafferty, Scott Somers, Rod Flood, Davy Dick and I with King Eric Cantona.

United Nations. Rick Adkinson, Hong Kong Branch MUSC, Alan Jackson, Carrickfergus MUSC, Stephen Ryan, Tokyo MUSC at the Toyota Cup in Tokyo 1999.

Tony Fisher and John Mahoney from The Daily Star, returning Big Lily.

Mick Murray and I doing our bit for public relations in Brazil.

Raul welcomes Lily to Madrid.

Big Paul and Alan in Tokyo.

Alex Best, Paddy Crerand, George Best, Denis Law and I at Evening With Legends.

*Lily the bridesmaid, Kyoto, Japan, 2001*

*What a team! Morrientes, Hierro, Raul, Canzaries, Wee Gary, me and Joel Taggart.*

*Having a laugh with Andy Cole in Brazil*

*Big Paul, Jamie, Alan, Tomoko and Kana at Asakusa shrine in Tokyo.*

# MANCHESTER UNITED

The Manchester United Football Club plc, Trafford Training Centre, Birch Road
off Isherwood Road, Carrington, Manchester M31 4BH

WEDDING CONGRATULATIONS

TO

## KEITH & YUKARI

COULDN'T LET TODAY PASS
WITHOUT ADDING OUR OWN
GOOD WISHES TO YOU ON
THIS SPECIAL DAY

21ST April 2001

HAVE A WONDERFUL DAY
AND
GOOD LUCK FOR THE FUTURE

*Alex Ferguson*

SIR ALEX FERGUSON CBE

AND FROM ALL THE
PLAYERS AND STAFF
HERE AT OLD TRAFFORD

Telephone: 0161 868 8700. Facsimile: 0161 868 8855
A subsidiary of Manchester United PLC. Registered office as above. Registered in England No. 95489. VAT No. GB 561 0952 51
www.ManUtd.com

*Speechless!*

*Big Lily at Champions League Final 1999
pic by Kenneth Ramsey*

Everton

22 May 2001

Keith Norris
6 Donegall Gardens
Carrickfergus
BT38 9LP

Our ref: WS/IN

Dear Keith

Glad to see you have met your match at last. I'm sure the Japanese language will
be no problem in future. Ethel and the boys send their regards to the newlyweds.

No problems at all about the book, which I hope will be very successful for you in the
future.

Obviously we look forward to meeting Mr & Mrs Norris either at Old Trafford or
perhaps Goodison Park next season.

Sorry for the delay in writing and I hope everything goes well in the future

Kind regards.

Yours sincerely

**WALTER**

*From the Everton Boss Walter Smith*

*Yukari, me, Keano, Treble and Big Lily.*

*Yukari.*

*Unbelievable gifts from Raul and Fernando Hierro.*

*Davy "Root" Nelson, Bilko and Faceman.*

*Lily playing in the Dog and Partridge.*

Michael McNally, Alan and I having a laugh with Mo Mowlam.

Having a laugh with Phil Neville.

United legend Paddy and I having a diet coke.

Yukari and I in Niseko Hirafu, Hokkaido, Japan - my favourite ski resort.

*Having a laugh with Roberto Carlos in Brazil.*

*Yukari and I with Raul and Hierro.*

*Yukari, her mother Nobue and me.*

*Nobuyuki, Masanobu, me and Kenshin with bridesmaid, Lily.*

"It's a tin whistle and a lucky charm, Raul".

Cockney Reds, Kevin and Jamie

Brian from Bray, Kevin Woodside, Kevin
Hannin, Wee Gary, Peter McMinn and me
having a laugh with Fernando Hierro.

Big Lily in Stretford End
pic by Manchester Evening News

*Nervously presenting Sir Alex*

*Taking over Barcelona*

*Playful outside Sam Platts*

*Visiting Yukari's ancestral shrine at Ginkaku Temple in Kyoto with Yukari's mum and grandmother, Nobue and Sizu*

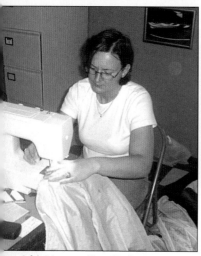

Having a laugh with Nicky Butt

Lily's Mummy - Karen Banks

King of the castle - Carrickfergus 2001

Flying high in Madrid

Jacko, Wee Gary, and I meeting Walter Smith

Lily at home

Lily in Turin

Neighbour and friend Jim Shields
packing Lily

*Lily with kids in Brazil*

*Alan, Tomoko, Big Paul and I chilling out in Ueno*

*Big Paul, United legend Kevin Moran, Jamie, Alan and I in Paddy Foley's*

*The charm that knocked United out of Europe*

*Jim Shields, John Daly, Jo Shields, Colodagh Miskelly, me and Marty Reid at The John Daly Show*

Lily outside Paddy Foley's in Tokyo

Real Madrid physio and good friend Pedro Chueca Remon at the Champions League Final in Glasgow, 2002

Wee Gary and me having a laugh with Walter. Wembley 1996

My new family - Masanobu and Nobue Fukushima

*Big Lily over East Antrim Motor Factors, October 2002 picture Tim Cully*

*Jacko gets all posh with Victoria Beckham*

seated in a lower corner of the stand and were initially reluctant to encourage Lily out. After leading off the singing of 'We're on our way to Wembley', we passed Lily along about fifty Reds and she made a wee trip up to the halfway line and back. The lower tier of our stand at Villa was much too small for maximum impact but I was satisfied that at least she had a decent 'run out'.

Teddy Sheringham, Ole Gunnar Solskjaer and Jesper Blomqvist were in the starting line-up replacing Andy Cole, Dwight Yorke and Ryan Giggs following the 0-0 draw on the Sunday.

"Yorke and Cole on the bench, did I hear that right?"

'Fergie's having a laugh, ain't he?' said big Paul.

Beckham scored early on and traditional FA Cup songs were sung with vigour:

"She wore …She wore a scarlet ribbon in the merry month of May

And when I asked, Why she wore that ribbon

She said it's for United and we're going to Wembley.

Wembley, Wembley

We're the famous Man United and we're going to Wembley"

And then:

"We're on the march with Fergie's army

We're all going to Wembley

And we'll really shake them up when we win the FA Cup

'Cause United are the greatest football team …"

Dennis Bergkamp levelled for the Gunners and they scored again through Anelka but much to our relief the linesman flagged and the goal was disallowed.

Roy Keane brought down Overmars and walked straight off, realising his fate following his earlier booking. Fergie sent on Scholes for Sheringham and it looked like we were heading for extra time - until, that is, Phil Neville fouled Ray Parlour and Arsenal were awarded a last-minute penalty.

'That's it, he must score, we've blown it now, Gary,' I said as I turned my back on the pitch.

'Schmeichel will save it sir, watch it, wee man.'

The Great Dane pulled off an amazing save that ensured we were going to have to endure extra time with only ten men - but we were, to say the least, extremely grateful.

Early in the second half of extra time, Ryan Giggs picked up the ball in midfield and embarked on a run which I can only describe as truly world class and the best goal I have ever witnessed live. Giggs beat four men and then unleashed a ferocious shot that left Seaman stranded.

Keano's sending off, the last-minute penalty save by the 'Great Dane' and Giggsy's 'Wonder Goal', all set the scene for an impromptu, yet friendly, pitch invasion.

'Wee man, we're going on the pitch; c'mon, bring Lily with you.'

Before I had time to think about it, wee Gary Callaghan had bolted down the steps and over the railing and on to the pitch, trailing Lily and me in his wake.

'Hold on, sir, wait to we get her the right way up.'

As the singing and dancing ensued, she endeavoured to unfurl herself on the pitch - about one hundred Reds lent their assistance and we were pleased to see 'Carrickfergus Reds' on the after-match analysis on Sky TV. Real success at last.

I must admit for a few days following the game and amid all the FA inquiry speculation Lily, Gary and I were concerned that we would get called to the inquiry and perhaps banned from attending games.

'Sir, it'll not be hard to trace us two wee men and Lily,' I uttered in a concerned manner.

'They wouldn't go that far, sure there was no trouble,' added Gary.

Thankfully common sense prevailed and Lily's invasion was seen as an expression of uncontrollable post-match joy and passion.

It had been one of those once-in-a-lifetime games and a crucial result in the end of season run-in. The 'Yip Yap Stam' song was given a very loud rendering and it was the first time that we dared even suggest a hint of 'The Treble'. Was it simply the sheer emotion of the night or indeed was the treble really on?

Several club members, already claiming ownership, rang me the following morning stating that they had seen 'Lily' or 'our flag' or the 'Club flag' on Sky television coverage.

## Italy Again

Lily's next trip would again take her back to Italian soil and the Stadio Delle Alpi in Turin as we prepared to take on the might of Juventus.

As kick-off time beckoned, the home fans started to beat their drums and wave their flags. Brian from Bray, my big mate Richard Herron and I assisted Lily out for her first look at the stadium, by now full of expectant and noisy fans. What a kick Lily got when she was given her most hostile reception to date. They hissed, booed and jeered as she was held aloft. What a great result - Lily had fulfilled her task again. That is the beauty of her. No two games are the same and while previously at Villa Park and Milan Lily was used for a celebratory purpose, this was pure 'in your face' provocation. Lily began to show more of her character, to show that she was not afraid of a confrontation.

But the pre-match tension swiftly became a mind-blowing start: Zidane took a corner to Di Livio who passed back for the Frenchman to find Inzaghi who scored at the back post. Andy Cole almost equalised in the next attack with a spectacular bicycle kick. This gave us hope and belief, which took a huge dent a few minutes later when Di Livio found Inzaghi whose shot deflected cruelly off Stam and over Schmeichel.

The Juventus fans went crazy for a second time in the space of five minutes. Drums, flags, flares and a frenzy of noise.

Initially stunned, the six thousand travelling Reds once more found their voice and got behind the shirts encouraged by a move involving a long clearance from Schmeichel, a header from Butt on to Yorke who was pulled by Ferrara just as he was about to unleash a shot.

'Penalty, ref!'

The ref dismissed the appeals to the chorus of 'Same old Itis always cheating' from the Red Army.

Then Beckham swung in a corner and Keane rose above the Juve defence to head the ball into the back of the net.

2-1 on the night, 3-2 on aggregate, a crucial away goal, we knew that if we scored again we would be in a winning position.

Roy Keane was booked for tackling Zidane. This meant that should we qualify our captain and leader would be suspended. However, we had no time to dwell on such thoughts as we had to get a result first. This was made more of a possibility when Yorke headed home a second goal after a cross from Cole.

'YEEESSSSSSSSSS!'

2-2, 3-3 on aggregate and crucially two away goals. Could it be?

This has to have been the most entertaining first half of a football match I have ever witnessed. From early despair; going two goals down to Keane's heartbreaking booking, renewed hope at pulling one goal back, to euphoria as Yorke scored the second to level on the night.

The second half was always going to be nervy as the game still hung in the balance. OK, we knew we had two away goals but you could never write off the Italians.

Juventus had a goal disallowed when Inzahgi was ruled offside after putting the ball in the net. What a relief!

'I can't watch this, Keith,' said Brian from Bray nervously.

'Relax, sir, we'll be all right, they have to score, remember,' I replied.

For the second time of the night Red heads went down as Scholes was booked following a dispute involving Deschamps, meaning that he, like Keane, would be banned for the Final.

We were now in full voice, the shirts were the better team and when Yorke was brought down by Peruzzi, we shouted for a penalty but Andy Cole followed up and scored from an acute angle to score and claim an historic victory.

'Yeeesssssss! - 3-2!'

'Aghhhhhhhhh, we've done it, we've done it!'

We should have scored again in the remaining few minutes but now we were getting greedy and entered celebratory mode once more.

"WE SHALL NOT, We shall not be moved

We shall not, we shall not be moved, just like a team that's gonna win the European Cup (Again)

We shall not be moved ..."

Followed by:

"If you're all going to Barca clap your hands
If you're all going to Barca clap you hands
If you're all going to Barca, all going to Barca
If you're all going to Barca clap your hands"

United had secured their first-ever win on Italian soil and a first appearance in the European Cup Final since 1968. We were euphoric, to say the least.

Although obvious rivalry existed between the supporters - and we were bombarded by the usual oranges and coins from the Iti fans above - there was equally a mutual respect, culminating in the Juve fans clapping United off the park.

We were kept in the stadium for at least an hour following the final whistle. What a reception Fergie received when he came back on to the pitch. The manner in which the shirts clawed back this result and overcame a stunned Juventus would probably have to rate as the proudest Red night of my life.

What a night! We took Lily to a rather posh restaurant for a celebration meal. As we struggled to find her a 'Cyril Smith' sized chair (she's a big girl, remember) the staff and locals were not too amused. We plonked down at a table close to the door and I ordered - again in my fluent Italian.

'A Diet Coke with iceo and strawo for big Lily sir, por favor. And douze water.'

Despite a busy day, Lily didn't appear to be terribly hungry. Time for another liquid lunch. Acting on Alan's advice, we dared not give her anything stronger than Coke - someone this size, sauced up, could do more damage than Bodie and Doyle.

Back at the hotel, the sun terrace, with its amazing view over the lake, was where Brian Merriman (from Bray) lived up to his name and we relived every moment of the game until sunrise.

'What a night, Keith, I honestly can't believe that we're through.'

'I thought when Keane was booked that he'd throw the head up.'

'Brian, we'll remember this night until we die, sir,' I chirped.

The headline in Corriere dello Sport the following morning read, 'Arrivederci vecchia Juve.' I didn't need to understand Italian to know that I had not been dreaming and that we were heading for Barcelona.

At about eleven a.m. it was time to visit our friends in BarPino for lunch. A nice family-run restaurant, we were highly impressed when the owner's wife, a pleasant, plumpish lady wearing a designer dress and many gold chains, produced a personally signed photograph of Ronaldo kissing the world player of the year award. In my broken Italian and on bended knee I offered to buy the photo for our forthcoming charity auction back home.

'Please, please, please, I pay, I pay mucho for Ronaldo,' I begged her.

'No, no, no, no, special for me, just look please,' she added in pidgin English.

'Ronaldo's mother, my friend, very special for me,' she reiterated as she pointed at the signature.

You can imagine my delight when just before we left she called me inside and presented me with her treasured picture as a gift.

'For you, my friend,' she exclaimed as she handed me the picture.

'No way, I couldn't take it, Lily.'

'Yes please, for you please.'

'How mucho?' I asked as I reached for my wallet.

'No, please, present, no money.'

Flabbergasted to say the least, I claimed the picture, thanked her profusely and kissed everyone of her family (paying particular attention to her twenty one-year-old daughter).

Genuinely humbled, we had nothing to give back other than a Carrickfergus Reds scarf.

'Here, Keith, do you want an Ireland shirt to give her?' one of the Cork boys asked.

We made a presentation of the Irish football top to the family and collected a substantial tip among us, which we gave to her son as a thank you.

Before we left, we unfurled Lily one last time. The next thing we knew we were being asked to pose for photographs by tourists and the local press. A memorable afternoon concluded with a vociferous rendition of 'Ohh Ahh Cantona' - much to the amusement of our audience.

The next day I was amazed to see the back page of the Guardian where Jim White wrote 'The banner passing over the Reds' heads read Carrickfergus Reds - a bit provincial-like Carrickfergus.' Although Lily was slightly upset by this, unwittingly Jim White (A top Red and quality journalist) had helped to make her even more famous and it was nice to see that the she did not go unnoticed in the national tabloids. There was not much point in arguing that 'Carrickfergus Reds' was not provincial. Quite simply it was. However, our Lily was deliberately provincial. She was already becoming a tool of togetherness for our supporters club and having an effect on the wider community.

On my return home, the first person I met was my friend Bilko. William 'Bilko' Rainey is a larger-than-life character. A well-known and likeable taxi driver with his Andy Capp tattoo, often unshaven and untidy, and sporting track-suit bottoms and dodgy T-shirts which he makes in abundance, Bilko is a gadget man - digital cameras, video cameras - and is the owner of a small and, it must be said, amateur company - Sil/Bas Productions who produce everything from Christmas cards, the aforementioned T-shirts and often incriminating videos.

He shares his passion for United with Waylon Jennings, Captain Beefheart and Willie Nelson.

'Wee man, you missed the best night ever in Carrickfergus,' he said. The Club had hired a large screen to watch the game.

'It wasn't bad in Turin either, Bilko!' I replied.

## Big Big Lily

Now with two Cup Finals coming up, I decided Lily needed some major cosmetic surgery. I rang Karen (Lily's Mommy as the papers called her) and asked her to transform the willowy, understated Lily to a mature, fuller-figured woman.

'I want you to make her three times bigger.'

'You're winding me up, aren't you?'

'Karen, I'm serious. Can you do it?'

'No problem, when do you need her for?'

'That's the problem. I need her in a fortnight. Is that okay?'

'Okay then, bring her up tomorrow and I'll get her sorted.'

Cue the FA Cup Final and Lily's most famous day to date. As we passed through the turnstile at Wembley, we were asked what was in the bag. At this point Alan took issue with the guy - 'Don't you mean who is in the bag?' The steward informed us we were only allowed flags the width of our outspread arms. In my case, four feet, in his case about six foot nine. He said, 'You cannot take her in, I will have to confiscate her.' Our hearts sank. So near yet so far.

'What am a going to do with her, sir?'

'C'mon, my man, please let her in, she's been specially made for today.'

All sorts of porkies were attempted: it's for a television show; it's for a documentary; it's for charity; it belongs to King Kong's wife. With great respect to him, when we gave him the 'sad eyes' he let us proceed. Lily was so pleased at being allowed to pass the hallowed Twin Towers, I had quite a task keeping her in the bag.

During the singing of 'Abide with Me' - as three years previously with 'Eric the King' (only this time we were in row 7 behind the goal) - Alan and I, along with approximately one hundred Reds, militarily organised the first unveiling of Big Lily to the world.

'Make sure she's the right way up, wee man.'

'Don't worry, sir, I have her sussed. Could you pass her over as far as you can on your side?' I asked Alan.

The secret of the success of this was the planning and the way in which, having fed Lily from her bag, we laid her at the feet of about fifty or sixty people in our row and then passed the top of her above our heads while holding tightly (for as long as humanly possible) to the bottom black strip.

This was truly an emotional moment for us as we looked behind to see her in full glory moving backwards over the heads of the Reds on a world stage, five-hundred million television admirers, ever the exhibitionist, only to be eventually confiscated by stewards as she neared the 'Barcodes'. Although concerned by her disappearance, we were more than pleased with her spectacular showing. 'I wonder did the camera pick her up?' was no sooner said when a text message appeared on Alan's mobile phone: 'Big Lily on TV'.

'That was class, wee man. She fair done her job that time,' Alan said smiling.

'I think I'll have a wee smoke to celebrate,' he added and pulled a Regal Kingsize from his inside pocket. Now I appreciate why the Yanks cheer and clap so hard after a successful space shuttle launch.

Early in the game, Teddy Sheringham replaced Roy Keane who had been injured in a clash with Gary Speed. Sheringham and Scholes combined, resulting in Teddy knocking the ball past Harper to put us one up. Party time again.

Just seven minutes into the second half, Alan and I and the rest of the United end were buzzing once more. Scholes scored with a great left foot shot. There was no way we were going to lose this now and stage two of this illustrious treble was nigh complete.

All Reds were now in full party mode once more, and thoughts switched to the biggest night in our lives on the following Wednesday.

"If you're all going to BARCA clap your hand

If you're all going to Barca clap you hands

If you're all going to Barca,

All going to Barca,

All going to Barca clap your hands …"

Men and boys on the day, a third domestic double in six years, we had won without Keano. Could we do the same on Wednesday?

Now I had to attempt to retrieve Lily. I asked several stewards if they had seen a flag anywhere. I was told to try Lost Property.

We walked around to the Lost Property Office and I asked a burly security guard could I enter to inquire about

Lily, but he refused. He was a cross between Tower Bridge and Mike Tyson. I thought I would play the sad, dejected wee boy and offered him a reward, sadly to no avail. I stood outside for approximately an hour and a half, asking every departing steward if they had seen Lily anywhere.

Eventually Tower Mike came over and took my name and contact details. I thought at first this was an effort to get rid of me but he was in fact genuine. By the time another twenty minutes had passed 'Tower Mike' had performed his duty. He walked over, blocking out the sun as he did so, with Lily safely wrapped in a black polythene bag. I offered him forty pounds as a reward but to his credit he wouldn't take a penny. What a great sense of relief to find her - better than Christmas again.

After the match, the Geordies in the Wembley Hilton lounge who were already somewhat aggrieved were incensed when the Cockneys, using their height advantage, not only got to the bar first, but also literally 'bought the bar dry' of bottled beer by the boxload. I remember 'Da Brian' showing us his tattoos and saying, 'I suppose I'll have to get another one now.'

Johnny Flacks and Paddy Crerand came to join us, as arranged. We greeted Paddy with an ironic chorus of, 'We want Fergie out. We want Docherty in'. His response could only be described as 'Gutter Glaswegian' so we changed the words to, 'We want Fergie out, we want Paddy in', followed by 'There's only one Paddy Crerand'. As we sang our hearts out, the mortified Paddy wrapped himself in the nearby curtain.

A great night ensued and I must pay respect to a few of the friendly Geordies whom I again met in the Trafford Hall Hotel prior to the Newcastle game in August 2000 and who gave us a safe passage to the hotel lift - shielding us from the by now 'baying lynch mob'. Obviously they saved their venom for Newcastle City centre on their return home. Two down, one to go!

# Barcelona

Back home for two days only, we repacked the bags for Barcelona. As Lily's bag had been lost, it was time to find a new 'carrier'. The only thing I had was a huge Salomon ski bag more accustomed to carrying boots and ski socks to the Alps. My good friend and neighbour Jim Shields had the task of folding and neatly packing Lily in preparation for her final trip of the season.

Were it not for my two great friends and neighbors, Jim and Jo Shields, I could not have travelled to watch the Reds so often. It is wonderful to know that my family of two dogs (Keano and Treble), three cats (Scholesy, Andy Cole and Andy's brother), thirty fish (the Red Army) and of course my home, are so well looked after. I could never thank them enough for what they do for me. They are my animal watchers, house sitters, video makers (Jim records all the games), housekeepers, security guards and best friends.

After our arrival in Salou, it was not long before any thoughts of an early summer holiday changed to the small matter of overcoming Bayern Munich the following evening. What a hotel! I had become very 'Lily conscious', so my first reaction was, 'What a marvellous balcony, oh, look at that, right over the foyer too,' I thought as I admired the 100ft high Romanesque columns. As we walked into reception, Gary, Brian and Richard looked over to me and smiled. They knew what was on my mind and, like me, that it wouldn't be long...

Sure enough, as the rooms were being allocated, Richard and I headed for the top floor and respectfully unfurled Lily around the towers, watching her roll slowly and majestically down to the foyer and reception area. We must have been spotted by a hidden camera because Security were on to us like a flash. Of course we simply pleaded ignorance.

'What are hotel foyers for, sir? Sure wasn't the hotel designed this way for a reason? C'mon, wee man, tomorrow is the biggest night of our lives, will you not let the big girl play?' This was just the beginning of Lily's wildest exploits so far.

Changed and ready for a 'night-on-the-town', we decided to take Lily with us as it was rumoured a vociferous battalion of the Red Army was about a mile away.

## Our Greatest Day Together

No matter how many domestic trophies we had won in recent years, we had never been anything other than partially satisfied. We yearned for 'real' success of a European nature. This may sound somewhat ungrateful, but at the same time, after previous results in Europe against Galatasaray, Dortmund and Monaco, a 'Were we ever going to win "It" again?' sentiment existed among the Red faithful.

The day we had dreamed of for so many years had finally arrived - 26 May 1999 - the European Cup Final. Up 'fresh' in the morning, Lily, Gary and I headed for breakfast and then out to catch a few rays before the coach journey to Barcelona. Lily was laid out in front of the hotel as usual and must have posed for at least one hundred photographs from all angles and for all kinds of people. Doc Keating and his mate had a photograph taken while they lay spreadeagled in the middle of her, like children in Legoland. Lily brings out the child in everyone.

The coach dropped us in the middle of Las Ramblas. It was refreshment time. I was getting some strange looks as I walked about in a T-shirt carrying a huge ski-bag, so I let Brian from Bray and wee Gary do the honours. Walking towards the stadium, we eventually found this quaint wee spot on the opposite side of the street to the bulk of the invading Red Army. With all provisions obtained, we set up camp and Lily was unfurled and laid her out along the pavement. As always, she created a stir and before long attracted a group of about one hundred Reds, and a Major League singsong ensued. You know the script.

What happened next brought a tear to my eye.

We crossed the street to the main throng of Reds outside the Inter-Continental Hotel. Lily was now in full flight, in her element, surrounded by hundreds of Reds, all holding, touching and kissing her.

The wind caught Lily and inflated her like a hot air balloon. For one split second, while I was underneath, making sure the entire adoring herd held her in the right position, I had an emotional moment to myself. This was it. This was our dream fulfilled.

I could sense everyone's affection for Lily. Several times I was handed bottles of ale with comments such as, 'superb flag, mate, respect, mate, saw it in Milan, held in Turin, cracker at Wembley, was that you on't pitch at Villa Park?' This was what Lily was all about. I may be lucky enough to be her 'keeper', but Lily belongs to every single match-going Red.

The next big challenge was to ensure we got Lily inside the Nou Camp Stadium for the biggest game of our lives.

If she is not properly packed, it takes two of us to carry her. We tried to keep her as inconspicuous as possible. Once again the Spanish police tried to provoke any Red they could. Why, with a stadium the size of the Nou Camp, were so few turnstiles open?

Joe Black and I were carrying Lily between us. After about an hour, we made it inside the first police line. I overheard one smartass say, 'Look at that dickhead with a suitcase.' Before I could give a response, a quick surge began towards the gate and 'bucket mouth' was out of sight. Eventually we got through the turnstile and guess who was standing just inside the gate waiting on his friends?

You've got it - 'bucket mouth'. I calmly walked over to him and told him in my finest public school English how nice his head would look jammed in the revolving turnstile. He apologised profusely. Thank goodness, as he was about six-foot tall and probably would have knocked me senseless.

We were into the stadium at long last and delighted with our position. Our seats were right behind the goal (row 7) in the United section. What an incredible sight. We'd been here before but never in the numbers as on this night. To witness the build up of the Red Army on this historic evening was an exceptional experience. An ocean of Red brethren and sisters, expectantly poised and me in a state of excited numbness. Not my usual chirpy and talkative self, lost in my own world of Red sentiment mixed with personal emotional memories of a lifetime. I wish my mum and dad could have experienced this special night with me. I had memories of all of my grandparents and my late Auntie Gertie. On one hand I was literally living my greatest ever dream by being here. On the other - maybe it was the fact that the dream was no longer fantasy - I didn't

160

want to discuss the tactics, the team, the atmosphere with anyone, bar none - even those good friends like Richard, Joe Black and Brian from Bray with whom I shared so much of my life in the past.

As the other 'Big Lily' (Montserrat Caballe) present on the evening started to chant 'Barcelona' in a tone resembling a sty of squealing pigs, Lily was released from her ski-bag home and unveiled.

She was quickly passed above the heads of the lower tier Reds and swooped right around the bottom section where the United supporters were located. This was it. Lily had once again made her appearance. As she passed along, I said my goodbyes. I could not see her coming home again, but what an exit, what an encore. I had been prepared for our separation but was still extremely emotional as the remaining part of her disappeared towards one of the exits.

'That's her now, sir, she's away for good, that's the end of the big girl.'

I honestly thought that it was a case of 'Big Lily - gone but not forgotten.'

This was it. I must admit I find it very difficult to articulate what happened next.

I was disappointed that the United fans were rather subdued or, at least, appeared to be, myself included. I can only suggest that it was due to being extremely nervous. My stomach was churning and my head pounding. It was difficult to be as vociferous as usual (although we should have been), especially after Bayern took the lead

David Beckham in midfield, Blomqvist on the left and Giggs on the right, 'Oh no, what's he at?' someone behind me exclaimed.

'What's he supposed to do?' another responded.

'Blomqvist's pass in Turin got Keano booked.'

I listened quietly to the debate and comments beside me. Who was I to question anything Sir Alex had done after the amazing weeks before Barcelona?

Ronny Johnsen tackled Jancker on the edge of the penalty area. The free kick was awarded to Bayern. Basler strode up and hit a curling shot past Peter Schmeichel's despairing left hand - 1-0 to Bayern Munich after just five minutes. Although an anaesthetized shell-shocked feeling prevailed, it was much too early to start panicking.

'This might be the best thing that happened, it'll bring us to life.'

'We always play better when we go one down.'

Come on, United, let's get at them!

Bayern had the better of the early exchanges and were playing well, too well for our liking. Jeremies, Basler and Zickler in particular all looked well up for it.

Blomqvist had a great chance to equalize when Giggs broke down the right. His cross only needed the slightest touch to be directed into the goal, but the Swedish winger ballooned it high over the bar.

'Blomqvist, you twat!' was heard among the disappointed groans around me.

'Unlucky Reds, that's better,' I encouraged as we clapped appreciatively.

With twenty-five minutes remaining, Teddy Sheringham was sent on by the Wizard in place of Jesper Blomqvist. As Teddy came on the Reds clapped, cheered and encouraged, begging him, willing him, to make a difference.

'Come on, Teddy son.'

'Go on, Sheringham, make a name for yourself.'

'Let's go, Reds.'

Cole attempted a bicycle kick, which went wide after more pressure from United. Becoming increasingly edgy yet hopeful, the Red Army found their voice again and shirts pushed forward in search of an equalizer.

'Look at the space they've got.'

'We're going to get caught here again, please no,' I uttered aloud as Mehmet Scholl almost killed us off totally.

His delicate chip had Schmeichel stranded, and mercifully bounced back off the post.

Ole Gunnar Solskjaer replaced Andy Cole and although we continually pressed forward, Bayern were resolute in defence.

'Come on, Ole son, you can do it, wee man.'

'Go on, Ole, do what you done to the Scousers in the cup, son.'

Schmeichel turned away a shot from Babbel for a corner. From the corner, Jancker athletically hit a spectacular overhead kick which thankfully rebounded off the crossbar.

'It's meant to be now, we will score,' someone behind me commented.

'I hope you're right, sir,' I added anxiously.

I daren't say that I didn't think we would, but I hoped against hope we would.

So much was at stake and as the game progressed I became more and more apprehensive. Looking at the clock which was displaying ninety minutes up, I have to admit I thought we had blown it, although eternally hopeful I thought it was going to be one of those nights.

Well, at least I saw them in a European Cup Final, I thought. Please God, let the Reds score, I prayed inwardly as I clenched my fist around my bar scarf.

'One last effort, lads; come on, get her up this end.'

With one minute to play, Teddy Sheringham miraculously rescued us from the brink of imminent defeat. Beckham's corner fell to Giggs on the edge of the area, he half hit a shot and Teddy steered the ball into the net. Unbelievable. Incredible. Inconceivable. Astonishing. Ecstasy. Fantasy. Happiness. Ultimate bliss as the Red Army kissed, hugged, danced and screamed simultaneously.

'We'll do them in extra time - it's ours now.'

'Come on, lads, you can beat the Germans now, they're finished!' the excited voice (the one who had been loud and positive all night) exploded beside me.

We were by no means finished yet. Another Beckham corner came in. Sheringham touched it on and Solskjaer guided it into the German net. Two goals in the space of a minute had won us the European Cup and the Treble.

'YEESSSSSSSSS!'

'YES!YES !YES!'

'I don't believe it!'

What a team! What a result! What a night! What a season! What a life! What a feeling to be a Red!

Goose bumps, sweat, tears, laughter, stress, trauma, elation, freedom, relief, euphoria ... I can't put that sensation into words. Deliverance, liberation, release, emancipation. Every possible physical sensation and every conceivable mental emotion imaginable - all at once.

The celebrations following the climactic sequence of events that unfolded during those amazing three minutes were, to say the least, momentous. I cried like a baby before, after and during the presentation. There they were - our team, my team, everyone's team, Alan and Gary's team, Davy Root and the Faceman's team, the Cockney's team, Bilko's team, the Reds, Brian from Bray's team, the shirts, the boys, the Red Devils, the Busby Babes, Fergie's Fledglings, the mighty Manchester United twenty feet in front of me, in front of me, in front us, the Reds, the Red

Army, blissfully celebrating with the European Cup we had craved for so long.

We met Kevin and Deirdre Woodside, then wee Gary and the rest of the lads. Everyone was embracing like long lost brothers and sisters. Our Red Family 'United' in celebration.

After watching the on-field celebrations for over an hour, the crowd slowly began to filter out. I guess it was the emotion of the whole occasion and I am a sentimentalist at heart, but my thoughts turned once again to Lily. I think a few of the tears I shed were actually for her, thinking she was gone forever. Joe Black, Brian from Bray and myself headed towards Lily's last-known location, asking many Reds if they had seen where the big flag had gone. We marched the aisles, jumped the seats and searched every exit, but to no avail.

'C'mon, boys, we better head back, she's not there, the stewards will have threw her out,' I said

'Keith, Keith quick, I think I see the big girl over there at the fence,' Brian from Bray excitedly exclaimed.

'It couldn't be, sir, that's not her, sure we were over there, weren't we?'

'That's her, my man, I'm telling you. C'mon we'll go over and take a look.'

Brian from Bray, Joe Black and I clambered over the rows of empty seats and jumped yet another wire fence and rushed towards the back of the lower tier.

You can imagine our delight when we spotted this huge pile of flag debris lying tucked behind the back row of the bottom tier right over the halfway line. There she was like an abandoned child, a refugee, an orphan. Only a small part of her was visible from where we had been standing a few minutes earlier.

'There she is, the big girl, I told you.'

'Brian, I love you, wee man. I don't know how you spotted her, sir.'

'Ah, Keith, you never lose the touch, sure I used to be a train spotter.'

I fell on top of her, hugging and kissing the biggest girl in my life.

Now it was Dr Dom Perignon time - big style.

Back to Salou, where we were informed that the hotel would provide food and keep the bar open for a few hours if we were quiet - aye, right.

In the hotel a bunch of about two hundred and fifty Mancs were on an official trip, including Charlie and Tony whom we meet regularly in the Amblehurst Hotel. All the guests in that evening were treated to a mock presentation ceremony. If before and during the match I had been poignant and uncharacteristically muted, my mood swiftly changed as it began to sink in and normal service was resumed.

'Lend us that big cup' - it was a large silver trophy - 'for a bit of craic,' I asked the hotel manager. 'We're gonna have a presentation like the one the boys done.'

We placed the borrowed large silver trophy on a table and set up a makeshift rostrum at the back of the hall. This was the greatest night in our lives and we had no intention of going to bed.

Everyone took their turn in quieting the exuberant crowd, Schmeichel-like, and then grabbing their own moment of glory on the rostrum with our own very special version of the European Cup.

What a day - what a night - what a season!

The champagne and San Miguel flowed, and the 'Happy Hour' lasted all night. Only one thing was missing. I sneaked up to my room and brought Lily down in wedding-train fashion. What a reception she received in the Red-filled lounge. At first she lay calmly enjoying the admiration of the vociferous Salford battalion of the Red Army and friends.

As the partying continued into the wee small hours, a huge 'Lily chain' began. Imagine the scene - Wee Gary Callaghan (who led Lily on to the pitch at Villa Park), started by rolling her up. We, in the chain, took the rolled-up Lily under our right arms, left hands on the shoulder of the person in front, giving the repeated refrain 'Red Army, RED ARMY'. I followed him, hand on shoulder, Richard, Brian from Bray, Joe Black and approximately another two hundred followed behind. This was the biggest and loudest Red Army chain we have ever witnessed. Round and round the room, outside the hotel, around the swimming pool and back again and again and again. Lily was without doubt the instigator of this jubilant high-spirited assault on the fabulous hotel, and the heart and soul of the party.

It must have been about six a.m. before the last of the stragglers headed for the sack. Gary and I along with a couple of our Southern Irish friends made our way to the roof of the hotel and proceeded to hang Lily over the side in full view of the Salou locals making their way to their places of employment.

The moon had long disappeared and Gary, Brian, Joe and I lay by the pool talking, wrapped in six thousand square feet of linen.

'What a day.'

'Awesome.'

'Lily was brilliant.'

'The best day of my life.'

'I thought we were chinned, sir.'

'When I saw that board go up I knew we'd do it, I just knew we would score.'

'We did it for Matt.'

'We did it for Eric.'

'And then to find Lily like that, unthinkable, Keith, unthinkable.'

We drifted off to a contented sleep. Rather fitting that after all her exploits and her travels Lily could even be used for something as humble as a sleeping bag.

## Paying Respect

Her next airing would be a little closer to home in Omagh Town and a charity game where the Reds were to pay their respects to a town that had suffered so much and to display the three trophies.

We arrived in the early afternoon and set up camp (as we thought) near the ground at St Julian's Road. We met up with a few Mancs and took Lily on a walkabout through Omagh Town Centre, much to the bemusement of the locals. As kick-off approached, we decided to walk back to where we thought was close to the ground, only to notice hundreds of fans walking in a totally different direction.

Eventually we were re-routed (now there's a much-hackneyed phrase in Northern Ireland) and pointed in the right direction by a local Red - to approximately two miles out of the town.

We arrived in the ground just in time for the one-minute silence. Having paid our respects, we began to unfurl Lily in the bottom corner of the Stadium. Taking Lily's enormity into consideration it was impossible for her to be fully extended as at Wembley and Barcelona. It would have covered the entire stand.

We left shortly afterwards, giving our four tickets to some deserving kids who had been locked outside. Charity games are not really our cup of tea, but a very worthwhile event in this case. It was fitting that Lily's last outing of the season was in solidarity with the people of Omagh.

# BIG IN JAPAN

## *'Full of dreams in Heaven and Earth': World Club Championship, Tokyo (30 November 1999)*

The prospect of a pre-Christmas week in Tokyo to watch the Reds play for the Toyota Cup and the chance to become World Champions was too good to miss - even if it would mean curtailment of future Euro aways. Many sacrifices had to be made in the form of Fiorentina and Bordeaux away before Christmas and the three-day trip I had planned to the Bradford game with the Faceman on Boxing Day. With so many matches in the restructured Champions League, it is impossible to go to every one unless you are a multi-millionaire or a fanzine editor.

Jamie, Alan, Paul and I had originally booked to fly to Tokyo via Istanbul or Pakistan but, when the travel agent increased the price and said we would have to stay at Karachi airport overnight, we pulled the plug.

That was it - now we were not going. It was a bitter blow, as Alan and I had been so looking forward to it. I telephoned a friend who works for British Airways and he gave me a very good rate of £339 return for the flights from London to Narita. This was a once in a lifetime opportunity (again) and there was no way we could refuse it.

Paul, Jamie and I were all booked. Alan was disappointed especially when he had been so up for it although already he had told Linda he wouldn't be going and, to be honest, he'd talked himself out of it, thinking our initial enthusiasm would expire.

Over the next few days I scanned the Internet for cheap hotels and any information on central Tokyo. 'The Red Issue' website is an excellent forum for United fans. The postings were all suggesting that most Reds would be making for the usual haunt on Euro aways - an Irish bar named Paddy Foleys, located apparently at the bottom floor of a tall building. No doubt we would endeavour to find it. On these trips getting to the Irish bar (if a city has such) is a must for most Reds.

Jamie had been friendly with two girls who had been working in London a few years previously. He said they had offered to put us up if we wished.

It was a nice gesture but to be honest I'm a bit odd (in fact, I'm as odd as a bottle of chips) about staying in other people's houses while on holiday, especially someone I didn't know or had never even met. I hate that awful feeling of awkwardness you get when you have to go to the toilet and someone is in it or even worse if you are in the bathroom and the owner of the house needs to go to the loo. I much prefer a hotel where I can create my own base camp and leave a mess, which a maid will clean. Thankfully big Paul felt the same way so it saved any uncomfortable moments.

I came across the Clarion Hotel in a district called Ikebukuro. It was fairly central if a little expensive at a price that worked out somewhere in the region of £70 per night each. The plan was to stay here on the first night and then look for something more affordable the following morning.

As the departure date came closer, Alan was really wishing he were going - it was obvious he was busting his gut to get away. Even the excuses that 'it was too close to Christmas' or the comforting thought that he would get to all the Euro aways in the New Year were more for his own peace of mind…I knew underneath that he was furiously trying to work out a way to justify the trip to himself, never mind to his wife Linda.

I plagued him with text messages on his mobile phone at almost hourly intervals. Messages like 'Life is short, We love you long time, Flied Lice velly good in Japan and You'll be big in Japan' were sent frequently.

My last throw of the dice was to call in on the Jackson household on the way home from work one Wednesday evening with a bottle of Dom Perignon (which I had got cheap) as a treat for Linda.

I acted as if I had accepted the fact that Alan was definitely not going and tried to adopt an 'I'm sorry, mate, I understand you can't make it' attitude, thinking this new approach would make Linda feel guilty …it always did.

The gesture was to prove successful. I'm not sure whether it was the effect of the Dom on Linda that made her decide Alan could get the much sought after 'pass out' but the result was the main thing: with hands being shaken and me promising not to tell the Cockneys that Alan was going - you know, like the Cilla Surprise Surprise show?

Alan and I are fairly close and he is an important part of most trips. He is well organised and great at looking after tickets and passports, which I am inclined to lose. Now we were all set for an adventure to the land of the Rising Sun, the home of Sumo, motorcycles, cameras and the Suzuka circuit.

When we confirmed flights to Tokyo for the Intercontinental Cup, Lily was my first thought. She had been involved at every stage of the Treble; surely I would have to take her to Tokyo.

Japan for me is one of the places I never expected I would manage to visit but added to this was the fact I was going to watch my team make even more history by hopefully being the first English team to win the coveted Toyota Cup and be crowned World Champions regardless of the new FIFA tournament to follow in January.

It was like a continuation of the Treble success. Where would this fantasy end? It was hard not to let it slip to Jamie and Paul as promised over the next few days but having secured Alan's flight with David we set about the quest for match tickets...

I had applied for tickets through Old Trafford but once again was told I was too late and they had all been allocated.

Jamie had got one ticket sorted out with his Japanese friend.

On the day before departure, in a desperate bid for three tickets, I even contacted Kate Hoey the Minister for Sport. To be fair, she honestly tried but to no avail although she did contact me again. A man from her office actually called me and said 'Kate has tried the two contacts who assure her that there are no tickets left whatsoever.'

The same day Alan suggested I fax Rick Adkinson whom he had met in Hong Kong. Rick was chairman of the Hong Kong Supporters Club and was a cert to be going.

I also sent an email to Stephen Ryan from the Tokyo branch of the Supporters Club who replied telling us to meet him in Paddy Foley's in Roppongi on the Saturday evening.

I made sure Lily was well packed into her itinerant home, the Salomon ski bag, for her longest trip to date.

Friday, 26th November was upon us. Up, washed, shaved and showered by five a.m. Normally it is a struggle to make it to work in the mornings but for a trip I bounce out of bed like a child. You have a real buzz on all match days but this was something special - this was even more than a match - an adventure, a fantasy, a dream.

We departed on the 0650 to Heathrow, made our way to Terminal Four in plenty of time to meet the Cockneys. Paul was to come in on the train and Jamie's sister was to drop him off.

Alan stayed in the background as a certain casual, complete with £300 Gore-Tex, designer baseball cap and customary pack of red Marlboro cigarettes in hand, approached from the train station.

Paul was shocked to see Alan - it wasn't really fair and possibly Surprise Surprise would have been better suited to schoolkids.

'What are you doing here, Jacko?'

'I'm only over to make sure the wee man gets away OK,' Jacko jested.

I felt a bit silly actually. Big Paul was gobsmacked but delighted.

We proceeded into the wee coffee lounge, already noticing a couple of well known faces as we sat waiting for Jamie. The big man arrived shortly afterwards as we were standing at the door just outside the main terminal. He too was shocked to see Alan.

'What are you doing here, matey?'

'We just thought we'd surprise you guys,' quipped Alan.

Big Paul said he had been like an eager kid all week. I knew how he felt. Sleepless nights, churning stomach, dreaming with excitement, nervousness, anticipation ... and endless trips to the toilet.

'You got Lily with you okay, Keith?'

173

'I bet you she's excited about all that sunshine and all.'

We had a couple of hours to kill before the twelve o'clock departure and it wasn't long before we were having breakfast in Harry Ramsden's.

Thankfully we had a spare seat between us on the flight - my friend from British Airways, David Gorman, had further ensured that our flight was as comfortable as possible by booking us a window and aisle seats, leaving a spare in between to act as bar, bed or wall. On our flight I estimated about sixty or seventy United fans. The British Airways waitress service was well used. Some airhostesses were noticed telling several Reds that not only had they consumed their quota but also the main cabin had run dry. To be totally diplomatic, considering some of the Reds bar bills, the fare at £339 was a bargain.

With a four or five-hour sleep, the twelve and a half hour flight passed fairly quickly. One well-known Red beside us was told by a Japanese girl as we were disembarking, 'You very noisy.' The Red nodded politely and said 'Thank you.'

Having cleared customs we were walking towards the exit when this throng of people and television cameras appeared. I spotted Alex Best standing near the door. I went over to say hello to her and she said they were out for a week to attend some functions with the Tokyo Branch. I wished her all the best - excuse the pun - and on my way back to the lads I pushed into the throng of journalists and reporters and shouted, 'George, Carrickfergus, what about you?'

George looked up and nodded in a friendly way before being totally swamped.

We travelled by train to Tokyo and eventually via taxi to the Hotel Clarion.

By this stage we were all absolutely knackered and immediately headed to four single rooms with a plan to get up in three or four hours, attempt to master the underground and search for a Red infested Irish Bar somewhere at the base of an office block.

I was awakened by the sound of high-pitched laughter coming along the corridor. As I went exploring I detected that the noise was coming from Jamie's room. Aye, aye the big man doesn't waste much time, I thought.

Jamie opened the door and introduced me to two beautiful Japanese girls, Tomoko and Kanakoyjo, or 'Kanu' and 'Tom' as they were soon christened.

Shortly afterwards we all met in the hotel lobby and soon we were on our way to the tube station, guided by our two new friends and, by now, adopted tour guides.

My first impression was of how clean and tidy the tube stations were. No cigarette butts, sweetie wrappers or newspapers. These walls were probably cleaner than our kitchens. There were thousands of people all seemingly walking towards us. Why does no one seem to be going the other way?

The tubes on time, the immaculately dressed guardsmen (shashou) complete with green jacket, army-type hat, white gloves and an amazing hand signalling action when trains were pulling to and from stations: these guys had pride in their work. The tube stations had many shops in them - kiosks selling everything from beauty products to lottery tickets.

It was pretty amazing walking into an Irish bar/restaurant in the middle of Tokyo. What was even more amazing was the guy behind the bar.

'How's it going, buddy?' he asked. 'Where are you from? 'Whitehead, Carrickfergus,' I replied.

'Do you know Buckets Haveron and Dee Jay?' he said in a North American accent.

I almost choked - this guy's Canadian sister had married a local guy whom I knew. The Buckets he was referring to was none other than Michael Haveron who not only was in the Club but also lived at the bottom of my street, was a regular visitor to my house and was my mate.

'Sure, Michael is in our Supporters' Club,' I said.

He extended his hand and said, 'I'm Kevin Haveron. Michael's cousin.'

'It's a small world, sir,' I added, shocked.

About thirty Reds were in the bar, many of them sampling the Black stuff at £6 a pint.

I had planned to meet Stephen Ryan from the Tokyo Branch. That is one thing about being involved in the Supporters' Club network: it opens up many new friends in different parts of the country and friendships continue for many years. Not only that but your own Red Family gets bigger. As I walked in the door I saw him sitting with four guys from Manchester.

The craic was good and the Japanese girls were urging us to sing a song.

You know how the atmosphere intensifies in a bar full of supporters? The Reds were not long in reaching full voice, singing all the old favourites: 'If the Reds Should Play in Rome or Mandalay, Eric The King up to the thirteenth verse, and the old battle cry of Reds Are Here Reds Are There'. I met a top Red and good friend wee Gary Newman and we debated some of the issues I like addressing to real fans.

We met a couple of boys, John and Paul, who were telling some stories from previous trips including Lodz away (which we didn't make). Some of them I cannot repeat. Sufficient to say they included some major 'jibs' including player impersonations in hotels when it came to bill-paying time.

And a tale of how they extended their 'jibbing' to include the previous night in a Tokyo hotel where electrical giants Sony were having one of their major product launches or a function of some sort. The lads approached the reception of the hotel only to be told they were not on the guest list.

'How can this be?' they enquired.

They asked for the manager and complained that they were not included on this list despite having flown especially from the UK for this conference. The security guards eventually let them through, apologising profusely for any misunderstanding.

About four hours later Paul was asked by security to take his friend 'Mr Sony' home as he had fallen asleep over a table.

'Jibbing' is a big part of fan culture. Stories of getting into grounds, trains, receptions etc without paying or getting invites are legendary among United fans. To be honest, I think more people talk about it than actually do it, although many stories involve masters of the jib, including the one in Brondby where a certain gentleman made it on to the bench with United players and most recently in Munich when Karl Power posed as United's twelfth man in the pre-match team photograph. In saying that, I know several masters of the jib and have witnessed many such acts both at away grounds in the Premiership and Euro Aways when tickets are scarce.

The next thing I know is that Paul, Jamie, Alan and the lads had 'done a George' and The Jibber and I are walking down the busy street. Workmen (or guardsmen) were directing traffic at the corner of the sushi bar, about five hundred yards from Paddy Foleys. They were all carrying police-like, foot-long, red illuminated batons for directing traffic.

I knew what was coming next.

'Jibber' John asked one of the workers if he could take a look at his baton, but the worker looked suspicious and his grip was getting tighter. Jibber told me to pretend to take a picture and walk back about ten feet.

I had no camera but made the action of picture taking and about ten seconds later saw John come running at me and shouting, 'Run for it, Keith,' (in a strong Manc accent).

I turned and made my getaway as fast as I could, down the street a hundred yards and then a sharp left up towards the main thoroughfare.

Jibber John had 'borrowed' the guy's illuminated blinking lantern (tenmetsutou) and we then took it on a tour of the nightclubs in the vicinity.

What a greeting the red lantern got - bemused looks from locals as if we were off our heads and cheers from the many Reds dispersed among the clubs. When we got back, Paddy's was long closed and, to be totally honest, I had no clue where in the world I was. With the rest of my crew away I tried to get a cab, but I had absolutely no idea where to tell him to take me.

All I knew was Hotel Clarion - same chain as the one in Carrickfergus. Yes, that would be well understood at three a.m. in central Tokyo …

I was sitting on a wall beside a pelican crossing outside Foleys's when one of the waiters from earlier asked me if I was okay. This guy took me back inside and I explained where I was staying.

'Well, Ikeboo hooor oo, or something I think.'

Kevin, who was still inside cleaning up, eventually got me sorted out and thankfully I arrived home all in one peace albeit with my wallet a lot lighter.

I honestly couldn't tell you if he charged me five pounds or fifty pounds but that did not even come into the equation. I had got home on my own somehow.

Quite an eventful beginning to the Far East.

Over the next few days, we took things easy. The lads had found new accommodation in Roppongi. Hotel Ibis was central, situated beside a tube station and a succession of restaurants, bars and shops. This would be home for the next six nights.

We had arranged to meet Kevin for something to eat in the Propaganda Shop Bar directly opposite where he worked, but he didn't make it and just as we were about to leave in walked several Mancs we knew and Rick and the Hong Kong boys whom we had met earlier. Our club CD was not long in coming out and once again the lads had a singsong.

'Mack', a well-dressed Red from Birmingham, was trying his best with a few of the local talent. Mack was obviously a lifelong match-going Red and was good craic but his mate, a Villa fan who had come to see United, was getting more than a wee bit tedious telling us how he loved United. This was fair enough but he kept changing his story so many times about whom he supported. Mind you if you had seen what he was drinking (some weird salt mixture) it would have come as no surprise he was having something of an identity crisis.

On Monday afternoon, Tomoko took us to the shopping district of Ginza mainly in search of a digital camera for my sister. We walked for miles past many tall department stores that were brightly lit with colourful, flashing neon signs, window shopping only - this was for the rich (Ginza is top of the list when it comes to the price of land and maybe that explains their extortionate prices). We took time out to visit the Sony building which was an amazing place: state-of-the-art in car entertainment, futuristic televisions, walking electronic dog (which was having some kind of launch while we were there) and the most amazing array of cameras you could ever imagine. Each floor was dedicated to a particular range of products. This was public relations at its best.

We walked past the impressive Pioneer building and then arrived at the Disney shop (Paul wanted to add to his Mickey Mouse collection) where we had our first encounter with Palmeiras fans before catching the tube back to Roppongi. We called in with Kevin to see what time he was opening on Tuesday. We advised him as early as possible because of the many Reds making the pilgrimage.

We had a bit of a lie-in on the Tuesday morning of the game and once again went to Paddy's about one o'clock, only to find it as yet unopened. Instead we decided that we should have a wee walk. Alan, who had gone for one of his mysterious walks on the previous night, attempted to retrace his steps because we wanted to buy similar souvenirs to the ones he had already purchased.

We walked round and round, in through people's gardens, peered through the window of a traditional Japanese restaurant and, without finding any of the shops again, landed at a quaint wee Italian restaurant beside a geisha girl parlour. The view was pleasant, the sun shining and the company excellent. We sat here for about an hour before going back to the Hotel Ibis both to change and to pick up Big Lily and about one dozen Carrickfergus Reds scarves that I had packed for the trip to the National Stadium.

Back around the corner and the short walk down the street to our adopted base, arriving at about two-thirty p.m. at the camp of Paddy Foleys once more, where we stayed for a couple of hours while many of the Red Army gathered.

I went back to the hotel to prepare Lily and change bags to make her easier to carry before going to meet up with other Reds in Paddy Foleys's. As we arrived, several Reds were producing flags for pictures outside the pub for souvenirs. I knew it would not be long before the big girl was out to play. A few faces from previous trips abroad were shouting over to me: 'You got the big flag this time?'

We stood in the corner watching the room fill with Reds. Lily could take it no longer - she had to come out. The bar was situated on a basement level, down a flight of steps just off the main road. We laid Lily out right outside the door. Instantly she became her usual spectacle. Passing locals on the street above were, to say the least, bemused. About twenty of us held Lily up for a photo session.

The Red Army were by now arriving in force and it wasn't long before the usual singsong started.

Stephen Ryan, big Paul and a few others gave us a hand to refold her in preparation for the game and then sorted us out with a taxi to take us to the National Stadium.

We left in plenty of time for the game by taxi. Jamie sat in the front and Paul, Alan and I in the back seat, while unbeknown to me, Lily reposed in the boot. As we pulled up outside the national stadium, the automatic taxi door opened and we jumped out. Alan and Paul, in desperation to go to the toilet, jumped the fence and relieved themselves behind a wall.

As the cab pulled away, I looked around for Lily.

'Who has got Lily?' I asked.

'She's in the boot of matey's cab,' said Jamie.

'You're joking, sir, are you winding me up?'

'Sorry, Keith, I forgot about her. I thought you or big Paul was bringing her.'

Panic set in as we realised that not only would Lily miss the match but also the chances of finding her from among the multitude of cabs in Tokyo (which, for you anoraks, boasts approximately sixty thousand taxis) were at best slim.

We stopped the next taxi, which had just dropped some more Reds off outside the ground. Paul, in his best cockney Japanese accent, tried to get the driver to radio through the details to the office (sounds so simple).

'Ere, matey, flag, bag, boot, lost, Lily, can you radio office?' he said, trying to gesticulate what he meant. 'We-have-lost-Lily,' he mouthed, speaking like a four-year-old.

'Ah, Lily ... asso.'

'You understand?'

Taximan nodded.

'Do you understand, matey? No he's having a laugh.' Paul looked back at us, sceptically.

Meantime, Jamie and I walked into the middle of the bustling street (which was four lanes wide on either side) like a scene from a movie, searching hopelessly for any resemblance of our cab driver who may have come back on the one-way system and passes us. Strangers in a strange land, we were looking for a Japanese taxi driver wearing a white shirt, driving the ubiquitous taxi.

However, if he had turned left after he dropped us off, we had no possibility of spotting him and we were on a major fool's errand.

Eventually Paul gave the helpful taxi driver whom we had stopped the number of our hotel and contact details. Onward to the game, a little despondent I must admit, but equally determined that this was not going to ruin our night and chances of becoming World Champions.

Jamie felt pretty bad, as it was he who had put Lily in the boot in the first instance. This was an accident we would laugh about - eventually.

We went into our section of the ground and it was not long before word had got to Rick, and the Hong Kong Battalion and his fellow choir members from Singapore Reds, swollen by several Mancs, broke into songs:

> 'Where's your famous flag?
> WHERE'S YOUR FAMOUS FLAG?'

and

> 'You left your flag in a taxi,
> Flag in a taxi,
> You left your flag in a taxi ...'

Lily had more than done her duty on her previous adventures and I was lucky to have kept her for so long, but I was truly emotional: it was like the death of someone you love - you never want it to happen and when it does you have to cope with it. The Palmeiras supporters were loud, colourful, passionate and were certainly not there just to make up the numbers.

The Palmeiras team, including former Newcastle favourite Tino Asprilla, were simply defied by a wonderful goalkeeping performance.

We were standing fairly near the back - about thirty feet from the noisiest Reds in our section, the battalion led by Rick and his Hong Kong and Singapore Reds mixed with a few faces. Every time we sang a song, the Japanese crowd would look at us in total astonishment, trying to establish what we were singing. Every now and again they would join in the songs we were attempting to teach them:

'Lion Gliggs, Lion Gliggs lunning down le ling ...' or 'Lere's only one Dabid Bleckham'.

This was without doubt Mark Bosnich's best performance in a United shirt. I think that because the sponsors had their mind set on 'Gliggs' or 'Bleckam', he was done an injustice by not being presented with the keys to a new Toyota sports car.

To be honest, we didn't play particularly well, with Keano taking the goal from Giggsy's pinpoint cross, but 'Champions of the World' still has a nice ring to it.

Ryan Giggs and David Beckham had threatened to run riot on the Palmeiras' defence but The Shirts failed to capitalise on their early domination and they nearly paid for this in the twentieth minute when Palmeiras striker Alex went close to scoring.

Then Giggs, once again, electric down the left wing, crossed to the back post where Roy Keane arrived and fired into the empty Brazilian net.

Palmeiras had most of the possession but failed to take their chances and Bosnich made a succession of world-class saves

Without a doubt we rode our luck and just about held on before being presented with two trophies - the Inter Continental Cup and the Toyota Cup.

I must admit that prior to kick-off I had not appreciated the historical aspect of this trophy properly.

I was standing beside Cockney Phil Walpole, a wee man of about sixty whom we had met previously along with his awesome digital movie camera, and who hugged me with tears running down his cheek as the final whistle blew. I must admit I felt almost embarrassed about not taking this seriously enough. Don't get me wrong, I appreciated we were the first English team ever to win this

184

coveted prize, but I was now going to appreciate it more and savour every moment.

Back to Paddy Foleys again - where even more Reds than before had packed into the two sides of the lounge. Big Paul's MUFC flag was draped up inside and we sang several new songs - ' Obladi Oblada Man United … Champions of Planet Earth'. This was the Reds in full-party mode.

United Legend Kevin Moran was in the bar and actually started a song after prompting from us, while Howard gave an emotional version of the 'Flowers of Manchester' on the karaoke microphone behind the bar. Tom was introduced to Kevin Moran who joined for us for a while. She had obviously no clue who he was, but when he was described as 'the first Roy Keane' she got the idea.

After a boisterous couple of hours, which included watching the game again on television, the Reds began to drift their separate ways. We walked across the street and into a dodgy-looking place called the Mowtown.

I had Paul's flag wrapped around me and danced around the floor as Alan danced with a few Palmeiras blokes and Big Jamie and Paul watched the amazing display of movement from the fit Brazilian birds.

As the club filled up it was obvious we were not the clientele the management desired.

Paul walked back to the hotel while we went looking for some food. We wandered on until we came to this office block with a lift on the front of the street with numerous plaques on the wall: the Comedy Club, Gentlemen's Club among others including two different restaurants.

'Let's go up and see what the craic is, there's bound to be a "Mackie D's",' said Jamie. These cockneys seem to live on McDonalds.

The first few floors had nothing interesting but on the seventh we read a sign saying: 'Come this way for a laugh' (the Comedy Club obviously). The door of the lift opened and I went to take a look in the window while the lads stayed inside. All was quiet and closed but outside the Comedy Club door were all sorts of goodies from the magic show. Now it was my showtime.

One by one the lift doors would open and close at Jamie's command. Each time I would demonstrate a particular magical accompaniment - hoops, rings, seats, hats, balloons, umbrellas, everything you could imagine you would find in a comedy club and then throw them into the lift where Jamie and Alan were still standing, bent double laughing. When everything was in the lift, I joined the lads and our new toys.

It is hard to describe the scene but if you imagine those ball pits that they have in children's playpens (usually at fast-food restaurants) - you know the feeling when you are covered in coloured balls and find it hard to move? The three of us were on the floor laughing and covered with what were obviously props from the magic show, which had long since finished. This was absolutely hilarious: three Reds stuck in a lift on the seventh floor of a deserted building in Tokyo having their very own magic show.

Jamie, always on the hunt for souvenirs, 'borrowed' a magic cushion and an umbrella that he unfurled even though it was not raining, much to the amusement of the Japanese locals.

Wednesday morning came rather early after our escapades the previous evening. Paul didn't believe the adventure until he tripped on the umbrella that had been left on the bathroom floor.

We set off for Akihabara (the supposed hub of discount electrical goods) at about three p.m. where we eventually found a digital camera at the right price.

We all overindulged in the usual tacky souvenirs and trinkets. I spent so much that I had to buy a bag for all I bought - like chopsticks fridge magnets and key rings.

We walked the length of the street and eventually came to Ueno, which could best be described as a huge outdoor market selling all sorts from fresh fish to oil paintings. This district was completely swarming with Japanese locals and Indian immigrants.

We were getting funny looks. No wonder - we were, after all, a bunch of either fat, tall or ugly blokes. And there was Jamie thinking it was the colour of our skin. In an effort to stop attracting attention we 'borrowed' four balaclavas from a street vendor's stall.

We were given green tea by a street vendor as a sample - how did he know we were Irish? People were courteous and friendly. Even if we did take bowing like nodding dogs to the extreme.

At the end of the market we stopped for another cup of tea and sat outside watching the locals watching us…

'Now we are getting real funny looks,' Big Paul said.

'It's you, big man, you're the first of that species they've ever seen,' joked Alan.

'Yeah, Paul, they ain't ever seen a baldie, matey,' added Jamie.

One old Japanese man walked up and out of the blue asked: 'Are you having a nice day?'

'What's the problem with matey there? Bleeding tourist,' quipped Paul. 'Yeah, what d'you want? Now sod off, yeah? Tomoko, how do you say clear off in Japanese?'

'Polite way is Noitekudasai,' she answered.

'What was that for? Clear off? What's the rude way then, Kanu?' insisted Paul.

'Usero.'

'What is it again, Kanu, Who-zero?' I asked.

'Uh sero?' responded Jamie.

'Yes, usero, but it is too rude to use, we do not use it,' Kanu replied.

'Really, I'll have some of that … Here, matey, why don't you just Ooh Sera,' Big Paul added, feeling proud that he had at long last conquered the language.

The Japanese man walked away, shaking his head in frustration, and muttered, 'Gaijain san warugiwanakatta, tada tomodachini naritakatta,' obviously in Japanese and further exclaimed in English, 'Foreigners! I wasn't being rude. I was just trying to be friendly.'

'He took that bad, didn't he?' said Paul.

'Yea, old matey really went in to one there,' added Jamie.

'Tomoko, what did that geezer say just now?'

'He say that he was just trying to be friend.'

'You're joking, Tom?'

'No really, he is really upset because Paul told him to go off.'

'Away after him, wee man, and do your bit for public relations,' Alan pleaded with me.

I walked towards him and began, 'Here, sir, sir, come here a wee minute, we meant no harm, we thought you were laughing at us.'

'No, me be friendly - he rude,' he added as he pointed to Paul.

'No, not rude, sir, he thinks you laugh at his napper,' I stated.

'Napper? What is napper?' he replied with a confused look on his face.

'Head, Kojak, no hair, bald - like him - napper,' I replied as I pointed to Paul's head.

'Hai, hai, soudesuka, no, not laughing at napper, be friend,' he answered as a smile broadened across his face.

Big Paul responded, 'Yeah that's all right, mate, no worries. I thought you was having a laugh at us.'

The local bowed apologetically to Paul and then to all of us individually. Like nodding dogs we repeated his bow back tenfold. As we continued to bow he continued.

'Please, you must stop bowing,' Kanu whispered.

'I ain't stopping until he stops, Kanu,' exclaimed Paul.

'Please stop first otherwise he never stop bowing,' Kanu further pleaded. 'Japanese man never stop bowing until you stop. He respect you. It is Japanese custom.'

'Yeah that's handy to know, I can see a right few nodding dogs over the next few days,' added Paul, smiling.

Ueno station ran above where we were sitting. Just across the busy street, Beer Monster Paul (as the two girls christened him) spotted a Japanese pub in the shape of a train. Now we would have to visit purely for cultural reasons.

As we took our seats by the window, which overlooked the hive of activity in the street beneath, there were about thirty of what appeared to be businessmen, all immaculately dressed in designer suits and ties, complete with briefcases and mobile phones, having a meeting in a glass-fronted room to the rear of the restaurant. As a speech ended, they all stood militarily and gave a tumultuous round of applause... with a difference. Every few seconds they would pause and we would think they were finished - then they would go crazy again with thunderous claps. Stunned by the sudden explosion of noise, we instantaneously joined in with them - adding a piercing 'UNI-TED' chant as they finished clapping.

You should have seen the looks on these guys' faces. Apparently it had been some sort of a retirement farewell meal. Just before they dispersed they gave another tumultuous round of applause. You could see a few of them watching nervously towards the group of foreigners by the window almost anticipating some contribution. We didn't let them down.

Normally on most trips you miss the local culture. We were all pleased and happy having seen a side of Japan tourists would not normally see. We ate a traditional Japanese breakfast consisting of rice, miso soup (which was made from fermented soybean paste), pickled vegetables and dried seaweed.

We had also learned a little of the changing shape of Japanese culture from the days of Emperor Hirohito to the Western influence of today.

Thursday, our final day was upon us. The girls had promised to show us the tourist sights before we went home. Although you get to see these on Euro aways, normally you are only in a particular city for one or two nights. This was the first time we had stayed anywhere for a full week having watched a match.

This is another aspect of football: it broadens your horizons. To be perfectly honest, we would possibly not have visited some of the locations United have played in our lifetimes if it were not for our love of the team.

The impressive Imperial Palace, home of Emperor Akihito, was the start of our sightseeing trip. The girls gave us our own history lesson. Apparently the Japanese treated Emperor Hirohito during the war like a god. He was all-powerful and almost worshipped. After defeat in the Second World War, Hirohito told his people he was only human and the role of Emperor became more like a figurehead with very little power.

190

We were then taken to Asakusa Shrine where we watched monks perform a service in a temple. Huge amounts of incense were burnt - you inhaled the smoke, which is said to nourish your brain and cure your ailments.

'Don't that sound familiar?' Paul asked

At the mention of this, Alan was next spotted running around the market looking for Rizzla papers.

Just when we thought we were taking a breather from football we spotted a couple of camera-waving tourists sporting Liverpool coats. This 'tourist' was with his girlfriend who was taken aback when Tom and Kanu, obviously two clued-up Japanese locals, approached him and greeted him with that well-known greeting, 'You Scouse barsteward!' The three of us fell about laughing. Paul, obviously an ex-language student, had been teaching our new Japanese friends some choice football songs and phrases with United connotations.

Although we had experienced much culture on this adventure, we still hadn't sampled a proper Japanese restaurant. The girls were in their element as we gingerly sat in the waiting area. Thankfully it was rather busy and I was not the only one to express satisfaction that the 'sit-on-your-knees, shoes-off section' was full. Instead we were guided upstairs to a normal seated section. It was not my choice, I must admit, but all of us - apart from big Paul - 'ate for Ireland', battered prawns and all.

We had already packed so much into one day but Tom and Kanu had another surprise in store. This would take the form of an amazing boat trip on the river past extraordinary landmarks, ships, a series of named bridges and arriving beside the awesome sight of the world-famous Rainbow Bridge and relatively new area of Odaiba, an amusement park called Joypolis including Sega World in which Kanu, Paul and I spent ages on a roller-coaster, tower drop, and the most amazing roller-coaster sci-fi simulation.

On the way to the park a guy was doing some paintings. I asked Kanu to see if he could write 'Manchester United' in Japanese. When the rest of the gang went on inside I ordered five of them as my wee gift to everyone. I was told that in Japanese Manchester United actually meant 'Full of dreams in Heaven and Earth'.

On Friday morning we took a bus to Narita Airport, passing Disney World on our right and leaving Tokyo with the unbelievable site of Mount Fuji ascending high into the clouds.

The Cockneys departed their separate ways on arrival in London. No big issue - shake of a hand and a hug, a genuine friendly hug hard to explain, like the parting of a loved one you're not going to see for a while. Alan and I made for the domestic departures lounge for the afternoon flight to Belfast.

'That was the best trip of my life, Jacko.'

'Wee man, I think you could stay there for a month or two alright.'

'I think it was the people, Alan, so genuine, weren't they?

'You'll end up marrying one of them wee Japanese girls, wee man.'

'Oh I doubt that somehow, sir, mind you, I could do worse. I'll tell you one thing for sure, I'll definitely be back again.'

Real friends are people you may not see for weeks on end and then pick up the phone as if it were yesterday. Nice people in this world are hard to find. Jamie and Paul, Kanu and Tomoko certainly fall into that bracket.

It was a great treat to be shown around Japan and the sights by the girls and, whether or not it is judged properly as such, we were there the night we became the first British Club to win the Intercontinental Cup.

My overriding memory from Japan will be Cockney Phil Walpole, who was standing beside me at the game and whom I have seen many times in the Dog but never spoken to, with tears streaming down his face at the final whistle.

'This is it, this is the one I have waited for.' This was the tournament of them all - world champions!

Before we had left the hotel, we asked a Japanese girl to ring all relevant bodies and yellow taxi offices giving details of our Hotel Ibis in Japan and contact details in Ireland. We also gave her the address of Jamie's friends, Kanu and Tomoko, who lived in Tokyo.

I was not very hopeful of ever seeing the 'big girl' again and was resigned to the fact she had come to an untimely and somewhat unceremonious end by being left in a taxi in the middle of Tokyo.

We addressed all avenues and I rang the Japanese Embassy in London on arrival home. I explained all the details, giving them Japanese contacts and my own details.

Amazingly, two hours later I received an email from Stephen Ryan stating that his hallway was now blocked with a huge flag in a Ralph Lauren bag. This was great news, but the only problem was how to get her home? Once again all fell into place nicely when Stephen said he was coming over for the Boxing Day game against Bradford and would gladly bring the bag with him. This he did and kindly left her at the Amblehurst Hotel in Sale for collection. Ta very much.

I seem to have said this a lot in my life and especially this last couple of years but this was a colossus of a trip. Little did I know at this stage that watching my team on the other side of the world would change my life for ever.

Having been so enthralled with Japan, its people and its culture, I posted a message on website requesting information about a shrine we had visited. Yukari kindly informed me that it was Asakusa shrine. We kept in touch via email and she decided she would come to visit whilst on a trip to Europe in August, 2000.

# MADRID GO NUTS IN BRAZIL

## World Club Championship: Rio de Janeiro (January 2000)

Having survived yet another near miss there was never any question of not taking Lily to the FIFA World Club Championship in Rio de Janeiro. This would be the chance for us to visit the spiritual home of soccer and the hallowed Maracana.

Of all the trips and all the matches throughout my life, the anticipation for this particular trip was something new to me. I must admit it has been a long time since I went as far on my own. The rest of the regular attendees were burnt out after so many consecutive Euro aways and Tokyo. Jamie and Paul and Alan were spent out. To be honest, I shouldn't have been going either. I just gave the credit cards what the farmer gave the peas - a damn good rodding! Life is short eh?

Normally I get the butterflies on the eve of the flight. All the media and club hype about how unsafe Rio was, as well as the fact that I had been knocked back for tickets yet again, made me all the more determined to go.

Ken Merrett gave an interview on television saying how dangerous and unsafe Rio could be. My personal gripe is that Northern Ireland gets so much unfair negative publicity. I detest when foreigners look at you as if you have two heads when you say you are from Northern Ireland. I was going to Rio to judge for myself. Besides, this was the home of football, the home of the Maracana and the birthplace of Pele, Socrates, Rivelino, Zico and Ronaldo. I'd heard about the beaches of Copacabana, Ipanema and Barra. The Statue of Christ - Corcovado - Sugar Loaf Mountain.

When I knew I was staying in the same hotel (The Intercontinental) as the players and especially my old friend Mr Crerand who was doing some work for MUTV, this put an extra spice into the equation. I have never been so nervous, anxious, excited, for almost three weeks. On the Monday prior I was still awake at three forty-five a.m.

I was having all these weird and strange dreams such as the Wizard himself, Sir Alex, being in the next-door room and he, Paddy and I sitting talking football half the night over a wee libation or two.

Then Fergie had to clamber back over the balcony, as not only were there armed guards on each floor but he had also set a curfew which everyone connected with United should adhere to, i.e. the playing staff and me. Inevitably this wasn't going to happen, was it? I guess all the pre-trip hype had my wee mind working overtime.

As I walked into the lounge at Gatwick, I immediately noticed a few faces from previous trips: Scotty and the boys whom I had met in Brondby and Howard (who gave the awesome rendition of 'Flowers of Manchester' in Tokyo) and Big Stuart. I'd seen him in Tokyo and on many trips but never actually spoken to him. I have been on a fair few Euro aways and each time you always come back with new acquaintances.

Having oiled our larynxes with a dose of good medicine in Weatherspoons, we headed through to the departure lounge and another boozer, which was awash with about fifty Reds.

Although you come into contact with many Reds from many European adventures you don't always have conversation with them. Normally the wee look, nod and 'all right, mate' suffices.

I was extremely fortunate in that I was upgraded to business class on the outward flight where I had one of those monster seats that move in about ten different directions. About an hour into the flight and a few champagnes later (well, it was free) I eventually got the seat to move backwards. Trying to look as if I knew what I was doing, I was more than a trifle embarrassed when I could neither get my personal television monitor out nor my seat back into normal position for dinner.

Picture the scene, my dinner on the tray in front of me, seat still reclined and me sitting like a perched budgie trying to look like I intended it that way.

As soon as I checked into the hotel in Sao Conadro, I got the shorts on and headed up the side of the beach, stopping frequently at the little shack type kiosks for a bottle or two of agua. I walked about a mile and then turned, walking back on the other side of the road. When I came to the last kiosk, I noticed a few faces having a few wee Skols in the afternoon sun. The next two or three hours were spent exchanging stories and tales from previous trips, favourite match discussions and debating the decline of the cockney Red specials, encounters with rival fans, the exploits of Millwest Travel who had shafted so many Reds in Barcelona and discussing the other teams in the tournament.

United were drawn in Group B with Necaxa, Vasco and South Melbourne. Group A consisted of Real Madrid, Corinthians and Al Nassr.

The teams were to play each other with the winners of each group meeting in the final on January 14.

I walked back to the hotel, had another shower and ordered a taxi to take me to the Maracana for about five o'clock for the game with Mexicans Rayos del Necaxa as I was advised to do. The traffic was chaotic, mainly with Vasco da Gama fans making their way to the game following ours. The anticipation of actually seeing the Maracana in the flesh was exhilarating in itself. I had never dreamed I would visit Brazil, let alone watch United play in the hallowed Maracana. As a kid I had read of the Maracana, its atmosphere and its history, venue for the 1950 World Cup Final and the location for Pele's 1000th goal in 1969.

The name 'Maracana' originates from a Brazilian bird, belonging to the 'arara' and parrot family, I was told by an English-speaking policeman as I stood gazing in a tranquil stupor.

A temple of soccer, a shrine, the epitome of world football and coliseum-like entrance, newly painted blue. Two huge walkways led to both tiers of the arena. Its sheer size and beauty was astounding, a spherical-shaped concrete mass hovering like an alien space ship.

'Sweating like a badger', as Brian from Bray would say, I arrived at half time and made my way to the United section in the upper tier only to be told the Shirts were one down and Beckham had been sent off.

Great start!

The incredibly passionate Vasco fans, almost all of them wearing the white replica shirts, were arriving in their droves and filling the top tier of the magnificent arena, beating drums, singing, dancing and waving huge flags - obviously happy with the first half proceedings and in anticipation of seeing their own team after our game.

Bosnich made a couple of great saves and Sheringham almost equalized with a shot that just cleared the bar. The Reds on the pitch were playing well despite the heat and humidity (37 degrees at kick-off). The Reds off the pitch in the white-seated upper tier were sweltered, sunburnt and consuming bottles of water and lemonade by the gallon.

'Keep drinking liquids, wee man, it stops you getting dehydrated.'

'I thought I was going to faint there a minute ago.'

'Away up to the shade at the back of the stand mate,' I was advised.

A few minutes later we were given a lifeline - one of their defenders handled in the area and the ref gave a penalty, only for Yorke's effort to be saved.

Sheringham and Solskjaer combined and the ball broke for Yorke who made up for his earlier miss: 1-1 and jubilation for us five hundred or so hot and bothered Reds high up in the stands.

The second half should have been comfortable, even though we were down to ten men. Solskjaer had a chance to snatch victory just before the end but again his good effort was well saved. The draw was probably a fair result.

I had shared a taxi with Howard and big Stuart back to the hotel via Copacabana where they were staying. Arriving at my hotel, I went straight to the lobby bar. The first person I saw was David Beckham walking towards the restaurant on the ground floor. He looked thoughtful but not downcast.

As I was sitting at the bar having another few aquas, a wee American girl started talking to me. I thought Doreen was waiting for someone but when she pulled a chair up beside me I thought, aye she could shorten my holiday. About an hour later, in walked Paddy, shook my hand and told me to order him a glass of red wine and he would be back in half an hour.

Martin Edwards walked in and spoke to big Kerry Wycherley and Paula from Wales and Brian Anderson and Anne Doherty from Belfast whom I would later befriend. Paddy came back along with a few of the MUTV crew who I must say were great lads with a thankless task in their line of work. Frontman Steve Bowers is a very amiable character and has gained the trust and respect of many players and Sir Alex. I had no tickets for any of the games and MUTV obliged. I told them how they were perceived by the majority of fanzine types. I also advised them to keep having the likes of Paddy C on the phone-ins and their credibility would rise. Admittedly MUTV had somewhat amateurish beginnings but the signs are there that it could be more than just a day-tripper channel. Recent exclusive interviews with Becks, Sir Alex and Keano are another step in the right direction.

Rob Darlington and a cameraman 'Ferdie', a tall unassuming Irishman, were also there. Rob had told me they were making a film about 'a year in the life of Manchester United' (which I later learned was to be Manchester United The Movie). He was particularly stressed after one day's filming when some of the players did not take too kindly to constant shots being taken of them. What stressed Rob out was the fact that they had been given the go ahead and the players had originally consented to the project.

Rai Van der Gouw, Quinton Fortune and big Jaap were also sitting at the table beside us watching the other game.

The night was mellow. The majority of the United non-playing staff including an extremely likeable and amusing character, Jesper Jesperson the chef, and another gentleman David Peters (the official Club photographer) joined us for a few wee Diet Cokes.

Paddy said he had asked Beckham if he had seen the player during the incident which led to his being sent off. Paddy insisted that even David's body language (he did immediately apologise and try to pick him up) suggested he had meant to flick the ball. Becks agreed with Paddy's interpretation. A little later a few of the United players watching the highlights of the game cringed when watching the incident again.

At the start of my stay in the Intercontinental Hotel I was in awe of the players, although I tried not to show it, but as the days passed I became much more comfortable and as my face became recognised by players and staff I felt as if I were a part of it all (Paddy had introduced me to most as the wee man from Carrickfergus with the huge flag)... You would meet the players in the lift, lobby, at the pool or on two occasions walking along the seafront beside the beach. A polite nod or 'How's it going, lads?' like the meeting with other Reds was enough for both parties. Getting into a hotel lift for the first time with Jaap Stam, Becks, Giggsy, Teddy Sheringham and Nicky Butt is a rather overwhelming feeling for a wee man from Northern Ireland who sells car parts for a living.

Although we were located about forty-five minutes from Maracana, there was no doubting this was football country: kids and adults playing continuously on the beach from seven-thirty a.m. to well after midnight. Even the barmen and the waiters had names like Ronaldo and Eder. A real sense of football was everywhere. Much has been written about the great spiritual home and you most certainly did get that feeling: a reverence, a respect.

The atmosphere was relaxing until three lads from Dungannon checked into the hotel: Mick, Paul and Ken were three sound blokes who knew how to party but didn't know when to sleep - and I knew we were in for a few lively nights.

My original feeling about the tournament was one of twelve days in the sun, watching United stroll to the final of the world's first World Club Championship. I honestly thought it was geared for a United /Real Madrid final.

Having drawn with the Mexicans (also staying in the Intercontinental) you now sensed a reality that United were here primarily for football and the game with Vasco would be crucial. The Necaxa game had whetted our appetite and, having witnessed the Vasco fans and the atmosphere they created, the pre-match nerves were already starting to build.

The morning of the Vasco game, I went for a walk along the beach up to my usual stop at one of the many wooden huts on the roadside and overlooking the beach. As I was walking, I spotted big Ned Kelly and the United squad all walking towards me. By now they recognised me.

'All right, Ned?'

'How's it going, Denis?'

'Hello, Roy, good luck tonight, sir.'

'Aye cheers,' replied Keano.

I nodded and wished them all the best for the Vasco game. I could see that they were all relaxed but focused as they enjoyed the relative anonymity of their beach walk.

The atmosphere against Necaxa was only enlightened by the arriving Vasco hordes. This was going to be something else.

I arrived about an hour before kick-off (having learnt my lesson) and already the atmosphere was starting to build. Firecrackers exploding everywhere. As kick-off approached, the energetic Vacsco fans bounced up and down with alternate rows dancing sideways, creating waves of ecstasy on a sea of passion. This was atmosphere. Flag bearers carried twelve large banners up from the concourse and along the front of the stand. With military precision they marched to their seats that were equally dispersed among the boisterous supporters to rapturous applause and emphatic vocal appreciation.

United started well with Solskjaer on the right, Giggs on the left, and Yorke in the middle.

Romario, once of Barcelona, and Edmundo - or 'Animal' as he is known - combined after a terrible backpass by Gary Neville to Bosnich, which resulted in Romario putting the Brazilians one up.

Minutes later, Romario was again the recipient of another Gary Neville error when the defender chested a ball into his path. This time Romario skipped past Bosnich and notched the ball into the empty net.

Just before half time, worse was to come. Edmundo with his back to Bosnich's goal received the ball at his feet, flicked it over his head, spun around past Silvestre and scored.

United were by far the better team in the second half but squandered opportunities to get back in the game.

Nicky Butt scored a consolation goal following a Cruyff free kick but by this stage the match was over as a contest.

A 3-1 defeat was a bitter disappointment, and effectively ended our tournament.

That night, Real Madrid arrived in the hotel (they had been previously staying in Sao Paulo for the group A games) and this was one of those things you normally dream about. The usual late-night 'relaxers' were being swallowed by the Dungannon lads, Brian, Kerry, Paddy and me. Steve McManaman walked into the bar and immediately began talking to Mick and Paul. McManaman swapped his Real Madrid T-shirt, as did Karembeu with big

Paul Falloon in exchange for a Guinness and a Dungannon Branch one respectively.

The Madrid boys were certainly living it up and in full party mode. As the bar emptied, only our table and one to our left remained occupied. Present were Chendo (Madrid legend, now involved with the players), Roberto Carlos, Raul Gonzales, Fernando Hierro, Fernando Morientes, Steve McManaman, the team physio Pedro Chueca Remon, and the Madrid lads began singing some songs in Spanish:

'*En Espana Real*
*En Europa Real*
*En El Mundo Real*'

As they finished their effort, we (Mick, Paul, Paddy C, Brian, big Kerry and MUTV Rob) broke into 'Oh Manchester is Wonderful'.

The Madrid lads were ecstatic and clapped and encouraged us as once again they broke into another tune.

'C'mon, Paddy, give us a tune,' gestured Steve McManaman as Raul and Roberto Carlos waved their hands implying we should continue.

This was too good to be true. We then gave them all a friendly choral acknowledgement in the form of 'Raul, there's only one Raul': 'There's only one Roberto Carlos' etc.

I then stood up beside the standing Raul and taught the Madrid boys the words to 'Yip Jaap Stam' one line at a time. We all (McManaman included) gave a vociferous rendition of the big Dutchman's tune. I even had Raul doing actions to Roy Keane's little ditty, often heard on the terraces (wearing the magic hat).

204

By this stage, I was in full flight and as I continued, 'Keanoooo - There's only one Keano, There's only one Keano', Raul, standing opposite me, raised his two hands and swayed back and forth singing with passion along with me.

'Keith, I don't believe you,' said Paddy, 'that was amazing, Raul singing about Roy - wait to I tell him tomorrow. Imagine that was the United players, the press would slaughter them.'

'Macca, what about Everton?' someone asked.

'Right, lads, let's give it Everton.'

We were on cloud nine already with what had already happened, but what I was about to witness was a shock. McManaman stood up on a chair and began singing, 'Everton, Everton, Everton' with venom. As he continued, we and the rest of the Madrid lads joined in.

Not long after, Chueca walked over to me and whispered in my ear, 'Watch for a surprise.'

'What do you mean?' I asked.

He made a gesture, putting his finger over his lips as if to imply 'keep it a secret'.

Sure enough about two minutes later this tall, completely bandaged character with horns and exaggerated manhood came skipping through the lobby and around the tables of the bar area.

Everyone was bent double and on the floor laughing.

It transpired that this was Morientes, the talented striker who had been bandaged, mummy-like, from head to toe, by Chueca for a laugh.

Eventually the Madrid players filtered away (well it must have been three a.m. and they had a game that night) with only McManaman left who cordially joined our company.

'How's it going, Steve son?' Paddy asked

For the next half hour or so Kerry, Brian, Paddy and I asked Steve many questions.

'Alex is a great admirer of yours, Steve,' stated Paddy.

'Could you ever see yourself playing for United?' I asked.

'What I always said was I could never sign for United from Liverpool although to be honest I couldn't sign for Manchester United.'

'Why not?' I enquired.

'Don't get me wrong, I'm jealous of them, all the trophies and that, I want that but I couldn't sign for them.'

'Why did you leave Liverpool?' someone asked.

'I just had to get out; there was a bad feeling about the place.'

'Was it Houllier?' I asked.

'I just had to get away,' he added without elaborating.

'How do you get on with the United players?'

'Yeah, all right, I just seen them earlier. Yeah all right, I see them at the England games and that. '

The question and answer session continued with Paddy and McManaman exchanging thoughts and views before he disappeared to bed.

We all may have booed him on numerous occasions and sung many a choice song about him (and for the record always will) but I have to admit he went up in my estimation big time after that night.

This craic continued well into the wee hours of the morning. We ordered room service for more refreshments, the bill coming to something like $88 which a certain member of our company signed for in the name of a very famous Real Madrid player who had by now gone to bed - that'll teach him.

We felt a trifle guilty, but given that he is living in abject poverty on sixty-eight-thousand pounds per week the person in question will hardly miss it.

This was one of the best night's craic I have ever had.

When I met Raul the next morning, he told me, in his pidgin English and with hand signals, that they had a special signed Real Madrid shirt for me. Sure enough, about half an hour later, Chendo, Hierro, Raul and Roberto Carlos walked into the lobby bar where I was sitting guzzling water by the gallon, and presented me with an autographed shirt with 'MANU' and the number 10 on the back, saying that he was not playing today. I, thinking he was a reserve team player, thanked him very much and it was not until later that night, when I showed the shirt to big Welsh Kerry, that we realised that he had had this specially made for me.

A nice gesture!

In our final game against South Melbourne, I chose to give Lily her debut in the most famous stadium in the world. I had originally brought her with me to the Vasco da Gama game but my clued-up and English-speaking cab driver advised me not to take her if I wanted to see her again. (Flamenco, Vasco's sworn enemy, wear the same colours as United).

Arriving at the ground early, I was third into the white-seated United section to make sure of no problems with police or security. It is much easier getting Lily in early rather than in the last-minute rush when the police can be particularly uncooperative.

As I set her out carefully in the white seats, I met Jamesy and Darwin whom I knew from Ballymena, tying up their own Ballymena Reds flag on the front railings of the upper tier. Even the stewards were going crazy to have their pictures taken beside my prodigy.

These are proud moments. You don't stand about to be known as the owner of the flag but it is a nice feeling and a great sense of inner pride to see so many people taking pictures of her. As usual, Lily lapped up the attention being lavished upon her. I had hoped she would at least make the television pictures back home as a means of a hello to Alan, Gary and the boys who were unable to make the trip.

I reckoned that if I set her on the seats, she would get to stay there until at least half time. Sure enough she sat among the travelling Red Army very peacefully and even later on in the second half the Vasco fans were spilling in for their game with Necaxa treated her with great respect.

Two goals from Quinton Fortune inside twenty minutes gave us something to cheer.

As I was folding Lily into her bag, I was helped by an English-speaking Vasco fan who said it was a pleasure to help me pack this 'important banner' away.

'Good work, sir,' I added appreciatively and gave him a Carrickfergus Reds scarf that I had in the bottom of my bag. This had been a major success and I headed back to the hotel and took Lily to our room.

The result meant that United would not have to play in the third and fourth place Final. I had heard it mentioned on the previous evening that United had already made flight arrangements, so no one was going to be too perturbed.

Throughout the ten-night stay I had many encounters with the players and got the opportunity to speak with most of them. Although at first they thought I was a journalist, they were very obliging and indeed polite. Stars for me in this department are Phil Neville, Denis and Keano.

I also had the pleasure of talking to the wizard himself, Sir Alex, on a few occasions. When I introduced myself as the wee man who had written this book, he smiled profusely and kindly gave me a very favourable comment to use on the back cover.

'Well done, well done,' he said. 'I enjoyed it.'

I had just read his own book and knew how he congratulated people in it with a simple 'Well done, well done'. It was sufficient and I took great comfort from this acknowledgement.

The next few nights were similar, only not as loud. On the United team's last evening (following the South Melbourne game) the majority of them were in the lobby bar partaking of a few quiet cokes.

I asked Phil Neville if the lads would mind signing a ball and shirt I had.

'No problem, bring it over.'

Kneeling, one arm on Denis Irwin's chair and one on Phil Neville's, and feeling very groupie-ish, I watched as every individual around the table autographed first the shirt and then the ball. Denis Irwin, Giggsy, Jaap, Gary Neville, David Beckham, Andy Cole and Phil Neville, all within six feet of me. You have so much you want to say, so many questions to ask, so much to tell, you can't and you don't. You think you know them, you don't. Even though you may know everything about them - their favourite food, their favourite television programmes - really they are strangers locked tightly among their own protective web.

As the team were leaving the Intercontinental Hotel the following afternoon, Mick Murray and I decided we would bring Lily out to the front of the hotel to see them off.

As we did so, about thirty local kids appeared on the scene and took immense pleasure from the sight of a monster flag opposite the main entrance of the hotel and beside the team coach.

'Do you boys want to hold her?' I asked them, indicating how they should.

They swarmed around Mick, Lily and me like flies.

Barefooted, wearing only shorts, these kids reminded me of the excitement when we used to help carry the cases of oil for my dad all those years ago.

I lined them up, schoolmaster-like. They held the flag open wide and as the team were leaving I exchanged two $10 bills, and gave the kids a dollar each. I'm sure they did not want to appear ungrateful; however one of the little skunks inadvertently left Lily homeless - he stole her bag.

This was Lily's farewell to The Shirts who clapped appreciatively and waved as they departed by coach. With no bag to carry Lily in, we left her in the lobby, relaxing at the bar.

Later that night, Mick and I were trying the piano cover for compatibility as a Lily carrier (purely for research purposes, you understand) when one of the wee waiters took exception - he thought we were seriously going to use this to carry Lily home.

United may not have come tops on the public relations stakes (although we'd certainly done our share with the locals) and we may not have set the tournament on fire but this was Brazil and we defintely went nuts.

# THE FINAL DREAM

The final dream was to have Lily make an appearance at Old Trafford. If this happened, then she would definitely be retired and I could concentrate purely on football again (well, that sounds good). She had more than surpassed our wildest dreams in what she achieved for community harmony and she was quickly gaining celebrity status.

In the week of the first game of the new millennium against the Scousers (March 4) I sent faxes to both Ken Merrett and Martin Edwards, requesting permission to unfurl Lily in the new East Stand Upper where we were to be seated.

Not long afterwards I received a telephone call from Old Trafford. Safety Officer Arthur Roberts stated that the flag should be fireproofed and have a fire safety certificate. He added that people were afraid of big flags and not only had they received many complaints about them but people had actually tried to set fire to them.

Sounded like a few likely tales … and a palming off.

I then rang Mr Merrett's secretary and Ken Merrett came on the line and promised to be more co-operative in future. He stated that the Liverpool game was high profile and it was unreasonable of me to ask only two days beforehand.

Considering what I had been told, I waited a few weeks and then sent a letter by recorded delivery, requesting Lily be allowed on to the pitch before the game or at half time on the day of the Chelsea game on Easter Monday. Surely this would answer all the safety issues unless the ball boys and Big Ned Kelly (former SPS security supremo) were more scared of 'The Big Girl' than they were of spiders?

I honestly believe that Lily enhances the atmosphere whenever and wherever she has appeared. Having dedicated much money and much of my life to my passion for Manchester United, of all the positive publicity generated at that time I did take, at this stage, the Club's stance most personally. To be fair, I received a letter a few days later stating that the club would try and accommodate Lily during the game against Chelsea on Easter Monday.

To me, Lily was a big part of the Treble. I loved taking her to these grounds but was gutted that she could not be displayed at Old Trafford. The fact that we would be celebrating our sixth premiership trophy in eight years was a chance for Lily to lead or, at very least, be involved in the celebration.

The draw for the quarter finals of the Champions League was made on Friday. Our prayers were answered when we were paired with the mighty Real Madrid. Lily was a cert to make this trip; to visit this ground was another dream. But worrying about getting into Old Trafford was put on ice for a few days. The following day Lily was to make yet another appearance in the April edition of the Official Manchester United magazine. With a 90,000 circulation, this had to be the pinnacle of her literary career.

# Back to Spain
## Champions League Quarter-final:
## Madrid (4 April 2000)

The mouth-watering quarter final Champions League draw against the mighty Real Madrid in 2000 was going to be another opportunity to take Lily to one of the most famous stadiums in the world: Estadio Santiago Bernabeu.

On the way home from the Supporters Club meeting, I called my friend and neighbour Jim Shields to ask him if he could help me pack Lily, as I was going to Madrid at six-thirty the following morning. As I arrived home about ten minutes later, there they were, Jim and Jo in my driveway, attempting to fold the big girl. The wind was strong and this was going to be a major task. Plant pots, bricks and bodies were required to control her and to prevent her from doing a parachute impression during the packing operation. Jo, dressed in her pink nightgown and wearing hair curlers, stood on one corner. A heavy Lobelia plant pot kept the other corner secure and I stood directly opposite Jim as he coordinated the folding with military precision.

I'm not sure what the neighbors thought was happening. Then again, I am renowned for skiing down my street when we get the slightest hint of a snowfall so the sight of a hundred-foot monster flag hardly came as a great surprise. Unless she is folded properly and all the air removed, it is almost impossible to pack her into a bag small enough to carry into a stadium.

With stringent safety regulations, stewards and police are wary of an oversized bag. Even though she weighs a healthy thirty-four kilograms and was well packed, she still looked like four stone of potatoes in a two-stone bag.

213

Although I should not have been going and should have concentrated on paying off my credit card bills, as the draw was being made I was already thinking of the arrangements for the game. After the exploits in Brazil, I had to go, especially as Raul and the lads promised that if we should draw Real Madrid, I would be a guest of theirs.

I had the phone numbers of the Spanish lads but could not speak the language. I tried faxing Chueca Remon at the Real Madrid Medical Centre but to no avail. I telephoned the British Embassy and explained my predicament. About an hour later I got a phone call from the Madrid Medical Centre. Chueca had received the message from Mary in the British Embassy.

'Hello, Mr Morris... Chueca Remon speaking.'

He instructed me to go to the training ground at twelve on the day following the game. When I asked about where to go he said not to worry, just walk into the Medical Centre and ask for him. He further stated that we might be going out for dinner with Raul and the boys after training.

'How do we get in through the gates?' I asked.

'No problems. I tell them you Manchester,' he reassured me.

It's hard to comprehend but very refreshing how legends such as these Real Madrid players would take time for a nobody like me. The brief relationship in Brazil was special to me and when Raul and Roberto Carlos presented me with the signed shirt I was genuinely overwhelmed.

On Monday morning Gary, Kevin Woodside and Kevin Hannin (two of my good friends from Whitehead) arrived at the airport in good spirits. Once again we were to travel with big Peter McMinn's company, Travel Solutions, who had arranged for us to stay in the four-star Hotel Mayorazgo in Flor Baja. I told the lads that I might have a wee surprise planned for them and relayed the tale about the Embassy and what Chueca had said. I don't think they believed one word.

On arrival in Madrid, we were transferred straight to the stadium where we were dropped off in the nearby coach park. It was about two hours to kick-off, but rather than attempt to find the much talked about Irish Rover pub I made my way directly to the turnstile.

Filled with trepidation, we approached the entrance. This is the worst possible moment of any trip. Thankfully the Spanish authorities showed no real alarm although they did make me unfurl Lily to ensure I was not concealing alcohol or weapons (as if!) which are strictly prohibited.

As soon as you get the green light, a weight lifts from your shoulders and you start to relax and savour the atmosphere these remarkable stadiums possess.

There is almost a reverence in these hallowed and celebrated places. Steeped in history and a major landmark in the footballing world, it is refreshing to see even the most seasoned campaigner's eyes light up as they get their first sight of an impressive arena.

Brian from Bray and I headed straight for the back of the steep, almost sheer stand where we unfurled Lily and tied her to the railings. In doing so, she floated majestically in the gentle breeze over the heads of the gathering Reds. I walked down to the lower tier and got a picture of her in full flight. This was mission accomplished - another feather in her cap.

Someone walked up to me and asked, 'Is that your flag, mate?'

When I indicated it was, he shook my hand and simply said, 'Well done. Top flag.'

This is what makes the effort of transporting and childminding her worthwhile.

The breathtaking Bernabeu stadium, the height at which we were above the pitch, a disappointing scoreless draw, a two-hour rendition of:

'Allo Allo, we are the Busby Boys

Allo Allo we are the Busby Boys

And if you are a City fan, surrender or you'll die

We all follow United.'

were my memories of the game.

How expectations have changed? A nil-nil away against one of Europe's finest teams and I was complaining. There was however a mood of 'We'll do 'em at Old Trafford'. I was nervous, I have to admit.

Although we did make a bit of a mess of trying to unfurl Lily just before half time, I was happy and she lay contented at my feet for the duration of the game. The two Kevins took great pride in packing her and carried her back to the coach park.

## Raul and Hierro meet Lily

The following morning we had to fulfil our appointment with the Real Madrid physio Chueca Remon whom I had become particularly friendly with in Brazil. We made our way via taxi to their training headquarters.

We drove by a pitch where we could see the players, including Anelka, training and being watched by a few hundred spectators including at least fifty photographers complete with those huge lenses. The fact this was his first day back training following his apology to Real Madrid officials had created much media interest.

At least twenty television crews were in attendance. Wee Gary, ever the publicist, suggested that this was the perfect opportunity to get Lily some major European exposure. Sure enough, as we unfurled her on the steps of the training ground, the paparazzi swarmed around the big girl in what I can only describe as a frenzy. For about ten minutes Anelka's comeback was forgotten. Lily stole the media attention yet again and we posed and gave interviews for all sorts of media, from *Sky Sports* television to Spain's *As* newspaper. It wasn't long before security approached and asked that the Big Girl be put away. Telling them we were friends of Raul and Hierro certainly brought a smile but they kept pointing to a stand behind one of the goals and saying something like 'Presidentey.' We were later told by Chueca that the Club President who had been watching proceedings was furious that a Manchester United flag should have the audacity to appear at his ground. If only he realised it was a harmless and friendly gesture by Lily. The big girl hasn't got a bad 'bone' in her body.

At two o'clock we ventured back down to the entrance of the medical centre where the players were beginning to disperse. As I walked through the gate, I spotted Fernando Hierro's large frame and he came over and hugged me like a long-lost brother. This was a special moment. Here was a legend of three World Cup campaigns, European Championships for Spain and Real Madrid, greeting a wee man as if I was the celebrity. Having introduced Gary and the rest of the lads, he told us to meet him in ten minutes in the Real Madrid coffee shop.

As I was walking away, I heard a voice shouting. Looking around, I saw Raul holding a mobile phone to his ear and waving me towards him with his other hand. Again he greeted me in the same fashion as Fernando had and said, 'Coffee shop, ten minutes.'

As we walked towards the main building, Gary said, 'Wee man, fair play to you, you can do it.'

The Real Madrid coffee shop was a restaurant neatly laid out with both reserved and unreserved tables, windows covered and several television monitors which I was told were to view the team training. We walked in and ordered refreshments and awaited the arrival of our friendly hosts.

Raul walked in first and immediately joined us at the bar.

'Ah Manchester,' he exclaimed as he hugged me.

As we were still embracing, I spotted the tall figure of Fernando Hierro approaching, immaculately dressed in a green designer suit and gleaming black shoes.

Having introduced all the lads again, I presented them with an Irish good luck charm (Leprechaun in a bottle) and a tin whistle, which Raul preceded to blow into as he and Fernando Hierro shared a joke.

Raul blew into the whistle again and Hierro sang 'Redondo, Redondo, Redondo'. I'm a great believer in reading someone's personality from their face and expressions. These guys were incredibly genuine and fun people to be around.

'Raul, what do you think the score will be in Manchester?' Gary asked.

Raul, dressed in casual but smart dark jeans and grey jumper with a thin gold bracelet and designer brown casual shoes, held up one finger in each hand and gestured to us 'One-one, Old Trafford.'

'I hope you score, Raul, but we will win,' I said, and held up my fingers indicating 3-1 to United.

'Three-one to United sir, Raul, sorry wee man.'

He smiled and again repeated his 1-1 gesture with his fingers.

Later, Chueca told me how Raul would visit children's hospitals on a regular basis beyond the glare of the media.

Even in team celebrations he would join in with the fans singing and partying.

'When Madrid win thee cup, Raul be singing and dancing with Madrid sapporter outside, how you say, in the street, outside Bernabeu. He take shirt off and wave it around above head with sapporter.'

I couldn't resist the opportunity to ask for a picture of him holding Lily. Chueca relayed the tale from earlier and Lily had been taking a back seat in the afternoon's proceedings following her exertions. Resting, yet ever attentive, Lily eagerly eased enough of herself out of her bag to greet the Spanish superstar.

'Raul, please say hello to Lily.'

'Lily?' he questioned, a shy smile on his face as he shook my hand and gently held Lily with his other hand.

'Raul, Lily is her name. Keith, Raul, Kevin, Lily.' I pointed to us and said our names. He now understood and a broad smile beamed across his face.

'Lily,' he repeated.

This afternoon was complete when we were instructed to go to a restaurant, Asador Donostiarri, ask for someone by the name of Chou (or similar) and tell him that Raul had sent us.

'Can I speak to Chou, please, we are friends of Raul?' I asked and showed him the piece of paper Raul had given me.

Sure enough, we were ushered through a queue and given seats in a secluded VIP area. Among the clientele that afternoon was another Real Madrid star, Guti, and we were informed that the Vice Chairman of the Club was in an adjacent cubicle.

We could do no wrong here. Even loud renditions of 'Ooh Ahh Cantona' and 'There's only one Arsene Wenger' went down well with the waiters and locals.

The rest of the day was spent milling around Madrid city centre spotting a few pockets of Reds like ourselves at a loose end, and talking about the return leg at Old Trafford. I was nervous. As much as we appreciated what the Real players had done for us, these guys were a quality team and not to be underestimated. I detected they were more than thankful of a draw (I reckoned they were expecting a tanking) and confidently predicted a one each draw at Old Trafford.

At the airport on the way home the following morning, someone suggested that we should buy a newspaper to see if Lily had made the headlines. Sure enough, there she was (in Spain's leading sports paper, *As*) with a nice story attached. What made this even more rewarding was the fact that the previous day the very same paper had run a story suggesting United fans were hooligans. Hopefully the Big Girl restored some credibility to the good name of Manchester United and their supporters.

Another momentous trip and Lily gained many more friends and admirers.

One of BBC Northern Ireland's top sports journalists, Joel Taggart, had accompanied our group to Madrid in a supporter capacity. Joel had been on previous Euro Aways during the Treble season and was familiar with Lily - in fact he helped unfurl her on many occasions.

As we sat in the lounge at Gatwick airport on our return journey, he made a few telephone calls and then stated that he would like to film Lily at our next Club meeting to be held as usual in the Quality Hotel.

The story basically was of how Lily had captured the imagination of United fans and was considered one of the biggest and most loyal supporters. I was interviewed and proceeded to tell the story of how Real Madrid superstar Raul had not only invited Lily to the training ground but

220

took time to pose with her. Well-known television commentator Jackie Fullerton finished the link from the news feature with the comment 'Will Lily be in the pink tonight' referring to our return leg in the Champions League Quarter final on 20 April.

Lily was anxious to go to Old Trafford, not only to renew acquaintances with her Spanish friends but hopefully to watch United progress to the next round. Unfortunately she would have to sit this one out, as we had not yet received her entry clearance.

To concede three goals to a team of Madrid's calibre - who were, however, in my opinion, lucky on the night - was just too much. We battled to the end and the disappointment among the Reds was not hard to spot.

'Now look what you've done, Keith,' said Gary.

'What do you mean, sir?'

'That lucky charm you and Lily gave your mate Raul, you've knocked us out of Europe.'

'Wise up, wee man, that was only a wee gift.'

'You gave him the lucky charm, wait to the Red Army hears about this.'

Argentine Redondo was awesome in defence and attack and Casillas, the young eighteen-year-old keeper, was truly brilliant.

Utter disappointment.

All Lily's plans for a semi-final and hopefully the final were dashed after her superstar friend knocked our team out of the competition. Although absolutely gutted, she had to take some solace in the fact that her friend scored two goals on the night and if we were to be beaten, better to have been beaten by a good team who played better football on the night.

# Old Trafford at Last?

Dear Mr Norris

Thank you for your latest letter. We will try and make arrangements for the flag to be displayed at our game with Chelsea and I will write to you nearer the time.

Yours sincerely

K R MERRETT

Lily, again expertly packed by neighbors Jim and Jo Shields, was apprehensive as we had received no confirmation from Mr Merrett that we would be guaranteed entry. As I had had no further correspondence and time was now up, I faxed Ken Merrett on Good Friday, asking for details as to where and when we should take her and gave all my personal contact details including mobile telephone number.

We set off full of hope on Easter Sunday for the Chelsea game the following morning in the knowledge we were already Premier League Champions and optimistic that Lily would be on show at Old Trafford. Although I had heard nothing since his letter dated 24 March, I remained hopeful.

Gary received a call at ten-thirty while we were still in the Amblehurst Hotel from Membership Secretary Barry Moorhouse. He asked if Lily was fireproofed.

This was a fair question and, of course, safety standards have to be met. However, I had already spoken in person to Ken Merrett (who was aware that the flag was not fireproofed) and he had promised to contact me in writing before the game and accommodate us possibly either on the pitch, before the game or during the half-time interval.

I was absolutely gobsmacked and decided that Lily was going to Old Trafford even if she was not allowed into the stadium.

About eleven-thirty we unfurled her walking down the Warwick Road (Sir Matt Busby Way, as it is called nowadays). I was then advised by the police to leave it with a badge seller I know, which I did, until after the game.

On the way back to the Amblehurst Hotel, we decided to stop in the Dog and Partridge where we could order a taxi and miss the bulk of the departing crowd. During the ensuing singsong (as was the norm in the Dog) Gary came up with his own little ditty: 'We won the Football League again, and Bestie's off the sauce, and Bestie's off the sauce…' (to the tune of 'Down by the Riverside').

As the rest of the lads present joined in the song, I began to unfurl Lily, helped by many willing aides. Eventually we had her out to her full glory and the assembled Reds serenaded her:

> *'We'll never die, we'll never die,*
> *We'll keep the Red Flag flying high.'*

The day, which had begun in disappointment and anguish, ended up being a joyous celebration with many of the hardcore Reds and the Big Girl's first visit to the Dog and Partridge.

On the Wednesday following the Easter Holidays I once more contacted Mr Merrett by fax, requesting a straight answer to the question: if I got Lily fireproofed would she be allowed in against Tottenham on the last match of the season?

223

The Friday before the final League game with Tottenham my mobile telephone rang. Mr Merrett was obliging and helpful. He explained he had been on holiday at the time of the Chelsea game and came back to work to see my fax lying on his desk. He instructed me to leave the flag with Barry Moorhouse in the Membership Office and he would either tie the flag up on the west stand for the duration of the game or have it displayed on the pitch prior to kick-off time (11.30).

Due to another ludicrous early morning kick-off, the traffic coming from Sale to Old Trafford was particularly hectic. I jumped out of the cab on the Chester Road and made it to the membership office about ten minutes to eleven … still in plenty of time, in my opinion.

Barry Moorhouse had telephoned Gary, asking where I was. He informed Gary that it was now too late.

I was disappointed, although I cannot blame Barry or Mr Merrett, that she was not displayed at Old Trafford, but took heart from the fact that both appeared to be genuine in trying to accommodate her. At the end of the day if they had received the flag earlier she would have had her greatest day at the Theatre of Dreams.

At the end of the 1999-2000 season, I decided to give Lily yet another facelift. Primarily a Manchester United flag, I felt it was time to update her image and have the old club crest inserted, as originally intended.

Flags are much more an integral part of the soccer scene at European away games.

Many people nowadays dislike flags with 'out of town' names on them. This has long been a part of football culture and my guess is that it will remain so. Recently there has been much debate about such flags and an encouragement that they should only be related to Manchester United or Mancunian music culture, or be devoted to jibes directed at opposing teams. I cannot disagree. It is time to lose the out of town no mark flags and for Old Trafford to be turned into a colourful Mancunian spectacle.

I make no apologies for the fact that Lily may have had 'Carrickfergus Reds' emblazoned across it and have been the biggest ever 'out of town' flag. I do not know how she will be judged in the history books but I genuinely hope people understand the significant role she played promoting harmony and togetherness in our club and in our local community. Her original purpose was to enhance the atmosphere and although she never deviated from this, there was more to her agenda than most could realise and that having been achieved, it was now time to return to pure football matters.

I contacted Barmy Charly the flagmaker and asked him the size of crest he could get on Lily.

'Oh, I'd say about nine feet square, Keith.'

'I want the old Manchester United Football Club crest, Charly, not that new Megastore one,' I pointed out.

'Don't worry, Keith, that's the only one I make,' he said.

'Can you get her fireproofed for me, Charly?'

'Yeah, there's this firm in Leeds I know does it.'

'Right, go ahead, sir, could you have her ready for the start of the season?' I meant August 2000.

I wasn't sure if I was being continually fobbed off. I had got no reply to my most recent fax requesting permission to bring Lily to the Bradford game.

But I'm not the sort to give up easily nor do I take no for an answer. Persistence and hard work always pay off in the end - ask Fergie.

I re-faxed Ken Merrett and sent an additional fax to Peter Kenyon and Sir Alex, requesting their support. The next morning (the day of the game) my mobile phone rang.

225

'Mr Norris.'

'Yes?'

'Ken Merrett, Manchester United. Mr Norris, I do not appreciate being bombarded with faxes regarding this issue, this is my responsibility,' he fumed.

Mr Merrett then instructed me to bring Lily to meet Arthur Roberts,

'The safety guy?' I asked.

At two-thirty Barmy Charly, Lily and I met with Mr Roberts and another gentleman from Trafford Council.

'Right, Keith, you're not getting Lily out tonight,' were Mr Roberts's first words.

Why was I not surprised?

The pair then examined Lily, who was lying solemnly in a huge sports bag, and took her safety certificate away with them. Mr Roberts stated that they would have to place an ad in the match programme asking whether there were any objections to Lily being displayed in Tier 2 of the Stretford End. He further suggested that we bring Lily to Old Trafford again so they could check her physical size and how best any unfurling could be coordinated.

Distraught yet again, we walked down to Samuel Platts and laid Lily reverently outside the main door to view her new nine-foot crest … and to let her relax for a while from the stresses and strains, which she obviously felt.

Carrickfergus Reds was replaced with STRETFORD END and Lily was now officially everyone's flag (although she always was). A fitting tribute that she should bear the name of the spiritual home of United fans.

# The heart of the Euro (24 October 2000)

Brussels, the home of the 'Euro', was to be the setting for Lily's next Euro away with Anderlect our opposition on October 24 2000 in the penultimate game in the Champions League qualifying stages. This was another trip that was to have a life changing effect on me. Before I had left home, I had 'borrowed' one of Yukari's rings under the pretence that I wanted to wear it on my chain around my neck as a symbol of my love. I had been toying in my mind about asking Yukari to marry me, so you can appreciate my mind was nervously working over-time.

I had never met such a beautiful woman, so kind, considerate, witty and loveable.

I was excited by the cultural fusion and the whole new dimension to my life. She knew about my United addiction. She knew my feet smelt on occasions, that sort of thing.

The atmosphere in Brussels was a trifle moody and the police were keeping a visible presence. Jamie and I took Lily into the Grand Place (the main tourist sight) in the town centre with the intention of giving her an airing and showing her the sights, but each time we made an attempt the police would quickly move in and make hostile gestures, implying that she was not welcome and we should refrain from bringing her out. A little despondent, we took her back to the hotel and left her in the sanctity of the bedroom for the duration of our stay.

Having had two draws and two wins in the first phase of the Champions League, we knew if we won in Brussels we were through to second stage and expectation was high.

Besides, the name Anderlect hardly scared the pants of us: when any Red hears that name they think of the club's biggest ever victory margin -10-0 against them in 1956.

The Tulip Hotel was right bedside the Sheraton Hotel where we had heard the team where staying. We stood talking with a certain well-known Red and United We Stand columnist, Mr Tony O'Neill.

As the team coach and the directors and friends' coaches arrived, we waited on Paddy to see if he fancied sampling the sights of the town.

'Some of the directors' friends are taking us all to dinner, lads, I can't make it, I'll call round next door tomorrow.'

We'd done the usual one-hour tourist bit - the Cathedral, the European Parliament - before heading off in search of more Reds.

A visit to yet another Irish bar, a mammoth singsong, all par for the course on a Euro away, ensued later that evening in Brussels town centre.

The Red Army were in fine tune and no hint of any trouble whatsoever - until, that is, a gang of Turkish youths appeared gesticulating throat-cutting through the windows from where they had gathered on the street outside.

'Right, matey, this is going to get moody and kick off here, let's get Lily back to the hotel,' Big Jamie suggested.

Anderlecht, inspired by a noisy home support, scored twice before half time.

Andy Cole was brought down in the area and Mr Dependable, Denis Irwin, forced home the penalty giving us a lifeline.

Desperate defending by the home team, unrelenting attacks by the Reds, Anderlect clung on to the tender lead and we were beaten for the second time in the group stages of our European travel.

Downhearted of course, but another top trip. Lily was especially disappointed, considering the weather had caused her to be confined to her room.

Jamie and Paul had flown home to London on an early morning flight meaning that I had a couple of hours to pass at the airport. By this stage I must admit that I had fallen head over heels in love with Yukari and had no doubt in my mind that I wanted to spend the rest of my life with her. She was the best thing that had ever happened to me and I didn't want her to go back to Japan.

Ever since I had woken that morning I had a gut wrenching nervousness about buying, or not buying, an engagement ring. I spied a jewellers just to the right of the duty free shop and awkwardly inched towards the glass fronted display cabinets, trying my best to scan the contents for something suitable. Feeling childishly embarrassed in case anyone knew what I was at, as if it mattered,  I at first shunned the assistant who asked, 'May I help you, sir.'

'No, I'm okay thank you, I'm just looking.'

'Were you looking for anything in particular?' she replied.

Feeling a little braver (not dissimilar to meeting the players all those years ago) considering   I had broken the ice with the assistant and there was no one else in the vicinity, I stuttered, 'No thanks, well, em, ah, actually I was trying, em, looking for your engagement rings?'

Phew…there said it…wasn't that bad was it, I thought.

'Oh yes, we have a good selection of finest diamonds, would you like to see? Do you know what size of ring you require?'

'I have a ring of hers on my chain.' Nervous and fumbling, I took off my necklace, removed Yukari's silver ring and passed it to her.

Oh no, I thought. Please have one. After all that embarrassment, and then my bravery, there was no way I could go through that again, not at another jewellers and definitely not at home where someone might see me.

'Do you have one a wee bit bigger, that I can get made smaller back home just in case.'

'Oh certainly sir? We have diamonds priced up to £50 000.'

'Not bigger diamonds! A bigger size I mean.'

'Oh sure, I thought you meant a bigger diamond, she added smiling. I detected that she was deliberately winding me up knowing I was as nervous as a bag of cats.

Feeling a renewed confidence, I replied , 'Behave your self missus, I only support Manchester United, I don't own them.'

'Oh, you are from Manchester?'

Don't you start too. No, I live in Northern Ireland but yes, I am Mancheter United supporter. We were beaten by Anderlecht last night.'

'And your future wife also?

'No, she's Japanese actually. It's a long story'

'How did you meet her?' she asked as she opened another tray or sparkling rings .

'I own a huge flag, Big Lily, which I take around the world. We played in Japan last year and hey presto...today I am going to ask her to marry me.'

'Wow, what a story. That's amazing. You should write a book.'

'I am,' I added smiling.'Any chance of a wee bit more discount now?'

230

'Okay, I'll give another fifty pounds off which ever one you choose'.

After about half an hour I picked one I thought Yukari would like, paid her, half in credit card, half in English notes and walked away feeling both relieved and accomplished…momentarily anyway.

On the flight home my galloping pulse was complimented by an aerobic brain. I had gotten over the first hurdle, now all I had to do was ask Yukari. That should be simple enough, shouldn't it? What if she says no? What if she just laughs or doesn't take me seriously? What words could I possibly say? What speech could I make in the despondent air of silent ineptness between question and impending answer? Avoiding embarrassing eye contact, do I pick a spot behind her head to stare at during this impending time warp? Restless, frequently moving position, rummaging through the seat pocket in front of me, I read the safety sheet, put it back, read it again, then examined the sick bag and scoured the pages of the in-flight magazine-all before we even took off.

Oh no, there's no way. Right, that's it. I'm not asking her. Definitely not. I can't. I'll just keep the stupid ring. No, I'll throw it away, and tell no-one, no-one in the whole wide world. It just never happened.

'Hot Breakfast, sir,' I was rudely interrupted as I stared trance-like out of the window.

'What! Oh, yes, sorry, thank you. Yes please,' as I pulled my tray down, beads of sweat of volcanic proportions forming and then abundantly flowing down my forehead in a relentless facial assault.

On my arrival home, still feeling as if stricken with some awful affliction, Yukari and I hugged on the doorstep, just inside the front door.

I could see my reflection in the mirror over Yukari's shoulder. We stood holding each other in silence. I looked woeful. Washed out, unslept, nervous-as if harbouring some terrible secret.

That's it. I'm going to ask her now…I can't live like this. If she says no then she says no. I'll worry about that then.

'Yukari.'

'Yes Keithy.'

'I've something to ask you.'

'What's wrong, Keithy?'

'Oh nothing's wrong, it's just something that has been bothering me for a few days.'

'Please tell me,' she said, sympathetically grasping my hand

'Will you? How would you feel about?'

'Feel about what, Keithy?'

'Will you marry me?' I blurted.

'What? Are you serious?' and laughed.

Oh No. Here we go. It's happened. Does she think I'm joking? Is this rejection?

'Look, I'm totally serious, will you?' I replied, reaching forward an opened box in my sweaty palm.

'Oh Keithy, I'd love to marry you.'

# City are Back! (18 November 2000)

Being an 'out of town' United supporter, I can never fully appreciate what it means to a Mancunian Red to participate in a derby match. I wasn't born with them. I didn't go to the same school or live in the same street as the bitters. I didn't grow up being called a 'Munich' or suffer their bitterness and massive jealousy directed at all things Red.

After a four and a half year gap as City plummeted to the depths of the Nationwide Second division, the eagerly anticipated derby was upon us. My seventh and the hundred and twenty-sixth Manchester derby was always going to be a highly charged occasion. If Lily could not get into Old Trafford, I was determined to take her to Maine Road and give her the chance to witness at first hand her bitterest blue enemies.

The singing among the Reds was humorous leading up to this much-awaited match:

*'And Joe Royle said is that a trophy in your cabinet, are you 'aving a laff, are you 'aving a laff?'*

Then:

*'You've got the tallest floodlights in the land coz City are a massive club*
*You've got Curly Watts as a celebrity fan coz City are a massive club'*

*'Twenty-four years, twenty-four years, twenty-four years, twenty-four years'*

Followed by:

*'You're going down, you're going down*
*You're going down, you're going down*
*City's going down with a Russian on the wing, a Russian on the wing.'*

Anti-City songs were all sung at recent European and Premiership games, more than anything I think in anticipation of this long-awaited derby. A new '24.5 YEARS' flag was unfurled at the front of our new home high in the rafters of the Stretford End.

'I'm anxious, boys, I've been nervous all week, it's getting out of Maine Road after the match is the problem,' said Alan.

'Don't worry, we'll walk back to town with the Firm into Piccadilly, they'll be plenty of Peelers about, we'll be all right.'

'I was speaking with Chris the other day. He reckons any City fan between eighteen and thirty will be looking a pop at a Red.'

'Wee man, I think you'd be mad to bring Lily with you tomorrow, you'll end up getting us all a kicking.'

'Sure they'll not pick on us three wee men.'

'Will they not? They'll slit the three of our throats and burn Lily.'

'Maybe you're right, sir, we'll see what the craic is in the morning.' I replied

The media hype had gotten to us, the Internet fanzine sites all proclaimed Armageddon, anyone you spoke to - even the staff - gave an opinion that there would be trouble everywhere.

234

An early night ensued in preparation for an eleven-thirty a.m. morning kick off (and hotel wake up call at eight a.m.). Although I had Lily with me in the reception area of the hotel and did want to take her, Gary and Alan persuaded me against such a move in case we inadvertently ran into any trouble.

Lily-less once again, we caught a taxi and got dropped off outside Maine Road.

Walking by, mixing in with the bitters, beside them, behind them, standing alongside them in their shop, watching them park their cars, many wearing replica kits and many bearing a forlorn smile and others wearing a 'this is the day' expression. Listening to their hopeful predictions of how they were going to annihilate the 'Munichs'.

'Munichs', as they call us Reds, is an abhorrent term referring to that fateful day in 1958 when eight of the Busby Babes perished. Throughout my football-watching career they are the bitterest 'supporters' and I can understand the hatred which Manchester Reds especially have for them.

The first twenty minutes were typical of a Mancunian derby - helter-skelter with the players looking to settle scores early on. Then Alf-Inge Haaland brought down Paul Scholes outside the City penalty area. David Beckham immediately placed the ball and curled it around a non-existent City wall. 1-0 to the Reds, Maine Road silenced by brilliance and the Red contingent behind the goal ecstatic.

The fifty or so of us at the top of the steps in the temporary 'scaffolding stand' laughed and danced uncontrollably in celebration. I looked over towards Alan and Gary and in doing so caught the eye of a stocky policeman who diplomatically winked and smiled.

Dwight Yorke should have had a first half hat trick.

City went close on occasions and Wes Brown made a miraculous goal line clearance.

> *'We've got Wesley Brown*
> *We've got Wesley Brown*
> *We've got Wesley, we've got Wesley*
> *We've got Wesley Brown.'*

1-0, three points secured and a satisfying victory over the bitters, normal service resumed.

'It was more special because it was the derby and there's no better way of quietening a crowd than when you stick the ball in the back of the net,' said Beckham after the match.

The 'Alfie Haaland is a Blue; he hates Munich's' chants, aeroplane gesticulations from men, women and kids at the end were cast aside as the Reds collectively broke into song:

> *'City are back, City are back*
> *City are back, City are back.'*

Did I hear the United fans singing 'City are back?' Paddy Crerand asked when he arrived at our hotel.

'Aye, Paddy, that was us all right, City are a massive club, aren't they?'

'It should have been five or six nil.'

'I hope we relegate them in April,' someone added.

Arsenal beaten by Everton, Liverpool beaten by Bradford - quite a weekend indeed.

A truly massive day.

# The Dream Fulfilled….partially

Following another meeting with Mr Roberts, Mr Ramsden, Mr Merret, IMUSA and Barmy Charly in November 2000, I received a telephone call from Charly stating that Lily would at long last be allowed in and for me to contact Mr Arthur Roberts directly.

I called Mr Roberts on 20 December, asking his permission to display her on New Year's Day against West Ham.

He was most helpful and agreeable and I now detected a genuine sense of accommodation.

'Meet me at two o'clock at the main entrance. I'm not sure whether we will walk around the pitch or have it displayed in Tier 2.'

'Good work, sir, I'll die happy when she gets out at OT,' I replied.

I'm not stupid enough not to appreciate the safety aspects and that Mr Merrett has many more pressing tasks in his job as club secretary, but I was chuffed that, after so much stress and rejection, perseverance had prevailed.

Lily, still resting peacefully and content in her 'Brussels bag', was elated when I broke the news to her.

'Lily, they're letting you in on New Year's Day.'

Faceman and I were gutted when our flight was cancelled due to the adverse weather conditions in Northern Ireland. Seven inches of snow had fallen in Belfast, the most for twenty years, and the airport was closed.

Our New Year pilgrimage had to be cancelled, as had the reservation at the Amblehurst Hotel and the meeting with Mr Roberts.

I didn't contemplate asking further permission until the Aston Villa game on 20 January.

I contacted Mr Roberts on the Thursday prior to the game, asking if there was any chance of bringing Big Lily to the game.

'Sure, Keith, no problem. Ring me at eleven o'clock and I'll confirm arrangements. Come to the players' entrance at twelve o'clock, security will be expecting you.'

Sure enough Gary and I, each carrying one handle of Lily's 'house bag', were welcomed by the burly SPS at the players' entrance.

As the players were disappearing down the tunnel after the warm-up, eight ball boys unfurled her in the centre circle of the hallowed Old Trafford turf. As the players completed their pre-match warm-up, the ball boys moved Lily around in a clockwise motion showing her to the Old Trafford faithful.

What a sight to behold.

'There she is, wee man, in all her glory,' I said as I continued to snap pictures as if 'shooting' a glamour model.

'Fair play to you, wee man, you got her in at long last.'

Alan Keegan, the stadium announcer, proclaimed, 'A very special welcome to the huge flag known as Big Lily, which has been seen across the world wherever United have played.'

Lily and I have had some special moments over the years but this beat them all, perhaps because of the fight for entry but more so because this was where she belonged - her audience was her family. She was one of them, part of them.

# THE KING AND I

## Valencia Away (Valencia, 12 February 2001)

Lily was particularly anxious to get to Valencia, especially as she had travelled to Brussels on her last Euro away but was confined to her bag. We decided to fly to Madrid and take in the Real Madrid/Lazio clash on the Tuesday, stay in Madrid and travel to Valencia on Wednesday via train.

As we sat in the blue seats gazing at the empty Bernabeu arena, I telephoned the Real Madrid medical centre in an effort to speak with Chueca.

'Can I speak with Pedro Chueca Remon, please?'

'Who is speaking, please?'

'Keith Norris from Ireland.'

'Mr Morris (as he calls me even though he knows it's Norris), I get your letter last night, I already spoke to Raul, he meet you after game.'

'Come to gate fifty at twenty minutes after game, I will meet you and take to players' tent.'

'Happy days, sir, thank you again, Chueca, see you later on.'

Following an exhilarating game of end-to-end football before a fervent Spanish crowd and a 3-2 win for Madrid capped by a last minute Figo penalty we made our way to the player's entrance.

'Come with me please,' we were instructed by security and led through high gates and past a vibrant Madrid crowd waiting for their heroes to depart in their cars.

As we walked down the incline leading to the inner sanctuary of the Bernabeu, we passed the Lazio team coach. Some players were sitting solemnly on board eating what looked like packed lunches.

One by one, the remaining Lazio players walked by us, Ravanelli, Crespo, Salas.

Ravanelli smiled courteously as I moved across and let him past me.

'Nice to meet you, sir,' as he proceeded to board the coach.

'Everything OK, Mr Morris? (another one having a laugh?)' Manuel, the English-speaking head of security asked as he walked by. 'Chueca will be out soon. Please stand here and wait for Chueca,' he added.

Chueca appeared, a broad smile lighting up his face. Shaking his hand, I thanked him for his and his staff's courtesy and he proceeded to lead us downward and inside the caverns of the Bernabeu. Past security through a narrow tunnel and then out into a larger room, fenced on one side with a crash barrier behind which must have been at least one hundred journalists. Lights flashing, television camera lights in active mode, the smell of expensive aftershave wafting as many of the players walked by.

'Keith, come here please, this is the boss, Julio Senn Gonzalez.'

I extended my hand to an immaculately dressed gentleman standing at the entrance to a small white tent.

'Thank you very much for all your hospitality, sir, you don't know what it means to us. What is your position with Madrid?'

'I am the Director General of Real Madrid,' as he presented me with a business card.

'Oh, sir, don't give me that, you'll regret it.'

'No problem, please take it. If you are ever in Madrid my numbers are on the card.'

'Right, lads, happy days, we're well in here, VIP next time and every time we draw Madrid,' I said as I glanced towards Brian from Bray and the boys standing about six feet away.

'He is the boss of Madrid, the big boss,' Chueca said. 'Raul is coming to see you soon, please follow me,' he instructed.

Chueca led the way into the white marquee/tent. As I followed behind, I had to stop to allow someone to pass by. It was none other than Fernando Hierro who smiled broadly and hugged me: 'Ah Manchester.'

I mumbled something in my usual gibberish and proceeded towards the centre of the room.

To my left sat Steve McManaman with three guests and to my right in the distance sat Roberto Carlos, Michel Salgado, Morientes and Ivan Campo, all of whom smiled in acknowledgement.

One by one Chueca called them all over and insisted they pose for pictures with us and sign autographs.

'Ah Manchester (as Hierro and Raul call me), Brazil - how are you?' Salgado exclaimed in perfect English.

Morientes, who was with family members, was reminded by me of the plaster of Paris in Brazil and proceeded to tell his company in Spanish about the night Chueca dressed him up in the Intercontinental Hotel, which was greeted by loud laughter from all concerned.

Raul, dressed in knee-length leather coat, walked in, smiling as ever and gave me a big hug. Chueca introduced us all again as 'my Irish family' in English and then reiterated in Spanish. I then presented him with an Irish crystal clock as a token of our appreciation. He seemed, as he always does, genuinely overwhelmed. Shortly after, Luis

Figo, sporting a smart grey suit walked in and immediately came over beside us and began speaking to Chueca who again introduced us all. I spluttered something to Figo like, 'You are a superstar, Figo - I mean Luis.'

'Thank you very much,' he replied in fluent English.

Boy, did I feel like a child.

Chueca Remon is more than the physio at Real Madrid. He is a character who is held in the highest esteem by all at the club. As Chueca joked, 'If you friend of Chueca, you friend of Madrid, I am the players' boss.'

As we were standing talking with Chueca, we noticed two lads walk into the tent and request, 'Two lagers please, mate,' in English accents. We thought nothing of it, assuming they were media or friends with some of the other Madrid players.

About five minutes later, security approached Chueca and asked if the two lads in question were with his 'Manchester United friends'. Chueca looked at me and then explained in English.

'No, these are my family, Mr Morris, Peter, Joel. No family,' he added and pointed to the two lads who were escorted from the tent smiling - after they had finished their lager.

Were they jibbing?

Shortly afterwards, Chueca called me over to meet someone dressed in casual but smart attire.

He introduced me, 'My friend from Ireland, Mr Morris.'

I stood talking gibberish in my Spanish/English for a few minutes to this gentleman who politely smiled back in my direction.

'Who was that, Chueca?'

'The President of Madrid, I tell him you meet Raul in Brazil and are friend of Raul and Hierro.'

'I wish you had introduced me to him, I didn't know he was President.'

'No problem.'

'I feel bad not thanking him.'

'No worry, he knows you,' he replied smiling.

'I can't believe I'm standing here with all these people, it's thanks to you, Chueca.'

'No problem, you are my friend, you are my family,' he continued.

'The King is here, you just miss the King.'

'The King? Eric Cantona?'

'NO,' he frowned, 'NOT Cantona, King Juan Carlos!'

'You're joking?'

'No, no joking, five minutes late, you miss the King.'

Chueca relayed the story of what I had said to the group of about eight, including Raul and Figo standing just beside us, who all laughed heartily.

'Mr Morris getting married to Japanese girl,' Chueca proclaimed and then added, shaking his head humorously as he spoke, 'Utah, Brazil, Manchester, Japan…crazy boy… my family are crazy.'

'Now we go to restaurant with Salgado and Roberto Carlos,' Chueca stated. 'Real Madrid restaurant, I will order taxis.'

Peter, Brian from Bray and I, all still giddy from the experience, jumped in the first taxi and Chueca and Joel Taggart followed in the next one.

Salgado, Roberto Carlos, their wives and friends had arrived before us. When the bill came we pulled out our wallets to pay our share.

'No, you no pay. Real Madrid pay, you are friends of Raul.'

I walked towards the bar and asked the manager if I could have the bill.

'You pay - I cut your throat,' the tall Spanish waiter gesticulated.

'No way, sir, we like to pay our way, it's not fair.'

'No. You friends of Real Madrid, you no pay - Real Madrid pay.'

We said our goodbyes to Roberto Carlos and Michel Salgado and proceeded outside with Chueca where two taxis were waiting to take us to our hotel.

It is hard to comprehend, yet heart-rending that on so many occasions not only did a man in Chueca's position but also the Madrid players, particularly Raul and Hierro, themselves take the time for United supporters like us.

## Rain in Spain

The early morning train from Madrid to Valencia was packed with many Red faces. Lily had never been on a train before. The two jibbers, Jimmy and John from Preston, who had been ejected from the players' marquee the previous evening, were on board.

'How did you get in there last night?' they asked

'Oh it's a long story, what were you guys at?'

'We borrowed a few Champions League bibs a few years ago and use them to make it to the players' lounges as often as possible. We've jibbed it about four times.'

Two masters of the jib no doubt. This was not a story. I saw it happen and if only I had sussed what was going on Chueca would have told security the lads were in our group.

It was a wet wintry day, followed by an even wetter night. We, along with Lily, stopped off at the team hotel just around the corner from where we were staying, to wish

244

them luck as they boarded the coach before making the short journey to the Mastellar stadium.

A fairly poor, rain-soaked crowd enjoyed a great end-to-end game which remained scoreless at the end of ninety minutes.

We'd have taken a draw before the game to be honest and although slightly disappointed (as always when we get to watch a nil-nil) you have to be realistic and appreciate that this was a good side we were playing and a draw was a fair result.

As is the norm on a Euro away, we were kept behind for about forty-five minutes after the final whistle. This was the most humorous part of the evening. The two pockets of Reds in two different stands in the empty stadium singing to each other such ditties as 'We can see you sneaking out' and 'Are you City in disguise'.

We headed back to the hotel via a little late-night restaurant before returning to Madrid the following morning in preparation for our flight home. Further disappointment for Lily but yet another momentous trip.

## The Real Madrid Connection

The connection between United and Real Madrid dates back to 1957. Insignificant as we supporters are, I am genuinely honoured and humbled by the mindboggling treatment I have received from everyone at Real Madrid as a supporter of Manchester United. I can understand now what Sir Matt Busby wrote about 'seeds of friendships' being sown in 1956/1957 and the 'lifelong bond' when they agreed to help the Reds out of financial difficulties which resulted from the Munich disaster, by playing a special game.

United were beaten 3-1 in Bernabeu in the semi final of the European Cup on 11 April 1957. Real were holders of the competition, having beaten Stade de Rheims in the inaugural final one year previously.

The Madrid line-up included the legendary Di Stefano and United lined up as follows: Wood, Foulkes, Byrne, Colman, Blanchflower, Edwards, Berry, Whelan, Taylor, Viollet and Pegg.

Real Madrid President Don Santiago Bernabeu presented United Chairman Harold Hardman with a statuette after the game.

A fortnight later on April 25, United played host to the Spanish giants. This game was unique because it was the first European Cup game played at Old Trafford and the first against foreign opposition played under floodlights.

The sixty-five thousand crowd was stunned by two first-half goals from Kopa and Rial and although the game ended 2-2 (goals from Taylor and Charlton) Madrid progressed and went on to win the European Cup for a second time. They remained holders of the competition until 1960, winning it a record - which I believe will stand for all time - five successive times.

In 1968 the teams were paired together again in the semi-final of the competition.

United won the first leg at Old Trafford on April 24 thanks to a George Best goal.

In the return leg in the Bernabeu on May 15, Madrid were 3-1 up at half time. David Sadler pulled one back after the break to make it 3-2 on the night and level on aggregate and with twelve minutes to go to full time, Bill Foulkes scored the all-important goal that clinched victory and put United through to the final at Wembley on May 29- which they won, beating Benfica 4-1.

United played host to Real Madrid for their Centenary game in August 1978. A side which included present boss Vincente Del Bosque was defeated 4-0 at Old Trafford.

Manchester United and Real Madrid are two genuinely legendary clubs with a mutual respect that continues to grow between them to this day. I would like to think in my own wee way that Sir Matt Busby would have been, and Sir Alex Ferguson is, proud of the association and bewildering friendship Lily and I have been fortunate enough to strike up with Real Madrid.

## Lily the Bridesmaid

Although anxious to make it to Greece on March 7 for the final away game against Panathinaikos in Athens (a city of nineteen thousand taxis by the way), I could not get the time off work. Lily was gutted. She had wanted to visit the Acropolis, the Parthenon and the home of the gods.

To make matters worse, I had to go to Japan on April 13 so I was going to miss the Bayern away and the Manchester City derby on April 21. From a Red point of view, this was the worst month I can recall for a long time. However, it was also the best month of my life. I was going to Japan to ski in Hokkaido for a week and then the small matter of getting married in Kyoto City to my beautiful fiancée, Yukari Fukushima.

'Is there anywhere I can watch the United match on television in Niseko Hirafu?' I asked Ben from Deep Powder ski tours on my arrival in Hokkaido. I had asked him previously via email and he was fairly confident, so I was pretty happy and prepared for what would be a memorable week indeed.

'If it is on satellite television there is a good chance if you travel to Sapporo.'

'Happy days.'

Lily was to perform yet another important duty at my wedding in Japan which was scheduled to take place on the same day. Although obviously delighted with yet another trip to Japan, she was extremely anxious because of her previous endeavours in the Land of the Rising Sun. She was disappointed that she would miss the crunch game against Bayern Munich and against City. However, when I informed her that I had been trying to locate an establishment which had cable television broadcasting the game live, she was more contented.

I had asked Lily if she would mind accompanying me to Japan as bridesmaid in the wedding ceremony, posing for some pictures with my in-laws. Because of her robust size and weight, and considering Yukari and I would have large amounts of baggage and ski equipment, we decided it would be better if Lily made the trip on her own.

On April 2, I sent her off to Kyoto in southern Japan to stay with Yukari's parents for a few weeks. This would afford Lily plenty of time to make acquaintance with Masanobu and Nobue (Yukari's parents) and give her the opportunity to see some of the wonderful attractions Japan has to offer, particularly following her getting lost in Tokyo in 1999. I would not see the big girl until the morning of my wedding.

I departed Belfast on April14; two days before my thirty-fourth birthday, four days before the Munich away clash in the Champions League and seven days before both the Manchester derby and my wedding on the 21st. If all went according to plan, we could send the bitters to the nationwide, scalp Munich and proceed to the semi-final of the Champions League and complete the week with a happy wedding in Kyoto.

The Bang Bang restaurant in the resort of Niseko Hirafu is halfway up on the left- hand side of the steep street leading to the base of the impressive ski area. OK, what has a restaurant and a ski resort to do with Manchester United?

We were eating in the quaint traditional restaurant, the three attentive staff dressed in traditional costume serving up such treats as chicken liver, chicken heart and crabmeat.

You learn a few words, you learn a few of their customs, you feel good - the Japanese appreciate any effort made.

'Konnichiwa (hello).'

'Arigatou gozaimasu (Thank you very much).'

'Sumimasen okanjyou kudasai (Excuse me can I have the bill?).'

'Where can I watch the Manchester United verses Bayern Munich game in Niseko?'

'It is not possible I think, only in Sapporo (about two hours away) but give me your telephone number and I will see what I can do,' Masanobu said.

Following skiing on the Wednesday, I returned to the hotel and was informed there was a message for me.

'I have satellite installed in my house, I will leave instructions on television. The game starts at 5.15 am. I will be away skiing in the mountain, I will leave door open for you, please enjoy.'

It transpired that Masanobu had his friend take his satellite system from his house in Sapporo, drive up to Niseko where we were and install it in his house adjacent to the Bang Bang restaurant. I couldn't believe it.

It doesn't matter where you watch a game of importance. Obviously nothing beats being there but you still go through all the emotions. A two-one defeat away to Munich ended any further European ambitions. Especially disappointing considering the manner in which I was able to watch the game at all.

Stunned by the lack-lustre performance of the shirts, Yukari and I returned to our hotel shortly after seven a.m, ate breakfast and headed off for another day's skiing. The mood of the morning was totally downcast. I was gutted. Yukari spotted this and tried to make me feel better as we sat on the chairlift taking us to the top of the mountain.

'So you not go to Milan, Keithy?'

'No, Yukari, no Milan, not this year, we just weren't good enough.'

'Disappointing, isn't it?'

'Yes, baby, I'm devastated but we'll be back next year. It's Fergie's last year and the final is in Scotland where Alex is from.

'No worries, Yukari, disappointing yes but we had another great season - we won the League three times in a row and seven times in nine years.'

'Very good team aren't they, Man United,' she added sympathetically.

'Yes, baby, we're the best aren't we? We must thank Masanobu again. I can't believe he had his mate from Sapporo install the satellite into his own house. What a pity we hadn't won after all that. Japanese culture is amazing, Yukari.'

# The Wedding

I often joked to friends that I would never marry an Irish girl and any possible wife would have to ski and have an allegiance to, or an understanding of, Manchester United.

I was always intrigued by diverse cultures and traditions when travelling in foreign countries and endeavoured to be an exponent of all things positive from Northern Ireland. I detested when people gave you weird looks because of your accent or when they heard Northern Ireland mentioned, made their excuses and left your company.

In truth, if it had not been for Manchester United, and for that matter, Big Lily, I would not have had the opportunity to travel and certainly would not have met Yukari.

The Takaragaike wedding chapel in Kyoto city, Kyoto prefecture, lies about a mile from the world-famous Kyoto international conference centre. Lily sat reverently at the back of the temple and, as I proudly turned to watch my stunning bride Yukari and her father walk up the aisle, I couldn't help thinking how pleased Lily looked for me.

A nerve-wracking forty-five minutes ensued, the ceremony in both Japanese and English taken by a French Canadian Priest who knew of, and spoke like, Eric Cantona.

Yukari looked stunning. Like a princess. Her Mother and Grandmother wore traditional wedding kimonos and Masanobo and her brothers wore smart black suits and white wedding ties.

At the rehearsal earlier I was instructed that as the important parts of the ceremony were in Japanese I would be given the nod by Eric's mate when I should say 'Hi Chikmas.' (I do)

Following the wedding service we stood and posed for pictures outside. As I approached the door, I noticed that the staff of the wedding chapel had opened Lily up to display the huge Manchester United Football Club Crest, behind which Yukari and I were to stand for the official

251

pictures. I was filled with emotion, having just married the girl I loved and having the other girl in my life as my bridesmaid.

Nobuyuki and Kenshin, Yukari's brothers, Masanobu, Yukari's father and Naho, Nobuyuki's wife, photographed repeatedly as only the Japanese can do as Yukari, Big Lily and I posed for all we were worth, smiling gleefully on this very special day in our lives.

Following the official pictures, my new brothers-in-law and father-in-law laid Lily out flat, exposing her truly colossal size in the small car park directly opposite the temple much to the bemusement of the many passing locals.

Lily was packed away once more, having performed her duties with dignity, and was sent back to Ireland with a courier on Tuesday.

I left Kyoto on Tuesday and returned home alone. Yukari could not return for another eight weeks until she received her marriage visa and entry clearance to the United Kingdom.

Lily arrived back on Thursday morning and we began looking forward to our next appearance at Carrington on Friday, May 4. It was hoped that Lily would be allowed to United's training complex to meet with her heroes.

Before I left, I had been speaking to Peter Brookes and Bob Farrer at MUTV who wanted to do a feature on Lily and a story about her role in the wedding.

Unfortunately I received no response from a second email I had sent to Diana Law, and Lily and I were left to anguish over what might have been.

# The Dream Fulfilled

All was not lost, however. Having sent an email to the editor of Rednews, Barney Chilton, requesting him to ask United PR guru Paddy Harverson if it was okay to unfurl Lily in Tier 2, I was amazed when I got the okay saying that Paddy Harverson had spoken to Mr Roberts who had no problem with Lily being displayed in the Stretford End.

On the morning of the game, I telephoned Arthur Roberts who organised security to permit Gary, Lily and me into Tier 2 to set her out at the back row of the stand so I could leave her safe and ready to be unfurled during the game.

Yet again, all did not go according to plan. My own seat in row 40 of block 3102 could not be used because one of the kids in the group understandably wanted to sit beside his father. In turn I had to sit in row AA of the South Stand, which meant no one was there to unfurl her. I tried telephoning a few members of our club who sit in the vicinity of row 40 but no-one wanted to be bothered.

Gary and I took our seats in the South Stand about ten minutes before kick off. When the game started I couldn't concentrate. I was stressed out big time.

'Wee man, this is serious, sir, Lily is lying up there all set to go out and she can't get out because them boys up there can't be bothered.'

'Relax, wee man, somebody will bring her out, wait there for ten minutes' Gary replied.

'I'll give it five minutes and then I'm going up to get her out.'

'They'll not let you in again, wee man, if you go out.'

'They will sir, I'll ask for Arthur Roberts, he'll get me up there.'

I could take it no longer so left my seat and headed for the back of the stand where I told a steward my predicament.

He radioed to the security and within a few minutes I was in the lift in the Stretford End. I made my way up to my seat in the back row where Lily was still lying anxiously waiting.

Having drilled those seated in the back row to unfurl the black section first, I led the bottom right-hand corner down the steep steps toward the front of the stand. As I did so, the crowd instinctively passed her downward, revealing her full size and broke into song:

**'We'll never die, we'll never die, we'll never die, we'll never die,**
**We'll keep the red flag flying high cause Man United will never die.'**

Emotional and sweating, I stood watching as she moved throughout the stand, dancing roguishly above the heads of the jubilant Reds in the Stretford End. I heard a buzz among the Reds - they were enjoying Lily, she was enjoying them and I was enjoying both.

She had been out playing for about ten minutes when she came back in my direction. I almost caught the corner but, teasingly, she moved backwards again and proceeded on her tour. I got the impression she was making sure the players saw her; she had fought for so long to get into the stand and she was making the most of it.

Eventually she came back towards me again. I enlisted the help of about twenty people around me to pull her in and the pair of us were escorted back to the South Stand. Lily was left in the old centre tunnel under the supervision of Ned Kelly and I returned to my seat beside Gary.

'Did you get any pictures, wee man? How'd she look up there in tier two?'

'She looked class, wee man, I got a couple of her,' Gary replied.

Together we satisfied the security and safety requirements, this was her final dream accomplished. All the previous stress and rejection was forgotten, the perseverance had paid off. She certainly increased the atmosphere and I was more than pleased.

Another day of celebration, tears and emotion. The seventh time in nine years I had watched my team lift the Premiership title. Lily's two year battle for entry, my recent marriage to Yukari and the fact that the Supporters Club was flourishing all combined to make it especially poignant.

You can never get tired of this and every time I get my sentimental 'tiny tears' (as wee Gary calls it) head on. This was to be no different. I didn't let him down.

Although beaten 1-0 by Derby County, no-one was overly disappointed - to be honest many including myself - were elated because it meant that Manchester City would require a miracle if they were to stay in the Premier League.

'We won the Football League again and City have gone down.' emanated from J and K stands of the ground.

Following the celebration the players were joined on the pitch by their families.

Victoria Beckham - or Posh Spice as she's better known - walked passed us where we were sitting in row AA in the South Stand.

'Victoria, I gave Brookyln his first scarf to David's mum.'

Victoria looked bewildered.

'The Carrickfergus one,' I added.

'Oh yes,' she beamed. 'Thank you very much.'

Not a bad wee weekend, sir, eh? Paddy's house, another league title, Lily up in Tier Two, City about to go down and Posh meeting us,' I smiled.

'Wee man, we've never had a bad one yet,' Gary replied.

As we walked out towards the exit, I heard this loud shouting of my name.

'Keith, Keith up here,' and to my utter amazement looked upward to see my friend Kerry Wycherley from Wales, whom I had met in Brazil, standing in the Directors' box.

Kerry signalled us up towards where he was standing, opened the gate and gestured that we should follow him into the Premier Suite where he introduced us to all and sundry.

'This is Keith, the guy who owns that big flag. This is the boy I was telling you about from Brazil. He had Raul and the Real players singing, "There's only one Keano."'

'Keith, I don't believe it. I was just showing Paula and the boys that video with the Madrid players and talking about you last night.'

'Kerry, you'll not believe it. We were up in Paddy Crerand's house last night reminiscing about Brazil and talking about you.'

'Come on upstairs a minute, Keith. I'll show you the manager's office and the VIP lounge.'

As we neared the top of the stairs, we found Sir Alex playing with one of his grandkids.

'Och, Big Man, how's things in Wrexham?' Sir Alex asked (Kerry was a big noise behind the scenes at Wrexham Football Club.)

Kerry proceeded to introduce us to Sir Alex once more.

Did I talk gibberish again? Yes.

'Hello, sir, did you get me letter?'

'What letter?'

'I sent you one about my wedding in Japan.'

'No, I didn't get a letter.'

Was I embarrassed? Yes.

Did I regret mentioning about sending him a letter? Yes.

I thought that either Sir Alex was not pleased at my letter or he was simply bamboozled by me going off in a tangent of gibberish in my usual star struck manner - then again I only posted it two days ago, so maybe he didn't - but he was much too diplomatic to say so - particularly as we were with Big Kerry.

After any noteworthy event while on our travels with United, I always send Sir Alex a wee letter with a few pictures. By his responses I know he is a genuine person, and is as passionate for United as we supporters. We feel he is one of us, fighting our corner himself, always under pressure from the PLC. Unlikely as it may be, one of my ambitions is some day to sit and have a sensible chat with him in English - and without going off at a tangent.

Three days later I received a letter with a Manchester postmark.

Wedding Congratulations to Yukari + Keith

Couldn't let the day pass without extending our best wishes and good luck for the future.

From all the players and staff here at Old Trafford

Sir Alex Ferguson, CBE

I was emotional and speechless.

# KIDNAPPED?

Following her successful display in Tier 2 at the Derby Game, the arrangement was that Mr Roberts was to contact me before the final whistle and Lily would be allowed on to the pitch with the players. When the call did not happen, Lily and I were not terribly disappointed, as she had fulfilled her ambition by appearing, eventually, in the Stretford End. Lily was left in the hands of security supremo Ned Kelly in the old players tunnel. I thought she would be safe enough. Besides, considering her immense size she was hardly likely to get lost.

I called a few days later to arrange collection. I was informed that Lily could not be found but someone would call me back when she was. When the call was not forthcoming, I telephoned the security office and spoke to Stuart Worthington who further advised me that he had exhausted all channels in his search for Lily's whereabouts.

I was most concerned. How can someone that size go missing?

How could Lily have disappeared from a secure area?

I spoke to Big Paul and a few other Reds asking their advice.

'What do they mean Lily has disappeared? She's done a Lord Lucan? Yeah, right. Yeah, she's probably living in some Greek Island with Shergar according to the PLC.'

'Keith, get your solicitor on to them and demand to find out where she is. It was in their control in a secure area and it just disappeared.'

'The suits have gotten rid of it, wee man.'

I contacted the fanzine sites, telling them what had happened and asking for their support.

The following appeared on the Rednews website:

# Cock-up?

Many of you will know of or have seen the huge Lily the Red flag owned by Keith of the Carrickfergus branch, which was centre-piece of the celebrations in the Nou Camp and subsequently altered to celebrate the Stretford End. It had been taken on to the centre of the Old Trafford pitch a few times last season. A good gesture for the club to allow such a great banner to be seen clearly before games.

That was until the last game of the season. The club following their own procedures had the banner and were due to give it back to Keith after the game. But they never did. Why? Because they've lost it. Unbelievable.

The suits were supposed to be looking after it - an item which has cost thousands of pounds to produce and of immense sentimental value. And all they can say is it has been 'lost'. We hope the many Utd employees who read this site will spread the word and do something about this. You can't just 'lose' such a massive flag. Anyone who knows of its whereabouts get in touch with us at rednews@compuserve.com and nice to know so much care and attention was put into looking after such a prized possession.

Red Issue further suggested a PLC conspiracy.

I instructed my solicitor to write to Old Trafford asking for Lily to be located and returned to me.

The media had a field day when they heard that Lily was missing.

'Man Utd Banner goes missing from Old Trafford' wrote the East Antrim Gazette. 'United fan unhappy,' proclaimed the Belfast Telegraph and 'Big Flag raises stink for Manu' wrote the Sunday World.

John Bennett from BBC Radio Ulster - who had now become an avid Big Lily fan since Yukari and I were interviewed in April prior to our wedding, interviewed me over the telephone and I relayed the tale of how she had become involved in yet another dramatic turn of events.

No amount of money or proxy flag could repay or replace my love for Lily.

For the third time in her short life she was lost. This time I really thought it was forever yet I remained hopeful. I knew a real United fan would not steal it; I certainly did not think that Old Trafford officials, no matter how much they may have detested Lily and me for that matter, would deliberately destroy or sabotage her.

There was obviously a possibility that a City fan or a Scouser had infiltrated the inner sanctum of Old Trafford security.

I received this by reply to the first solicitor's letter.

June 22, 2001

Dear Sirs

We acknowledge receipt of your letter dated June 18 and have asked our Stadium Safety Officer's deputy to look into this matter and give it his urgent attention.

Once we have anything positive to report we will write again

Yours sincerely

K R Merrett
Secretary

This deputy referred to was the same one that informed me that he had exhausted every avenue and told me there was nothing they could do.

Feeling extremely disappointed at the treatment by certain Manchester United Officials, my thoughts were that they were happy to use Lily in their merchandising regime, yet, when it came to accepting responsibility, she was cast aside.

The plan to take Lily to The Far East once again where the team was to play matches in Kuala Lumpur, Singapore and Bangkok was put out of my mind. If they can't be bothered about Lily why should I bother about them were my sentiments. Besides, Yukari and I had promised to go to visit her parents on July 24, which coincided with the pre-season tour.

# Thailand August 29th 2001

I could not bear the fact that United were playing only a five-hour flight away from Japan. While I did feel aggrieved with certain officials, my love for the team and the club never floundered. I told Yukari I simply had to go to Thailand. She agreed to come with me if we took her mother so they could spend some time together.

'Happy days,' I said and the next morning we flew to Bangkok from Osaka.

The Radisson Hotel was bedecked carnival-like with much United insignia including a huge club crest in the lobby entrance and enormous yellow and red ribbons adorning the check-in area.

A city of ten million people, one hundred thousand taxis and some twenty thousand tuk-tuks which make a noise like something from the Flash Gordon series.

262

Towering skyscrapers, huge express ways, street vendors, endless markets, aroma of cooking, diesel fumes and raw sewage leave a lasting impression.

We had a wonderful three days, beginning with a City tour that included visits to the famous Temples and witnessed The Golden Buddha, The resting Buddha and a canal tour on the Chao Phraya River which feeds a network of canals and floating markets.

A stroll through the crowded street markets revealed much of what you expect in such countries. Fake Rolex watches, bootleg brand name clothing and Premier League shirts and merchandise in abundance. United, Arsenal, Chelsea, Leeds were all well represented. I even spotted a City shirt-wearing local who tried to hide in embarrassment when I snapped a picture of him.

The United hierarchy relaxed often in the hotel lobby bar sharing jokes and wisecracks. Messrs. Kenyon and Draper were relaxed and obviously enjoying themselves in the pleasant ambience.

Throughout the duration of our stay the hotel was swamped by autograph hunting kids and many others including a taxi-driving Buddhist monk. Everyone was signing autographs. I was even asked to autograph a shirt or two myself.

I purchased a ticket from a tout and proceeded to watch a United 2-1 victory in the Rajmangala Stadium.

Giggs opened the scoring before Thailand equalised through Sripan and a very lean looking Dwight Yorke scored the winner.

Following the game, an estimated ten thousand people, in a scene resembling the Treble celebrations, lined the street to say farewell to the team coach.

I arrived back in the hotel long before the team and rested in the lobby for about half an hour before being joined by Paddy and a few of the MUTV crew quenching our collective thirst as we drooled over Veron and Yorke in particular. Shortly afterwards Martin Edwards, Paddy Harverson, Peter Draper, Peter Kenyon et al joined our company.

I was feeling mildly embarrassed and a little unsure of myself given that they had just received two solicitors' letters from me concerning the club losing Lily on final day of last season. Then again, they didn't know me so if I kept quiet there would be no discomfort.

When Paddy Crerand introduced me to them as: 'The wee man who takes that big flag everywhere' I nearly swallowed my glass whole.

'You know that big flag you see everywhere? This is the silly bugger that carries it. Keith is from Carrickfergus…'

'You're the flag man then?'

'Big Lily?'

'I didn't know you were the flag man.'

Paddy Harverson stated, 'Big Lily, we've lost it on you, I believe. I got the emails about it (from Barney at Red News). I think it has been locked away somewhere by mistake, I think we'll find it okay. If not, we'll sort you out,' he added.

'We've lost his flag on him?' questioned Peter Kenyon.

'Yes, we've lost it on him' replied Paddy H.

'Looks like we're buying him a new flag then, doesn't it?' he responded.

I was pleased to hear that they admitted responsibility although I had not the courage to tell them I did not want a new flag. I wanted Lily back.

However, I did feel relieved that they now knew that I was the flag man and I became much more relaxed and entered into conversation with Martin Edwards and Peter Draper about subjects such as marriage and club merchandising. Oh, don't worry, I did pose the question to Peter Draper about the marketability of a huge flag on more than one occasion.

A female fan appeared requesting the lads' autographs and brandished a picture of Martin Edwards kissing her on the club's previous visit to Thailand some four years earlier.

'The News of the World would love that picture, Martin,' joked someone.

Later in the evening most retreated to the lounge on the top floor where many of the party joined the singsong with the resident Elvis impersonator.

A top evening, potentially embarrassing introductions notwithstanding, and some of my apprehensions about 'The Suits' and their attitude towards supporters proved unfounded...or maybe I was just glad that Lily had received official recognition.

I returned to Japan for a further five days, the highlights being a visit to the famous Temple where Yukari's ancestors are buried and a BBQ at an exclusive restaurant which ended in me teaching my in-laws and about thirty enthusiastic Japanese locals the words to Ooh Aah Cantona.

A freshness was required, which we could all see coming. We longed for genuine quality to add to our squad. This we now have in abundance and following The Treble hangover this pre-season, there was a genuine excitement amongst all Reds.

It gave you a feeling of roll on Fulham on August 19.

I was so disappointed that Lily was not there in person but it felt good to know that I had the Manchester United Directors and officials referring to her as Big Lily and the Chief Executive at least promising to address the situation.

I received no further word from Old Trafford and unfortunately had to send a third solicitor's letter asking for a response within seven days before we initiated legal proceedings. I didn't want to get involved in a legal battle with the team I loved but at the same time I was not going to sit back and let them forget about Lily.

Few know the depths of my feelings for Lily and it would have been unfair to sit idle while she was cast aside.

I racked my brain regarding all possible permutations.

If only I knew where she was or what happened to her, I could at least try to come to terms with my grief. I was dumbfounded.

## Reward for Lily

I had asked the United fanzines to make representation to Paddy Harverson. He consequently telephoned me to give his assurance that he would endeavour to bring this to an amicable conclusion. I was pleased to read in the Official Match Programme on Saturday September 22 2001 (home game against Ipswich):

'Changing subjects entirely, I would ask if anyone out there knows the whereabouts of Big Lily. For those who don't know, Big Lily is a huge red, white and black United flag that makes regular appearances on the big occasions. It is owned by Keith Norris of Carrickfergus, and after it was unfurled at the final home game last season was temporarily stored in the old players' tunnel in the South Stand. It has not been seen since, and we are very keen to track Big Lily down and return her to Keith. If anyone has any information, please contact me at the club. A small but meaningful reward is on offer.'

By Paddy Harverson
Communications Director

Following this announcement the on-line and print media frantically scrambled for any quote, from me or Paddy Harverson, or information which they could use.

'What size does Lily fold up to, Keith?'

'She folds up to the size of a "young goat", sir.'

I knew this would attract more attention and it certainly did. Red Issue, Red News, Fa-Premier.com, Annova.com and several local and national newspapers all covered the story. United had, for the first time, acknowledged Lily officially and had offered a reward for her safe return. Wherever she was, Lily would have been delighted with this news.

'Wee man, you're having a laugh with this aren't you?' asked the Faceman.

'Now that Paddy Harverson has addressed the problem, I'm happy that the club have, at least, acknowledged Lily. Obviously they realise how important she is and that I will not go away. I am hopeful.'

The Daily Star ran a story by John Mahoney entitled 'Keith Waves Goodbye to Footie Flag' on Saturday September 29 and even passed comment in it's The Daily Star Says column under the title of, 'Flag flap'.

'Manchester United nut Keith Norris has had his football flag stolen. It cost £3,500, measures 100ft by 60ft and answers to the name of Big Lily. Keith has taken the flag all around Europe and even made it bridesmaid at his wedding. Talk about getting wrapped up in your hobby.'

While I greatly appreciated Paddy Harverson's efforts, I was still no further forward. If, as he suspected, Carling staff may have inadvertently dumped her surely more pressure could have been put on them to replace Lily or at least offer some compensation as a goodwill gesture.

The Daily Star article certainly cast Lily into the national domain. Later that evening I was interviewed on

Talk Sport radio by Hawksby and Jacobs and the following morning on Channel 4's The Big Breakfast.

'Keith, you're a Manchester (spits) United supporter?' asked the presenter, called Squeaky,(who I had been informed was a City supporter) smugly.

'And you're a Bitter aren't you?' I replied.

'Keith your flag is a huge flag isn't it?'

'Yes, it's MASSIVE.'

The 'Massive' jibe is of course a favourite of United supporters directed at City and made famous by Red Issue forum user 'Moboss' on a national telephone 'Phone-in' to Adrian Littlejohn.

If I managed only one 'massive' on Channel Four's, The Big Breakfast, I certainly made up for it on Talk Sport later that evening when interviewed by top Red Dominic McGuiness -who was feeding me the bait for bitter bashing.

According to Rednews.co.uk news the following morning the editor stopped counting at seventeen mentions of 'massive' during the interview.

## Liberation

Thursday Oct 4, 12.10 p.m. my office telephone rang.

'Is this Keith Norris?'

'Who's this?'

'John Mahoney, Daily Star, I think I've found Big Lily'.

'You're joking? Where? Who's got her? Where is she?'

'Was it made by a Karen Banks?'

'Yes, her name is on one of the corners, she is Lily's mommy'.

'Okay, I'll get back to you later'.

I received another call from John stating that they had liberated the big girl and were bringing her back to home soil via the 2.00 p.m. flight from Manchester to Belfast.

Frantic negotiations with local authorities bore fruit when permission was granted to unfurl Lily over the battlements of our historic Carrickfergus Castle at 5.00 p.m.

John Mahoney and a photographer, Tony Fisher, arrived in a taxi.

'Where is she?' I asked anxiously.

'Don't worry Keith, she's in the boot.'

'Aye aye, I've heard that before,' I joked.

John opened the boot and unveiled a huge army type bag.

I couldn't believe it and lovingly hugged and kissed her. Lily was back and all was well with the world.

Twelve friends, including my Japanese in-laws, assisted in this and after the photo-shoot which was attended by Deputy Mayor Eric Ferguson the only council representative to show any interest and who has since become an avid Big Lily fan. I took Lily home for the first time in five months.

Mystery still surrounds the circumstances of her disappearance but I didn't care. She was home and that was all that mattered. Apparently a season ticket holder from North Wales, who requested no publicity, had Lily in his roof space since finding it on the steps of a pub on the Chester Road and having read John Mahoney's article contacted him, wishing her to be returned to me.

'Flag flies home...thanks to The Star' was the article header in The Daily Star on October 10.

Lily and I were guests on The John Daly Show on BBC 1 on Friday October 12 and her growing celebrity status was reinforced when she was unfurled over the heads of the studio audience.

Gary, Alan and I went to Sunderland happy the following morning where we met up with Pete Boyle, Southy and the lads before the game at the Stadium of Light.

'Big Lily's back, Big Lily's back, Big Lily…' sang Boylie, who like the rest of the lads had seen the Daily Star and the Manchester Evening News.

The following Saturday (October 20), although we were disappointingly beaten by Bolton Wanderers, Lily once again featured on page fifteen of the official match programme.

'Finally, on a different note I am delighted to say that Big Lily aka the Pride of Carrickfergus, has been found and returned to her rightful owner, Keith Norris. After my appeal in an earlier programme for information on the flag's whereabouts, the Daily Star newspaper helped track it down to a loft in North Wales, from where it was shipped across the sea to its spiritual home. We look forward to welcoming Lily back to Old Trafford sometime this season, when I hope Keith keeps a firm grip.'

By Paddy Harverson

Permission was granted (thanks to Paddy Harverson) and Lily was successfully unfurled in Tier 2 again on January 13th 2002 when we were disappointingly beaten the Scousers.

'Wee man, that's twice in two games that Lily has been here that we have been beaten…she's bad luck,' complained Gary.

'That will be her final appearance for a long time, sir,' I replied.

'What's the next stage in her career, wee man?'

'If I said she was going to star in a Hollywood movie, you'd probably laugh your head off, sir.'

'Wee man, you are right. I would laugh my head off but that doesn't mean I don't believe you.'

'I'm going to meet Mark Huffam tomorrow.'

'Who's he when he's at home?'

'One of Speilberg's sidekicks…he was a producer of Saving Private Ryan and that Captain Corelli's Mandolin.'

Alan and Gary did, as usual, laugh their heads off.

I did meet Mark Huffam who was so enthralled with Lily's story that he wanted to take a three year option on this manuscript with a view to making a movie. He even suggested he would bring me on board as a Producer.

I had already received a written offer of an option from Velveteen Films in New York and although I was a wee bit out of my depth, I was extremely heartened by the fact that both producers, one of whom especially was a major player in the industry, wanted to obtain the rights. I had further meetings but decided I would wait and see if and how the book sold.

Yukari had gone to Japan for a holiday in January 2002 and I joined her there at the end of Feburary. This had been the first time since we were married that we were apart for such a length of time. Sure I managed to get to a few more matches but I have to admit I missed her terribly.

I had gotten so used to her being there to welcome me home. I was missing her laughs, making me take off my shoes and teaching each other different words and phrases in our respective languages.

We were sitting on the floor of the living room the day we returned (February 2002) both still groggy with jet-lag when Yukari dropped a bombshell on me out of the blue.

'Keithy, I think I'm pregnant.'

'What? What do you mean you think?'

'Yes, I think I am pregnant but I should go to doctor'.

'Isn't there a test or something you can do?'

'Yes, I did it, two times.'

'And?'

'It says yes.'

'What do you mean it says yes? You better go to the doctor to make sure. I'll ring for an appointment. Who knows?'

'Nobody, just me.'

'Okay let's not panic…let's wait and see'.

Sure enough two days later it was confirmed and we were expecting a child. Big Lily was going to be an auntie in October, 2002.

# UNITED for UNICEF

Following the media exposure, I offered Lily's assistance to the 'Kick Racism out of Football' and the 'UNITED for UNICEF' campaigns. Being married to Yukari, I have witnessed at first hand the scourge that is racism, even in my hometown. This was an opportunity to highlight this campaign and keep Lily in the media spotlight.

Having observed the faces of Brazilian kids when Lily was unfurled and watched programmes involving UNICEF, I wanted to offer Lily to UNICEF as a promotional tool but also something which would bring happiness to kids.

I contacted Louise Stewart who inserted the two crests for the two good causes and Lily was once more granted permission to appear at Old Trafford at the Champions League semi-final first leg against Bayer Leverkesun. The following evening she appeared in the Manchester

Evening News, in another documentary on MUTV and on RTE in Ireland.

If Lily ended the season 2001/2002 on a high, the same could not be said about United. Beaten by Arsenal at home and drawing away to Leverkusen meant that we were not going to win four premiership trophies in a row and were not going to Glasgow to play Real Madrid (who had beaten Barcelona) in the Champions League Final.

In the premiership, whilst we were certainly gutted by the fact we were beaten by our closest rivals' most Reds I spoke to felt that we had been beaten by a deserving Arsenal team who consistently played attractive attacking football, remained unbeaten away from home and scored in every game. We lost six premiership games at home during the season. As Sir Alex himself said, "We didn't lose the league at home to Arsenal. We lost the league because we lost six games at home over the course of the season. That's not good enough. We should not lose six games at home."

For the first time in ten years we finished outside the top two positions in the league. Some of the muppets and so called United supporters who telephoned radio phone-ins complaining about tactics or players such as Juan Veron only brought shame on United. It's not the United way to boo or criticize. It had been an excellent year as far as I was concerned with Ruud Van Nistlerooy's impeccable goalscoring, the form of our club captain Roy Keane and in particular some great United comebacks.

# Irish Good Luck stones

Wee Gary and I however were fortunate enough to get two complimentary tickets from Raul and Hierro for the Champions League Final and spent three glorious days in the Cameron House Hotel at Loch Lomond.

Spain had been over to play Northern Ireland in a friendly match a few weeks previously. I had taken Yukari to meet them for the first time and she presented them with Irish rugby shirts, a Scottish rugby shirt for Chueca Remon and a special gift from Next for Raul's two year old son, Jorge. I was so proud introducing Yukari to the lads and we all posed for a picture together. I didn't give the guys gifts to get anything in return (besides the treatment and gifts I have received from these two could never be repaid) but was overawed the following afternoon when Fernando Hierro said that I would be getting his and Raul's match shirts after the game against Northern Ireland and absolutely gobsmacked when, as they departed the stadium, both shook hands saying, 'See you in Glasgow'.

We had arranged to meet the lads at the Gleddoch House Hotel on the Tuesday afternoon. As Gary and I pulled up in a taxi two security staff rushed towards us ushering us away stating, 'sorry lads the hotel is closed to the public'.

'We have to meet some friends here, sir'.

'I'm afraid not, sir' he replied, 'the hotel is for Real Madrid staff only'.

'That's why we're here, sir' I retorted.

'Who might that be?' he added sceptically.

'Raul Gonzales Blanco, Fernando Hierro and Pedro Chueca Remon. Why don't you give them a ring and ask them to come down?'

Gary and I stood in the small cloakroom at the entrance to the reception as our ever efficient friend proceeded to check his paper work. A few seconds later Chueca appeared and waved us past security and into a plush lounge(the hotel was once the home of Glasgow shipping baron Sir James Lithgow) with dramatic views across the River Clyde to Ben Lomond and the surrounding hills beyond.

'Raul and Hierro are eating. I go join them and we be back in thirty minutes,' he instructed.

Sure enough about twenty minutes later most of the team appeared. Several of the players acknowledged us in the corner, particularly those whom we had previously met. Others just looked confused. Raul and Hierro walked in smiling as usual and sat at our table. We exchanged the usual elaborate greetings as the boys ordered some coffees.

'Raul, do you get excited on big games?'

'Yes, on the day of game. Fernando, one week before'.

'Hierro on the toilet one week before big game?' I joked and made the obvious sounds to much laughter.

I reached into my bag and produced some Irish wishing stones.

'If you make a wish with these stones you (Raul) will score and you (Fernando) will lift Champions League trophy'. Both placed the stones in their palms and wished for all they were worth. Fernando Hierro left the room and appeared a few minutes later brandishing two tickets.

'Raul, the Germans attack like a big wave,' I said gesturing with my hands, 'All Madrid players must have big hearts like Roy Keane and David Beckham for us (United) and you two have for Real Madrid to beat them'.

Raul and Hierro know our passion for United and understood what I meant.

'Wee man, who do you think you are? Del Bosque-Norris?' Gary interjected and as we all laughed heartily we were joined by Roberto Carlos.

Before we left for our hotel, the lads suggested we go to Glasgow Hilton Hotel for the after match dinner party as their guests.

The lucky stones certainly worked. Raul scored the opening goal, Madrid won and Hierro lifted the cup. No wonder they welcomed us with open arms and introduced us to their wives at the Hilton and then invited us to the private party in the Gleddoch House.

One of the funniest things I have ever seen in my life was the sight of my accomplice and friend, Gary Callaghan, attempting to bribe one of the Madrid hierarchy to go and waken the President (who we were informed was sleeping with the European Cup) and tell him to bring it down to the lounge so we could take a picture.

'C'mon, sir, please. Away up and get him down with the cup for a picture with me and the wee man,' Gary pleaded, even resorting to offering him forty quid from his bulging wallet. Chueca had taken a picture of us with the cup a few hours before which didn't come out properly. In an effort to appease him (Gary hates being told he cannot have something) we were promised we would get a picture with the cup at the Centenary game in Madrid in December 2002.

I told the lads that they must now take the stones to the World Cup and if they did so Spain would win and Raul would be top goal scorer.

Sky Sports La Liga pundit and El Mundo journalist Gulliem Balague covered the story of the stones and how they helped Spain proceed, even knocking Ireland out in the process, to the quarter finals before the luck eventually ran out with two disallowed goals against South Korea. I was even interviewed by Mary Harboe on Radio Onda Cero International in Southern Spain about the story of lucky stones and the World Cup.

Two United players who epitomise what the Red cause is all about -Gary Neville and Roy Keane- didn't play in the World Cup Finals in Japan and Korea for varying reasons. True United Reds like Paul Scholes, Nicky Butt and David Beckham enjoyed a successful campaign in my wife's homeland and another of Lily's friends, Roberto Carlos, won a World Cup medal as an entertaining and deserving Brazil beat Germany in the final. At least the stones worked for him!

# Undying Love

Little did I know that I was creating what hopefully will be a legend in United folklore. One that would not only appear on television at the games but would also appear on TV news, be a star in a documentary entitled 'The World of Manchester United', shown on Sky Sports 1, star in 'Green and Red' documentary, shown in the Granada region and on RTE in 2002, feature twice on Eurosport's Review of the Champions League (Milan and Turin), feature once in a two-page spread in the Sun, regularly in The Daily Mirror, a full page picture in The Daily Star appear repeatedly in local newspapers Sunday World and Sunday Life.

Lily would also have her own Internet site (www.mybiglily.com), appear in the Official Manchester United Season Guide, the Official Manchester United magazine (twice), numerous magazines and frequent appearances in the Official Match Programme and MUTV, star alongside George Best, Norman Whiteside and Roy Keane in the official club video, The Irish Connection released in August 2000, be criticized in the Guardian; but, perhaps most importantly of all, be adored and kissed by thousands of Reds.

Big Lily became probably the most famous fan icon in the history of Manchester United Football Club. The Daily Mirror on July 7 called her 'Football's most famous flag.'

I am proud to have been her keeper and travelling companion over these last five seasons. Together we have visited three continents and travelled some sixty-five thousand miles. Lily is now in her fourth year. She has matured into a fine figure of a woman and has begun to notice the opposite sex - particularly those hot Latin flags like the one at Deportivo La Coruna. She keeps mentioning that 'big boy' belonging to the Corinthians' supporters whom she met previously in Brazil.

Some may look upon Lily as only a flag. That's like saying Buckingham Palace is only a house or the QEII is only a boat. However she has been imbued with an actual personality and has won many friends among the Red faithful.

Lily, for our own Carrickfergus Reds, became a symbol not only of togetherness but also of hope for the future.

Thank you, big girl. We all love you!

To all the people, all around the world, who understand our feelings and thoughts about our club and the team we love, I hope that a little piece of Big Lily stays with you in your heart. Lily will, without doubt, continue her unequivocal support and if you ever happen to meet her, be sure to say hello to her ... she'd like that.

# A RED EPILOGUE

The fact that United are the biggest club in the world means we are going to have more of everything. More 'suits', more executives, more tourists, more daytrippers and more of a 'firm' (just a wee bit quieter these days, but still there).

We have to accept, whether we like or not, that Manchester United are a cosmopolitan team with much global appeal. There is room for all sorts at Old Trafford but let's get things in perspective and let's continue to pursue the atmosphere, ticketing and safe standing issues with vigour.

Supporters are the lifeblood of Manchester United. Okay, elements within the Plc may want customers and clients rather than supporters nowadays, but we can make a difference.

Are we victims of our own success? 'Spoilt rotten' and in danger of becoming comatose? If our ambivalence over the match atmosphere is the result of our success, then bring back failure. Bring back the days when we had such a will to win that we supported our team with total passion as in the pre-1990 era when a few FA Cup final appearances (good as they were) were the highlight of two decades. However, it may indeed take a few barren years to rid the Big Red Lady of some of the unwelcome baggage she now attracts in droves.

All that any Manchester United fan wants is for our club to be successful on and off the pitch. We all wish to increase the atmosphere and be proud of our team in all respects. We all have a responsibility in this department. Some people criticise my good friend, United folk legend and songster Peter Boyle, but he, and those like him, need support and encouragement. It is also important to remember that a successful Manchester United team is good for all of our rival teams. When Liverpool were the 'kings' of European Soccer, all the major British soccer teams benefited as a consequence of greater representation in UEFA competitions. After Heysel, all of our teams were banned for five years. The intense rivalry between the supporters of various clubs is what gives the adrenalin rush but in the wider sense, all of us will stand or fall together.

The partial reclaiming of the Stretford End and the work done by the Vocal Fans Campaign is to be applauded and while obviously welcome we now must push for reconfiguration of the stand so those like-minded people can be together, whether it is through safe standing areas or seated.

We may indeed have been the first billion pound club, but what does this really matter if the Club is slowly losing its soul? Relations between club and supporters, for so long practically nonexistent, have moved considerably onwards. The right sounds have been coming from within the club but it is now time for action and substance.

We all dread when Sir Alex really does step down in 2005. He has proved to be a master in man management, implemented the squad rotation system like no other could and has the uncanny knack to know when to let stars leave - even if we at the time disagreed - Ince, Pallister, Bruce, Hughes, Stam, to name but a few.

Even with the vast wealth of Manchester United, there is no one formula for success. Fergie instigated a second to none youth policy, training facilities and nurtured talented individuals into an incredible squad.

The Master of them all, thank you, Sir Alex.

For all that we give United through time, energy and financial expenditure, what we receive is gigantic in return. I gave United a lifetime of devotion. In return I gained unimaginable satisfaction and fulfilment, lifelong friends, memories and the ultimate gift any man can only dream of - my beautiful wife, Yukari. For what I have gained out of my allegiance to United, I am eternally grateful.

The troubles and tribulations of this part of the world need no revisiting. Faceman and I are neither statesmen nor politicians, just two lads crazy about football who along with our prodigy Big Lily hopefully, in our own way, made a small difference and perhaps, who knows, set some kind of example for troubled and divided communities across the world. I'm still a Protestant and proud of my heritage and upbringing. Faceman's still a Catholic, proud of his heritage and upbringing. But you know what? We are still best friends and better than that, we share a common bond that superficially is about a football team but is deeper and more enduring possibly because of the sterile background to the setting of this story. The vast silent majority are still there and still silent.

Meeting Yukari was the best thing that ever happened to me. Since she came here permanently, we have been unbelievably happy. Then again, being happy when you are around Yukari is easy. She is so gentle, remarkably friendly and humorous. We love to laugh and spend many hours in our Japanese Garden with the dogs. She has settled down in Ireland much better than I thought possible and I have been to Japan more often than I would have dreamed. Yukari has given a totally new dimension to my life and thankfully, she appreciates what a big part United are in it. There is a tinge of sadness I suppose in the fact that life can no longer simply be an homage to the Reds. I have come to realise that a life dedicated to the support of football alone would eventually become a sterile and unfulfilling existence. My footballing trips around the world are now fewer than I would have foreseen. Other priorities occasionally dictate where and when I can continue my extra-marital love affair with United. I've made my bed of roses and am enjoying the company immensely.

Even my diet is looking up.

Daily meals for me now include bountiful supplies of rice, natto beans, kimuchi, miso soup and sea weed. I have got my cholesterol on the run. My low density lipoproteins are scattering before the divine winds of omega-three fatty acids. No more Ulster Fries with their saturated animal fats. Bring on the sushi.

We have many laughs as we discover our cultural differences. The Japanese have little nasal hair. They don't like wearing shoes indoors but do shave their eyebrows. They don't use cotton buds to clean their ears but rather employ a foot long lump of wood with a ball of fluff. The first time I saw this it quite frankly scared me stiff. Nose blowing is considered to be extremely rude but slurping soup or noodles they consider normal. Anyone dropping litter in the street is frowned upon by Yukari, often leading to bad moods when witnessed. Seaweed stops you going grey, soya bean paste is good for the brain.......

Lily has definitely settled down and matured. In her youth she was a playful child with roguish characteristics, ever the exhibitionist wanting to go everywhere and do everything, thinking she could cure the world. She is now more selective, more focused and more in control of her destiny. She more than accomplished her original goals for this generation of the supporters' club. Hopefully this trend will continue.

The premise was to help mend past historical and cultural differences in our community. History certainly was not on her side but I believe she more than fulfilled her original objective. As we are led on different paths in life, so Lily's also deviated.

Our memories will always be with us. It's been a huge roller coaster ride. The obvious highs and lows, many of which I cannot articulate. All Reds will have their individual memories of seasons past. If I helped rekindle these, then this effort has been worthwhile. These are my recollections - from childhood including the 98/99 season when we landed the 'Holy Grail' of European Soccer. As I write at this moment all is well with the world, the stars revolve in their courses and the planets weave their way around the Sun. I am excited about fatherhood, what the future may bring and Manchester United being back on top of the Premiership in 2003.

Faceman, my best mate, the source of my inspiration and motivation, and I were talking the other night. As so often happens on these occasions, we were soon reminiscing about the team's achievements. Naturally our thoughts soon turned in the direction of Big Lily and the state of affairs of our Supporters Club.

'Wee man, it's been like a dream, hasn't it? ' said the Face.

'Aye sir, I think we did ourselves proud, I even got myself a wife out of it.'

'Aye, sir. You got yourself a wife because of Big Lily and I lost mine because of her.'

'Faceman, some of the things our wee team has achieved, you couldn't dream half of them nor invent the other.'

'Being a Red is like living a dream isn't it, … one big Red dream!'

In a small, dusty building not far from North Road in Carrickfergus there are three, large cardboard cartons. Each of these contains a vast amount of material suitable for the manufacture of parachutes. In one box the contents are red, in another a scrap of white peers upward from a tear in a corner and the last box sits waiting with its black folds ready for the stitchers needle.